ASTON VILLA
REVIEW 2000

Published by Sports Projects Ltd

ACKNOWLEDGEMENTS

Aston Villa Review 2000
First published in Great Britain, June 2000,
by Sports Projects Limited

© 2000 Sports Projects Limited
188 Lightwoods Hill, Smethwick, Warley,
West Midlands B67 5EH.
email: info@sportproject.u-net.com
web site: http://www.sportsprojects.com

ISBN 0 946866 54 6

Printed and bound in Slovenia
by Mladinska knjiga

Editors. Jeffrey Prest and Vic Millward.

Photographs: Bernard Gallagher and
Neville Williams.

Design, layout and graphics: Vic Millward,
Bernard Gallagher, Phil Lees and
Nadine Goldingay

Special thanks to: Rod Evans, Mike Beddow,
Pam & Dave Bridgewater and Tony Leighton.

KEY

❏	Player booked
■	Player sent off
32	Figure in goals column indicates time of goal
†56	First substitute and time of substitution
†	First player substituted
‡56	Second substitute and time of substitution
‡	Second player substituted

Notes:

● *Players are listed in squad number order, except for the goalkeeper, who is always at the top of the list.*

● *Substitute goalkeepers are in squad number order, with (Gk) after their name.*

● *In friendly games, where several substitutes may have appeared, additional symbols are used in the following order: #, §, ††, ‡‡, ##, §§, ≠.*

Also available in this series:

Aston Villa Review 1993
ISBN 0 946866 09 0   Price: £7.95

Aston Villa Review 1994
ISBN 0 946866 19 8   Price: £8.95

Aston Villa Review 1995
ISBN 0 946866 23 6   Price: £8.95

Aston Villa Review 1996
ISBN 0 946866 32 5   Price: £8.95

Aston Villa Review 1997
ISBN 0 946866 39 2   Price: £8.95

Aston Villa Review 1998
ISBN 0 946866 46 5   Price: £9.95

Aston Villa Review 1999
ISBN 0 946866 50 3   Price: £9.95

With the Cup to hand, we die of thirst

1999-2000 at Aston Villa will go down as the season when only flares and the FA Cup failed to make a comeback.

If it seemed a little presumptuous that the supporters of the losing Cup Finalists could look so stunned at failing to emerge triumphant from an occasion their club hadn't graced since Bill Haley topped the charts, it was only because the stage had seemed so perfectly set.

As time stepped from one millennium into the next, Villa had left behind the Nervous Nineties and emerged as the Heroes of the Zeros, a team that put furrows into the brows of anyone who faced them.

Dion Dublin was back from a potentially tragic neck injury, well ahead of schedule, and had scored the penalty that sent his team to the Final.

David James was back from the scourge of paralysis-by-analysis on Merseyside, paving the way for Dion's magic moment by saving two penalties in the shoot-out that decided the semi-final.

Paul Merson was back with a vengeance, having initially struggled just to be part of the team.

Benito Carbone was back from a season that had looked to be going horribly wrong up at Hillsborough.

By the time Ian Taylor made it to the Final, despite a hamstring injury that had looked set to finish his season, Villa and its personnel had come back more times than Sinatra. Had this been Hollywood, their case for a happy ending would have been inexorable. Unfortunately, this was north London. Venue of legends and crushed dreams

If the mission of restoring self-respect after the previous season's dramatic decline was achieved with room to spare, Villa's next objective will be to find the killer instinct when it comes to reaping the harvest of their labours.

For in their three biggest matches of the season – the second leg at Leicester, the semi-final with Bolton Wanderers and the Final with Chelsea – they produced three of their tamest performances, each unrecognisable from the exciting football with which they had earlier resuscitated their season.

With two good cup runs and their fifth straight finish in the Premiership's top seven behind them, the platform is in place for them to move onwards and upwards next term, and while reflecting on Chelsea might not come easily at present, there are worse examples a team could follow.

Gianluca Vialli's men were on the brink of taking nothing from a season that had promised everything, when they lined up at Wembley. Popular opinion had predicted that they would succumb either to nerves or post-Champions League apathy. In the end they did neither. They went resolutely about their work and found a way to get the job done. As winners will always do.

They may have denied Villa the FA Cup but hopefully they also handed out a lesson which will stand John Gregory's team in good stead when it looks to come back once more in the 2000-01 season.

Jeffrey Prest

CONTENTS

CONTENTS

Saturday 7th August 1999 • St. James' Park • 3.00pm

NEWCASTLE UNITED 0 ASTON VILLA 1

Half-time 0-0 • Attendance 36,376

Referee Uriah RENNIE (Sheffield)

Referee's Assistants A. BABSKI and R. BOOTH

Black and White Striped Shirts, Black Shorts	Goals	Claret and Blue Striped Shirts, Claret Shorts	Goals
13 Steve HARPER		1 David JAMES	
2 Warren BARTON ❑		3 Alan WRIGHT	
3 MARCELINO †		4 Gareth SOUTHGATE (c)	
4 Didier DOMI		5 Ugo EHIOGU ❑	
5 Alain GOMA ❑		6 George BOATENG †	
8 Franck DUMAS		7 Ian TAYLOR	
9 Alan SHEARER (c) ❑ ■71		9 Dion DUBLIN	
11 Gary SPEED ❑		11 Alan THOMPSON ❑	
14 Temuri KETSBAIA		12 Julian JOACHIM	74
15 Nolberto SOLANO #		24 Mark DELANEY ❑	
21 Carl SERRANT ‡		34 Colin CALDERWOOD ‡	
Substitutes		*Substitutes*	
7 Kieron DYER †45		10 Paul MERSON	
10 Silvio MARIC ‡75		13 Michael OAKES (Gk)	
16 Laurent CHARVET		17 Lee HENDRIE †56	
23 Lionel PEREZ (Gk)		20 Najwan GHRAYIB	
28 Paul ROBINSON #84		26 Steve STONE ‡87	

BEFORE	P	W	D	L	F	A	pts	AFTER		P	W	D	L	F	A	pts
Villa	0	0	0	0	0	0	0	5	Villa	1	1	0	0	1	0	3
Newcastle	0	0	0	0	0	0	0	18	Newcastle	1	0	0	1	0	1	0

FACTFILE

Steve Watson misses game through suspension... Only Villa's 13th league win at St James' Park in 62 attempts and their first in the Premiership, after six straight defeats... They win their opening game in a season for the first time in four years... First away win to start a campaign in five attempts.

Shearer dismissal aids winning start

Perhaps we should be grateful to referee Uriah Rennie. After long summer weeks where 'player power' has become the buzz phrase *ad nauseam*, the new season has barely begun when he changes the record and shows us 'ref power' in all its crippling horror.

He will go down in history as the man who finally shattered Ruud Gullit's cool. The Newcastle United manager has to be restrained from confronting Rennie on the field, having watched his team's promising start punctured by incessant blasts of the whistle, and his captain Alan Shearer sent off for a second bookable offence.

Calmed down by the time of the post-match press conference, Gullit nevertheless remains insistent about the cause of his wrath.

His beef is not with Rennie, but with what he sees as football's increasingly pedantic idealism as to how games should be policed, which he believes has reduced referees to fussy mother hens.

"Never in my career have I seen a referee be as much of an influence as he was today," says the Dutchman. "The ref has to guide a game, not become a major part of it. There was no fluency. If these are the new restrictions then the game will be destroyed and I owe the game too much to watch this happen."

His claim that football's physical element is being slowly neutered is valid: less so his belief that United lost solely because of the referee.

Villa are also left scratching their heads at a game that yields six bookings in addition to the two that lead to Shearer's dismissal, without even coming close to being nasty, yet they deserve credit for absorbing their opponents' impressive start in front of 36,000 impassioned supporters, before gradually clawing their way

into the game and picking off United in the 74th minute.

Mark Delaney seals a promising run-out in the right wing-back position when he crosses from the right to the near post. Almost in slow motion, Julian Joachim's head nudges the ball inside the far post.

The goal comes three minutes after Shearer's departure for a nudge on Colin Calderwood that is the crowning offence in what the referee sees as an overly-physical performance by the England captain.

It's a sour finish to an afternoon that started so sweetly for a United team that parades its four new signings. While there will be more prominent days to come from ex-Ipswich Town midfielder Kieron Dyer, Spaniard Marcelino and French duo Alain Goma, particularly Franck Dumas, look good acquisitions.

Less notable is George Boateng's first Premier-ship game for Villa, but David James is in sparkling form, particularly after the break, when the Newcastle attack revolves around Temuri Ketsbaia for the opening 10 minutes. Twice, James has to stop the Georgian's drives from the edge of the penalty area.

In the first half, it had been the turn of Nolberto Solano and Gary Speed to torment the opposition defence, the pair linking up twice for the Welsh international to head over and then see his shot deflected wide.

Julian Joachim gives chase to Franck Dumas

Wednesday 11th August 1999 • Villa Park • 7.45pm

ASTON VILLA 3 EVERTON 0

Half-time 1-0 • *Attendance* 30,337

Referee Graham BARBER (Guildford)

Referee's Assistants C. BASINDALE and A. WILLIAMS

Claret and Blue Striped Shirts, Claret Shorts	Goals	White Shirts, White Shorts	Goals
1 David JAMES		13 Paul GERRARD	
3 Alan WRIGHT ❏		3 Michael BALL	
4 Gareth SOUTHGATE (c)		4 Richard GOUGH	
5 Ugo EHIOGU ❏		6 David UNSWORTH	
6 George BOATENG †		7 John COLLINS ❏ ■50	
7 Ian TAYLOR	85	8 Nick BARMBY	
9 Dion DUBLIN ‡	57	9 Kevin CAMPBELL	
11 Alan THOMPSON #		10 Don HUTCHISON (c) ❏	
12 Julian JOACHIM	8	11 Scot GEMMILL	
24 Mark DELANEY		14 David WEIR	
34 Colin CALDERWOOD		21 Mitch WARD	
Substitutes		*Substitutes*	
10 Paul MERSON ‡61		12 Mark PEMBRIDGE	
13 Michael OAKES (Gk)		15 Richard DUNNE	
17 Lee HENDRIE †57		16 Danny CADAMARTERI	
20 Najwan GHRAYIB		17 Francis JEFFERS	
26 Steve STONE #67		35 Steve SIMONSEN (Gk)	

BEFORE		P	W	D	L	F	A	pts	AFTER		P	W	D	L	F	A	pts
5	Villa	1	1	0	0	1	0	3	1	Villa	2	2	0	0	4	0	6
9	Everton	1	0	1	0	1	1	1	16	Everton	2	0	1	1	1	4	1

FACTFILE

Villa open their Premiership account with back-to-back wins for the first time since 1995 and consecutive clean sheets for the first time since 1972... David Unsworth plays at Villa Park for the first time since his brief sojourn as a Villa player at the start of last season... John Collins' sending-off is his first ever.

Lacklustre Toffees swept aside

What starts as Eclipse day ends as Groundhog Day, as Villa comfortably dispatch a 10-man Everton side with three unanswered goals, just as they did in the corresponding fixture last season.

If Everton show little of the fight with which they salvaged a point against Manchester United three days earlier and Villa aren't exactly clinical in their approach work, the hosts find three goals of great panache with which to whet their supporters' appetite.

It's now very much business as usual for Julian Joachim, as he follows up the deft header which defeated Newcastle, with a confident strike that sets his team on their way after only eight minutes.

Showing every sign that he and Dion Dublin are now firmly tuned in to the same wavelength, the diminutive striker's anticipation leaves the visitors' defence for dead when Dublin beats Richard Gough to a header and knocks the ball into the path of Joachim, who calmly advances and strokes the ball past keeper Paul Gerrard.

Far from the game being opened up by this, it settles into a stalemate of pretty patterns that go nowhere in a congested midfield. With both equally keen to be lord of the manor, Alan Thompson versus Don Hutchison looks odds on as the evening's flashpoint, yet the unravelling of Everton comes from an entirely unexpected source, as John Collins gets the red card after 50 minutes, following a mistimed tackle on Mark Delaney either side of the half time break.

One less body on the pitch seems to unclog the game and after David James' sole mistake of the night, a fluffed punch following a Hutchison free kick, Thompson sweeps the ball out to Alan Wright, whose cross is volleyed home with aplomb from the outside of Dublin's right foot.

Only Hutchison appears to harbour any hopes of an Everton fightback and with the arrival of Lee Hendrie, Paul Merson and Steve Stone from the subs' bench, Walter Smith's men are swamped. It is cruel luck on Hutchison that his should be the clearance intercepted by Ian Taylor with five minutes left, setting up a one-two with Joachim which Taylor converts into the top right-hand corner.

Villa will face much tougher opponents this season, but they have at least shown some flamboyance to go with the resolve that sustained them at St James' Park.

Joachim's pace is now allied to a determination to shoot on sight more often and after a good performance from Dublin, it is disturbing to see the latter hobbling in the latter stages with what is later revealed to be a back injury.

After the game, there is a telling commentary on the Premiership's current 'card culture' from John Gregory, who has seen 16 cards of either hue brandished in just three hours of football this season.

"I thought of taking Ugo Ehiogu off when we were 3-0 up and he was on a yellow, even though I'd already used all my subs," reflects the Villa boss. "I didn't want to appear disrespectful to Everton, though."

Alan Thompson gets to grips with the Everton midfield

Monday 16th August 1999 • Villa Park • 8.00pm

ASTON VILLA 2 WEST HAM UNITED 2

Half-time 1-1 • *Attendance 26,250*

Referee Mike RILEY (Leeds)

Referee's Assistants A. BUTLER and R. BONE

Claret and Blue Striped Shirts, Claret Shorts		Goals	White Shirts with Navy and Claret Trim, Navy Blue Shorts		Goals
1	David JAMES		1	Shaka HISLOP	
3	Alan WRIGHT ❏		3	Stuart PEARCE ❏	
4	Gareth SOUTHGATE (c) og7		4	Steve POTTS	
5	Ugo EHIOGU		8	Trevor SINCLAIR	90
6	George BOATENG †		10	Paolo DI CANIO	
7	Ian TAYLOR		12	Paulo WANCHOPE	
9	Dion DUBLIN	5,52	13	Marc-Vivien FOE	
11	Alan THOMPSON ‡		15	Rio FERDINAND	
12	Julian JOACHIM		16	John MONCUR ❏ ‡	
24	Mark DELANEY		18	Frank LAMPARD ❏	
34	Colin CALDERWOOD		20	Scott MINTO †	
	Substitutes			*Substitutes*	
10	Paul MERSON		7	Marc KELLER †45	
13	Michael OAKES (Gk)		9	Paul KITSON ‡82	
17	Lee HENDRIE †45		21	Michael CARRICK	
20	Najwan GHRAYIB		22	Craig FORREST (Gk)	
26	Steve STONE ‡88		26	Joe COLE	

BEFORE		P	W	D	L	F	A	pts
1	Villa	2	2	0	0	4	0	6
9	West Ham	1	1	0	0	1	0	3

AFTER		P	W	D	L	F	A	pts
2	Villa	3	2	1	0	6	2	7
9	West Ham	2	1	1	0	3	2	4

FACTFILE

Dublin's goals are the first between these teams in three games... He scores two in a game for the first time since his memorable brace against Arsenal last December.

Clever Trevor nicks a point

West Ham wing-back Trevor Sinclair ends the first half hobbling off for treatment after a crunching collision with former Blackpool team-mate Alan Wright. An hour or so later and he's entitled to reflect on football's flickering fortunes, as he pops up to collect a dainty back-heel from Paulo Wanchope and bury a 93rd minute equaliser that breaks Villa's hearts.

His revival mirrors that of his team, who looked ripe for the taking when John Gregory re-jigged his midfield at half-time and a transformed Villa went 2-1 in front just seven minutes after the interval.

While George Boateng seems to be finding his feet more with each game, he had none of the fuel-injection that his replacement Lee Hendrie introduces. Villa's best passage of the game occupies the first half-hour of the second half, as their play sparkles with pace and one-touch football, setting the Hammers back on their heels and suggesting that it is merely a matter of time before the edge given to Villa by Dion Dublin's second goal of the game becomes something more permanent.

There is an inspirational quality to Dublin's goals that echoes the lift he gave his new club when scoring seven times in his first three games last season. It's hard not to feel good about Villa's prospects when the 30-year-old leaves Rio Ferdinand for dead with the game just five minutes old, rolling off his talented marker to collect a ball knocked in from the left and fire Villa in front from an acute angle.

It needs a freak occurrence to cancel that effort out just a couple of minutes later – Gareth Southgate's valid attempt to intercept an optimistic diagonal shot by Marc Vivien-Foe, parking the ball in his own net, past a wrong-footed David James.

Villa need the rest of a pedestrian first half to get that one out of their system, but once Dublin benefits from a goalmouth melee at a corner early in the second half, thumping a shot high into the net from the edge of the goal area, they seem set fair to monopolise the points.

As the match enters its final 15 minutes, however, a clock strikes 12 deep in the Villa subconscious and their evening turns pumpkin-shaped. As quickly as it came, their flow departs and hesitancy returns, coupled with an inability to string passes together; the sign, perhaps, of a team not yet into its stride this season.

This plays right into the hands of a West Ham side whose season began three weeks sooner, thanks to their InterToto Cup commitments. Under the cosh they may be, but unlike Everton five days earlier, they don't relinquish their ambition whenever they find the ball at their feet.

Constantly driven on from midfield by Foe and Frank Lampard, they rouse Paulo Wanchope from his mid-game slumber for his point-blank range header to force an instinctive save from David James in the 75th minutes. 18 minutes later and the Costa Rican employs his heel to more telling effect and Sinclair sweeps in the equaliser.

Dublin blasts home to put Villa 2-1 up

Saturday 21st August 1999 • Stamford Bridge • 3.00pm

CHELSEA 1 ASTON VILLA 0

Half-time 0-0 • Attendance 35,071

Referee Neale BARRY (Roxby, North Lincolnshire)
Referee's Assistants M. NORTH and K. HAWKES

Blue Shirts, Blue Shorts	Goals	White Shirts with Claret and Blue Sash, White Shorts	Goals
1 Ed DE GOEY		1 David JAMES	
2 Dan PETRESCU †		3 Alan WRIGHT	
3 Celestine BABAYARO		4 Gareth SOUTHGATE (c)	
5 Frank LEBOEUF ❑		5 Ugo EHIOGU	og52
6 Marcel DESAILLY		7 Ian TAYLOR	
8 Gustavo POYET ❑		9 Dion DUBLIN	
9 Chris SUTTON ❑ ‡		11 Alan THOMPSON †	
11 Dennis WISE (c)		12 Julian JOACHIM	
17 Albert FERRER		17 Lee HENDRIE	
20 Jody MORRIS		24 Mark DELANEY	
25 Gianfranco ZOLA #		34 Colin CALDERWOOD ‡	

Substitutes		*Substitutes*	
4 Jes HOGH		8 Mark DRAPER #88	
12 Bjarne GOLDBÆK †76		10 Paul MERSON †70	
18 Gabriele AMBROSETTI #86		13 Michael OAKES (Gk)	
19 Tore Andre FLO ‡76		15 Gareth BARRY	
23 Carlo CUDICINI (Gk)		26 Steve STONE ‡77 #	

BEFORE	P	W	D	L	F	A	pts	AFTER	P	W	D	L	F	A	pts
2 Villa	3	2	1	0	6	2	7	4 Chelsea	3	2	1	0	7	2	7
7 Chelsea	2	1	1	0	6	2	4	5 Villa	4	2	1	1	6	3	7

FACTFILE

Villa's first defeat of the season and first game in which they are held scoreless... They have now scored own goals in consecutive games twice in their last seven Premiership outings... Chelsea's fourth straight win over Villa, who have beaten the Londoners just once in their last eight meetings.

'Negative' vibes hit Villa

John Gregory deflects most jibes that come Villa's way with a wry smile and a pointed one-liner, but the manager is genuinely irked by the brickbats that follow today's post-game press conference, when he outlined the game plan that came closer than any he employed last season to thwarting Villa's blue-shirted nemesis.

Against any opponent, he points out, the first objective must be to stop them playing. Against Chelsea's assortment of virtuosos, that objective is at a premium.

Had these sentiments followed a game in which Villa found the net, his remarks would have been little more than a footnote in the next day's newspapers. After a performance in which the visitors again rank second-best to Chelsea in the creativity department, however, 'negative Villa' is too convenient a label for the back pages to ignore.

This is a little harsh on the visitors, who have progressed markedly from the team that was taken to school by Gian-luca Vialli's cultured side on two occasions last season. Despite missing the injured Didier Deschamps, the Blues still glitter in the afternoon sun, but this time they must work hard for every opening as their opponents hound them relentlessly.

Villa can even take some perverse comfort from the fact it needs one of their own to score the game's only goal. Author of an afternoon's torment for Alan Wright, Dan Petrescu deserves a break, but

Ugo Ehiogu

he's still indebted to Ugo Ehiogu, whose sprawling attempt to intercept the Romanian's drive across the face of goal only succeeds in poking the ball into his own net after 52 minutes.

Cursed luck it may be but it's a fair reflection of the teams' respective promise in front of goal. While Villa's attacks end up in cul-de-sacs, the Blues repeatedly find the open road through their opponents' back line.

Chris Sutton and Gustavo Poyet spurn chances to open the scoring after being put clear by Petrescu, and Ehiogu has a 26th-minute reprieve to bear in mind next time he feels harshly treated by referees, when his foot goes in search of the ball as Zola cuts into the box, only to find the Italian's leg. Even Gregory admits he'd have given it...

Zola is denied recompense two minutes later when David James tips away the Italian's free-kick as it curls towards the top corner.

With French World Cup duo Marcel Desailly and Frank Leboeuf majestic at the heart of Chelsea's defence, Villa must look to the flanks for hope, and Mark Delaney's reputation continues to soar as he roasts makeshift full-back Celestine Babayaro.

His team's scope for optimism broadens with Paul Merson's arrival in the 69th minute. He brings Villa a vision they have lacked up to this point and with Chelsea suddenly going off the boil, two sides whose previous games were transformed in the final minute, brace themselves for a repeat.

Villa remain one key short in their bid to unlock the Chelsea defence, however, and that, rather than their strategy, is the afternoon's principal negative.

Tuesday 24th August 1999 • Vicarage Road • 7.45pm

WATFORD 0 ASTON VILLA 1

Half-time 0-0 • *Attendance* 19,161

Referee Steve BENNETT (Orpington)
Referee's Assistants J. ROSS and P. NORMAN

Yellow Shirts, Red Shorts		Goals	Claret and Blue Striped Shirts, White Shorts		Goals
13	Chris DAY		1	David JAMES	
2	Des LYTTLE		3	Alan WRIGHT	
3	Peter KENNEDY		4	Gareth SOUTHGATE (c)	
4	Robert PAGE (c)		5	Ugo EHIOGU	
5	Steve PALMER		7	Ian TAYLOR ❏	
6	Paul ROBINSON		9	Dion DUBLIN	
7	Michel NGONGE #		10	Paul MERSON †	
8	Micah HYDE †		12	Julian JOACHIM	
9	Tommy MOONEY		17	Lee HENDRIE	
19	Clint EASTON ‡		24	Mark DELANEY	69
32	Mark WILLIAMS ❏		34	Colin CALDERWOOD	
	Substitutes			*Substitutes*	
16	Nigel GIBBS		2	Steve WATSON	
20	Johann GUDMUNDSSON ‡79		6	George BOATENG †80	
24	Alex BONNOT †79		13	Michael OAKES (Gk)	
33	Dominic FOLEY #79		20	Najwan GHRAYIB	
34	Herwig WALKER (Gk)		22	Darius VASSELL	

BEFORE		P	W	D	L	F	A	pts	AFTER		P	W	D	L	F	A	pts
5	Villa	4	2	1	1	6	3	7	2	Villa	5	3	1	1	7	3	10
9	Watford	4	2	0	2	4	5	6	11	Watford	5	2	0	3	4	6	6

FACTFILE

Villa's first-ever league win at Watford, after two draws and four defeats... Mark Delaney's first goal for Villa... Villa and Graham Taylor are involved in the same game for the first time since Villa visited Everton on 5th May 1990; Taylor's last game as Villa boss before taking over as England manager.

No room for sentiment

It's a lesson all visitors to the House that John Built learn fairly swiftly. No matter how many mikes and flash-guns are pointing your way the day you sign for Villa, from that point onwards you're just one cog in the engine.

After all the plaudits that have accompanied a highly impressive start to his Premiership career, it's reality check time for Mark Delaney, 45 minutes into Villa's first visit to Vicarage Road in 13 years.

"We gave him a telling-off at half-time because he was playing like a tart," says that arch-feminist John Gregory afterwards. Far from breaking the spell for the young Welsh wing-back, however, the blunt assessment is merely the spur for his return to football utopia.

The game is 69 minutes old when Dion Dublin heads on a cross from Alan Wright and when Watford's defence can only clear as far as the edge of their area, Delaney hits an angled shot high into the far corner of the net.

"When he smashed that ball he must have seen my face on it!" his manager observes later.

The goal is the saving grace of a scrappy contest that sees Watford boss Graham Taylor up against the club which provided him with his stepping-stone to the England manager's desk.

The newly-promoted Hornets set out to do to Villa what Gregory's men had attempted to do to Chelsea three days earlier and stifle their opponents. After a promising start, the visitors struggle against the unceasing attention of the opposition, who also manage to create openings of their own.

It means a chance for David James to showcase his talents against the club with which he began his career. With impeccable timing, two days ahead of Kevin Keegan naming his latest England squad, the Villa keeper pulls out a blinding save to tip away a shot from ex-Villa junior Tommy Mooney two minutes from the end of the game.

Earlier, he had again been at full length to deny the hosts, when Belgian striker Michel Ngonge's looping header in the first half seemed destined for the top corner.

The game slips beyond the half-hour mark before Villa managed a response, Julian Joachim seeing his shot from the edge of Watford's area grabbed by Watford keeper Chris Day.

Lee Hendrie nearly has his reward for a busy first-half performance shortly afterwards when he collects an Alan Wright cross and evades his marker, only for his shot to be deflected wide of goal for a corner.

Villa resume the offensive seven minutes after the restart, when Dublin heads a Delaney cross narrowly wide of the post.

The quality of the decisive goal which follows can't mask the fact that, as at Stamford Bridge, it is not a vintage Villa performance. There will be other days for putting on the Ritz as far as their manager is concerned, however. For now, he is simply happy that their toil has, on this occasion, earned its reward.

"My boys showed a lot of character," Gregory says. "They got on and rolled their sleeves up."

Match-winner – Mark Delaney

Saturday 28th August 1999 • Villa Park • 3.00pm

ASTON VILLA 1 MIDDLESBROUGH 0

Half-time 1-0 • *Attendance* 28,728

Referee Mark HALSEY (Essex)

Referee's Assistants G. TURNER and P. CANADINE

Claret and Blue Striped Shirts, Claret Shorts		Goals	White Shirts with Purple Trim, White Shorts		Goals
1	David JAMES		1	Mark SCHWARZER	
3	Alan WRIGHT		4	Steve VICKERS	
4	Gareth SOUTHGATE (c)		6	Gary PALLISTER	
5	Ugo EHIOGU †		7	Robbie MUSTOE	
7	Ian TAYLOR		9	Paul INCE ❑	
9	Dion DUBLIN	5	10	Brian DEANE	
10	Paul MERSON		14	Philip STAMP	
12	Julian JOACHIM ‡		16	Andy TOWNSEND (c) ‡	
17	Lee HENDRIE		19	Hamilton RICARD †	
24	Mark DELANEY		27	Robert STOCKDALE	
34	Colin CALDERWOOD		29	Jason GAVIN	

Substitutes			*Substitutes*		
6	George BOATENG †66		12	Alan MOORE	
11	Alan THOMPSON		18	Andy CAMPBELL †70	
13	Michael OAKES (Gk)		20	Alun ARMSTRONG	
20	Najwan GHRAYIB		22	Mark SUMMERBELL ❑ ‡76	
22	Darius VASSELL ‡77		25	Ben ROBERTS (Gk)	

BEFORE	P	W	D	L	F	A	pts	AFTER	P	W	D	L	F	A	pts
2 Villa	5	3	1	1	7	3	10	2 Villa	6	4	1	1	8	3	13
4 Boro	5	3	0	2	7	7	9	10 Boro	6	3	0	3	7	8	9

FACTFILE

David James registers his fourth clean sheet in just six games, one game fewer than Mark Bosnich required at the start of his Villa career... Back-to-back wins go some way towards reducing the flak Villa took for what some perceived as a negative approach against Chelsea.

Villa toil against weakened Boro

Whatever their views on Paul Gascoigne, there can't have been many neutrals who wouldn't have welcomed his presence as this pedestrian encounter struggled towards its conclusion.

Gazza, however, is part of a damaging Boro injury list that also deprives the game of the Teessiders' newly-signed German ace Christian Ziege. Both would have given their club at least a fighting chance of nullifying what turns out to be the game's only goal, scored by Dion Dublin after just five minutes.

Both would also have brought a better performance out of the hosts, who seem to be dragged down to the same limited level as their opponents, having started so promisingly.

Paul Merson admits before the game that he wouldn't have fancied facing his former club last season, with Middlesbrough nerves still so raw after his move to Villa. While his reception from the visiting fans is anything but amicable this time, though, he serves up the perfect response.

It's his pass from the outside of the foot that releases Alan Wright on the left flank with the game barely into its stride. The wing-back sends over a cross to the near post, where Dublin, hardly troubled by his marker, flicks a perfect header to the far corner of the net to open Villa's account.

Merson comes close to another feather in his cap with 10 minutes gone, when his free kick from the left flank finds Ugo Ehiogu, who has managed to get the better of Brian Deane at the far post. Falling as he makes contact, however, Ugo can't get over the ball enough and his header, which lacks power, lands on the roof of Mark Schwarzer's net.

The visitors threaten a response 10 minutes later, when Deane's header from a Paul Ince cross is fumbled by David James in the Villa goal. Fortunately for James, the ball drops at his feet, but he still needs treatment as Hamilton Ricard thunders in to try and capitalise.

James is glad of his defenders later in the half, when he is stranded after attempting to cut out a cross and Colin Calderwood blocks a shot from Ince just feet off his own goal line.

With Deane and Ricard linking well, Boro are refusing to let the game get away from them, although they enjoy a slice of luck on the stroke of half-time, when Alan Wright, possibly overcome at the thought of just his fourth goal in 165 appearances for Villa, miskicks horribly with the goal at his mercy, after the ball arrives at his feet from the left wing.

Far from bruising the hosts' confidence, it serves only to remind them how comfortable they should be against under-manned opponents. They dominate the second half of the contest, prompted repeatedly in the early stages by Julian Joachim, who forces a fine save from Schwarzer before having another shot denied by the woodwork, all in the space of three minutes after the restart.

Boro, however, avoid the ultimate setback when Schwarzer saves a stinging shot from Merson after 63 minutes. Missing your current stars is one thing; receiving painful reminders from your old ones is something else.

Boro's Paul Ince and Gary Pallister try to close down goalscorer Dion Dublin

Saturday 11th September 1999 • Highbury • 3.00pm

ARSENAL 3 ASTON VILLA 1

Half-time 1-1 • Attendance 38,093

Referee David ELLERAY (Harrow-on-the-Hill)

Referee's Assistants D. DRYSDALE and I. BLANCHARD

Red and White Shirts, White Shorts	Goals	Claret and Blue Striped Shirts, Blue Shorts	Goals
13 Alex MANNINGER		1 David JAMES †	
2 Lee DIXON		3 Alan WRIGHT	
3 Nigel WINTERBURN ❑		4 Gareth SOUTHGATE (c)	
4 Patrick VIEIRA		5 Ugo EHIOGU ❑	
5 Martin KEOWN		7 Ian TAYLOR ❑	
6 Tony ADAMS (c)		9 Dion DUBLIN #	
9 Davor SUKER †	45,49	10 Paul MERSON ❑	
10 Dennis BERGKAMP ‡		12 Julian JOACHIM	44
11 Marc OVERMARS #		17 Lee HENDRIE ‡	
15 Ray PARLOUR		24 Mark DELANEY ❑	
18 Gilles GRIMANDI ❑		34 Colin CALDERWOOD	
Substitutes		*Substitutes*	
7 Nelson VIVAS		6 George BOATENG	
14 Thierry HENRY #83		11 Alan THOMPSON ‡63	
16 SILVINHO †68		22 Darius VASSELL #70	
24 John LUKIC (Gk)		31 Jlloyd SAMUEL	
25 Nwankwo KANU ‡75	83	39 Peter ENCKELMAN (Gk) †52	

BEFORE		P	W	D	L	F	A	pts	AFTER		P	W	D	L	F	A	pts
2	Villa	6	4	1	1	8	3	13	5	Arsenal	7	4	1	2	10	7	13
6	Arsenal	6	3	1	2	7	6	10	6	Villa	6	4	1	2	9	6	13

FACTFILE

Villa have a solitary point to show for their last five games in London... Joachim's first goal in four games... Villa have now gone seven games since their last win at Highbury... Suker is the first man to score twice in a game against Villa since Tore Andre Flo in Chelsea's win at Villa Park on 21st March.

No answer to Suker-man

How ironic that after catching the eye already this season with his prodigious throwing and kicking, David James' inability to do either on a sunlit afternoon at Highbury should lead to Villa's second fruitless trip to the capital in the last three weeks.

The Villa keeper finds a knee injury sustained in training coming back to haunt him at a critical time in a finely-poised game. Having had treatment on it during the first half, he is reluctant to kick as Villa advance upfield early in the second.

Perhaps not realising the extent of his plight, none of his team-mates hang back sufficiently to provide an outlet for James to throw the ball, leaving him caught between a rock and a hard place.

He stays there too long in the opinion of referee David Elleray, who whistles for time-wasting, leaving Arsenal with the juiciest of free-kicks, right in the heart of Villa's penalty area, no more than eight yards from goal.

There is much complaining about the severity of his judgment from the Villa camp afterwards but a word for Gareth Southgate as the Villa skipper lingered over a first-half free-kick, had already put the visitors on notice that punctuality was the order of the day.

Villa's cavalry charge from the goal line as Arsenal take the free kick is a magnificent sight, bettered only by ano-ther one; a precise drive from Davor Suker that sends the

David James - knee injury

ball high into the net, well clear of the onrush of bodies.

His debut penalty-miss at Anfield is now a distant memory for the newly-signed Croat striker, who had already struck in injury time in the first period to snuff out Villa's short-lived triumph at taking the lead.

A ball to Dennis Bergkamp, loitering just out-side Villa's area, was exquisitely flicked into the path of the advancing Suker, who evaded Gareth Southgate's lunge just enough to blast home the equaliser.

It limits Villa's happy time in their last three hours at Highbury to just two minutes. Beaten here rather more emphatically than a 1-0 score-line suggests, in last season's finale, they have their reward for an improved performance this time around when Paul Merson turns on the style against his old club, keeping the ball air-borne with several taps from the instep, while turning through 180 degrees to prod a pass through to Julian Joachim, who smartly tucks it home in the 44th minute.

Unfortunately for Villa, that gem eats up their inventiveness quota for the afternoon. They might make a better job of blunting Arsenal's advances that on their last visit but they offer barely a hint of a counter-punch and when Suker's brace leaves them trailing as much on the scoreboard as in the creativity department, they look sunk.

James makes way for Peter Enckelman, who performs creditably for a man making his debut in front of the North Bank, but there is an air of inevitability about Arsenal's third goal, Nwankwo Kanu side-footing home with ease from a Marc Overmars cross, seven minutes from time.

Tuesday 14th September 1999 • Deva Stadium • 7.45pm

CHESTER CITY 0 ASTON VILLA 1

Half-time 0-0 • *Attendance* 4,364

Referee John KIRKBY (Sheffield)

Referee's Assistants A.R. BROWN and I.D. SHAW

Blue and White Striped Shirts, Blue Shorts	Goals	Claret and Blue Striped Shirts, Claret Shorts	Goals
1 Wayne BROWN		39 Peter ENCKELMAN	
2 Ross DAVIDSON		2 Steve WATSON	
5 Martyn LANCASTER		5 Ugo EHIOGU	
6 Matthew WOODS		7 Ian TAYLOR ❏	
7 Andy SHELTON		10 Paul MERSON †	
8 Nick RICHARDSON (c)		11 Alan THOMPSON	
9 Goran MILOVAIJEVIC †		12 Julian JOACHIM	
10 Luke BENNETT		15 Gareth BARRY	
11 Neil FISHER		17 Lee HENDRIE	78
15 Darren WRIGHT		20 Najwan GHRAYIB ❏	
18 Matthew DOUGHTY		34 Colin CALDERWOOD (c)	
Substitutes		*Substitutes*	
13 Neil CUTLER (Gk)		6 George BOATENG	
14 Jonathon JONES		8 Mark DRAPER	
16 Danny CARSON		13 Michael OAKES (Gk)	
23 Paul BERRY †84		22 Darius VASSELL †67	
26 Steven MALONE		31 Jlloyd SAMUEL	

Hendrie spot-kick spares blushes

FA guidelines on non-provocative use of the PA system don't seem to have filtered down as far as Division Three.

"HOW LUCKY CAN YOU GET?!" booms the wholly-impartial match announcer, as Villa trot back to the half-way line after scoring the only goal of the night. If it's not *de rigeur*, it's a reasonable assessment of the kind of fixture Villa could have done without, so soon after being picked apart by Arsenal on national television.

Chester City's American chairman Terry Smith has brought hands-on management to the team he saved from administration, playing the role of head coach and preparing dossiers on opponents, before spending the game by the dug-out, brandishing a sheaf of tactical notes ("We reckon they're glued to his hand," observes one of his players).

Big on motivation, he will have had an easy time of it in the run-up to this game. Villa are currently a victim of the ludicrous demands of modern football - besieged by criticism despite being sixth in the league - and City's players must surely sense a chance for glory.

It certainly seems that way, once the hosts withstand a bright Villa start and begin to realise that reputations not withstanding, really it is just eleven versus eleven.

What follows is an even fight, the gulf between the teams pared away as Villa's self-doubt and Chester's nothing-to-lose ebullience meet somewhere in the middle.

With City's fans buoyed by an enduring 0-0 scoreline and the travelling support increasingly restless, Goran Milovaijevic's wanton handball following a 78th-minute corner is a lifebelt to a drowning man.

Hendrie steps up for the resultant penalty kick, which Wayne Brown saves smartly, diving to his right. He can't get a grip on the ball, however, and Hendrie stabs at the rebound to put his team in front.

The goal is a calming influence on the visitors and they might have had more, when the arrival of Darius Vassell's fresh legs starts tearing holes in City's defence late in the game.

It is Villa, however, who are left counting their blessings as Andy Shelton, son of former Villa player Gary Shelton, cuts in from the right touchline with 92 minutes on the clock and hits a dipping shot from 30 yards which Peter Enckelman just manages to tip over.

It is far from his only task of the evening. With the newly signed Milovaijevic as their fulcrum, the Blues overcome some robust defence from their opponents and manage to test their visitors.

A shot from lone striker Luke Beckett is just too high in the 34th minute and Neil Fisher narrowly fails to curl a free kick in at the near post four minutes later, while everyone is focused on the throng at the back.

Villa have their moments, but despite solid performances from the ever-reliable Ian Taylor and the returning Gareth Barry, their lack of cohesion makes this a game to survive rather than to revel in.

A goal down and Villa Park to come, however, Terry Smith's second-leg dossier will still need to be a beauty.

Najwan Ghrayib joins the Villa attack to put Chester under more pressure

Saturday 18th September 1999 • Villa Park • 3.00pm

ASTON VILLA 1 BRADFORD CITY 0

Half-time 0-0 • Attendance 28,083

Referee Stephen LODGE (Barnsley)

Referee's Assistants R. BOOTH and J. ROSS

Claret and Blue Striped Shirts, Claret Shorts	Goals	White Shirts, White Shorts	Goals
39 Peter ENCKELMAN		1 Gary WALSH	
2 Steve WATSON		3 Andy MYERS	
4 Gareth SOUTHGATE (c)		4 Stuart McCALL (c) ❏	
5 Ugo EHIOGU		5 David WETHERALL	
6 George BOATENG ❏ #		9 Lee MILLS †	
7 Ian TAYLOR		10 Gareth WHALLEY	
9 Dion DUBLIN	71	11 Peter BEAGRIE	
11 Alan THOMPSON †		14 Andrew O'BRIEN	
12 Julian JOACHIM ‡		15 Dean WINDASS	
15 Gareth BARRY ❏		18 Gunnar HALLE	
17 Lee HENDRIE		28 Dean SAUNDERS	
Substitutes		*Substitutes*	
10 Paul MERSON †55		2 Stephen WRIGHT	
13 Michael OAKES (Gk)		13 Matthew CLARKE (Gk)	
22 Darius VASSELL ‡64		20 John DREYER	
26 Steve STONE #85		22 Wayne JACOBS	
34 Colin CALDERWOOD		29 Bruno RODRIGUEZ †45	

BEFORE	P	W	D	L	F	A	pts	AFTER	P	W	D	L	F	A	pts
5 Villa	7	4	1	2	9	6	13	4 Villa	8	5	1	2	10	6	16
18 Bradford	6	1	2	3	3	8	5	18 Bradford	7	1	2	4	3	9	5

FACTFILE

Villa's unbeaten run at home this season extends to four games... Dublin's fifth goal in eight games... Steve Stone returns to action after missing four games due to the back injury he sustained at Chelsea... Villa's first game against Bradford since Villa won 1-0 at Villa Park on 2nd May 1988.

Dour Bantams almost hold out

"I hope you're going to criticise their manager the way you criticised me at Chelsea." He doesn't miss a trick, this John Gregory.

The Villa manager makes this remark to the waiting reporters in the post-game press conference, after his team have made hard work of breaking down a Bradford team that made no secret of its limited ambition, massing its defences in a bid to stifle its hosts. Villa's containment role at Stamford Bridge last month looked ornate in comparison.

For ex-Villa man Dean Saunders, it means a lonely and fruitless afternoon up front – "I think Ugo did more attacking than me!" says the Bradford striker of his marker and former team-mate – but the ploy almost works, with Villa having to rely on a late goal from Dion Dublin to separate two sides.

Substitute Darius Vassell puts his pace to work on the right flank with 71 minutes gone, before cutting into the Bradford box and pulling back the ball to Lee Hendrie, whose shot is blocked by goalkeeper Gary Walsh, but only as far as the waiting Dublin, who tucks home one of his easier chances.

In terms of possession, it is just reward for the hosts, who have switched to a 4-4-2 formation in a bid to open up more attacking options. Their best one comes with the introduction of Paul Merson from the bench, however. Once again, he adds a spark to Villa's game and they threaten to run riot with the calming influence of a goal behind them.

Dublin slips when poised to shoot following a Steve Watson cross and Hendrie then warms Walsh's fingers with a low shot, yet it is ironically their besieged visitors who almost have the last laugh.

Former Leeds United player Gunner Halle

moves inwards from the right flank with the game in its final minute but Dean Windass can only head his cross over the bar.

A more telling finish doesn't bear thinking about for a Villa side playing in front of a sub-30,000 crowd for the third time in four Premiership fixtures.

Much of what they see, in truth, provides precious little incentive for them to hurry back. Once again, Villa plough through an hour in which their territorial advantage is squandered by a lack of imagination – their attacking strategy being based too heavily on pressurising the Bantams' defence with Julian Joachim's fleet of foot.

Their manager is in combative mood afterwards, responding to questions about his team's waning pulling power at the box office with a reminder that at this level, everything is secondary to results.

"I'm not here to entertain; I'm here to win," he insists.

Bradford, now in the relegation zone and looking likely still to be there after 38 games, would shake their heads in disbelief if they knew what passes for a crisis down Trinity Road way.

Villa old-boy Dean Saunders is well covered by Alan Thompson and Ian Taylor

Tuesday 21st September 1999 • Villa Park • 7.45pm

ASTON VILLA 5 CHESTER CITY 0

Aggregate score 6-0

Half-time 2-0 • Attendance 22,613

Referee Scott MATHIESON (Stockport)

Referee's Assistants J. HOLBROOK and G.B. TURNER

Claret and Blue Striped Shirts, Claret Shorts		Goals	Yellow Shirts, Yellow Shorts		Goals
39	Peter ENCKELMAN		1	Wayne BROWN	
2	Steve WATSON		2	Ross DAVIDSON	
4	Gareth SOUTHGATE (c)		5	Martyn LANCASTER	
5	Ugo EHIOGU		6	Matthew WOODS	
6	George BOATENG	17	7	Andy SHELTON †	
7	Ian TAYLOR †	32	8	Nick RICHARDSON (c)	
9	Dion DUBLIN #		9	Goran MILOVAIJEVIC ‡	
11	Alan THOMPSON	50	10	Luke BECKETT	
15	Gareth BARRY ‡		11	Neil FISHER #	
17	Lee HENDRIE	46,47	15	Darren WRIGHT	
22	Darius VASSELL		18	Matthew DOUGHTY	
	Substitutes			*Substitutes*	
10	Paul MERSON †49		13	Neil CUTLER (Gk)	
12	Julian JOACHIM #60		14	Jonathon JONES ‡63	
13	Michael OAKES (Gk)		16	Danny CARSON #87	
26	Steve STONE		23	Paul BERRY †52	
31	Jlloyd SAMUEL ‡53		26	Steve MALONE	

FACTFILE

Villa score five goals in a game for the first time since beating Wimbledon 5-0 at home on 22nd December 1996... Their biggest margin of victory in a League Cup tie since beating Peterborough United 7-1 over two legs in 1995... They draw Manchester United at home in the Third Round... Hendrie's three goals over the two legs is the best haul by a Villa player in a round of this competition since Nii Lamptey's three over two legs against Wigan Athletic in the Second Round of the 1994-95 competition.

Midfield the best form of attack

While two-legged cup ties may increase profit margins, they considerably diminish the scope for giant-killing. Whatever dreams Chester may have harboured after a spirited first leg left them just one goal down, they are to perish inside 20 minutes as reality kicks in at Villa Park.

What starts out as a contest ends as a benefit night for the Villa midfield. Rarely at its best so far this season, it provides all five goals tonight, as Lee Hendrie, Alan Thompson, Ian Taylor and George Boateng fill their boots against their Third Division opponents.

As proof that the spell was well and truly broken when the final whistle blew at the Deva Stadium a week earlier, Chester are even denied a consolation from the penalty spot, when encroachment by several of their players forces the kick to be retaken, after Luke Beckett had slotted home his original attempt with aplomb, sending Peter Enckelman the wrong way with a powerful shot to the corner of the net.

His second attempt clearly reflects his disenchantment, a tame attempt that is saved with ease by Enckelman. The only blessing is that, by now, it is purely academic.

Lee Hendrie had killed off any Chester hopes when he hit both his goals within two minutes of a half-time interval that had seen Villa 2-0 in front on the night.

The second half is just 29 seconds old when Hendrie converts with a low shot, after Ross Davidson fails to deal with Boateng's cross. Hendrie is scavenging again a minute later, when Steve Watson's centre comes to him after being only partially cleared, and a deflection takes his 12-yard shot over the stranded Wayne Brown in the City goal.

Alan Thompson completes the evening's goal-count when Hendrie turns provider in the

50th minute. The Geordie collects a pass which he guides past three defenders before clipping the ball past Brown from an awkward angle with his right foot.

Earlier, it had taken Villa just 17 minutes to start erasing the memories of their unconvincing performance on their visitors' own ground. After Darius Vassell, making his first start for the first team, and Dion Dublin both go wide in the early stages, Hendrie beats his man on the left to send a deep cross towards the far post, where Boateng rises to direct a header into the far corner and open his account for his new club.

It's the head of Taylor that extends Villa's lead just 15 minutes later, as he heads home an inswinging left wing corner from Thompson at the near post.

With Vassell continuing to threaten, Chester may have felt a certain relief at their damage limitation skills as they went in at half-time, but by the end of the night they are relieved not to have conceded seven or eight goals, so telling is Villa's domination.

It may be against lowly opposition, Chester are currently 92nd in the Football League, but Villa have won in style this evening, showing some glitter to go with the goals.

"A good night's work," as their manager succinctly puts it.

The cavalry arrives as Lee Hendrie threatens the Chester goal

Saturday 25th September 1999 • Filbert Street • 3.00pm

LEICESTER CITY 3 ASTON VILLA 1

Half-time 1-0 • *Attendance* 19,917
Referee Jeff WINTER (Stockton-on-Tees)
Referee's Assistants R. BONE and J.J. ROSS

Blue Shirts, White Shorts	Goals	White Shirts with Claret and Blue Sash, Claret Shorts	Goals
1 Tim FLOWERS ❑		39 Peter ENCKELMAN	
3 Frank SINCLAIR		2 Steve WATSON ❑ †	
6 Muzzie IZZET	40	4 Gareth SOUTHGATE (c) ❑ ■65 og48	
7 Neil LENNON		5 Ugo EHIOGU	
9 Emile HESKEY		6 George BOATENG	
11 Steve GUPPY		7 Ian TAYLOR	
14 Robbie SAVAGE ‡		9 Dion DUBLIN	73
15 Phil GILCHRIST		11 Alan THOMPSON ‡	
18 Matt ELLIOTT (c)		12 Julian JOACHIM	
24 Andrew IMPEY		15 Gareth BARRY	
27 Tony COTTEE †	55	17 Lee HENDRIE ❑	
Substitutes		*Substitutes*	
20 Ian MARSHALL †81		10 Paul MERSON	
21 Graham FENTON		13 Michael OAKES (Gk)	
22 Pegguy ARPHEXAD (Gk)		24 Mark DELANEY †63	
29 Stefan OAKES		31 Jlloyd SAMUEL	
37 Theo ZAGORAKIS ‡86		34 Colin CALDERWOOD ‡66	

BEFORE	P	W	D	L	F	A	pts	AFTER	P	W	D	L	F	A	pts
4 Villa	8	5	1	2	10	6	16	6 Villa	9	5	1	3	11	9	16
11 Leicester	8	3	2	3	11	10	11	7 Leicester	9	4	2	3	14	11	14

FACTFILE

City continue as Villa's bogey team, having avoided defeat against their midland rivals in their last nine meetings... Dion Dublin's sixth goal of season... Villa's first sending-off since Steve Watson's against Charlton Athletic in May... They have lost each of their last four games in which a Villa man has been red-carded.

Nightmare time for Southgate

By far the lowest ebb of Villa's season so far is epitomised by Gareth Southgate, as he uses up his quota of misfortune for the season inside 65 minutes.

The Villa captain won't forget Emile Heskey in a hurry. The big Leicester striker sells a convincing dummy at a Leicester free-kick, three minutes into the second half, and as the ball enters the Villa penalty area, Southgate sticks out a foot to block its progress, only to stab the ball into his own goal, with Peter Enckelman off balance. His team now 2-0 down, Southgate stares at the pitch with the weary resignation of a man who's been here before.

With 65 minutes gone, his afternoon hits rock-bottom as he is sent off for the first time in his career. Previously booked for a foul, he becomes embroiled in a dispute with Heskey over the same piece of turf as the ball heads towards them. Heskey goes down in a flurry of arms and a disbelieving Southgate finds himself staring at a red card.

It's not much consolation but with Villa 3-0 adrift as he departs, at least his dismissal can't be regarded as pivotal. Villa simply have no answer to a busy Leicester side which almost seems to be drawing strength from the feverish boardroom battle currently in progress at Filbert Street.

With hardly any service of note for Dion Dublin, the hosts monopolise the first half scoring opportunities and have their reward five minutes before the half-time whistle, when a Lee Hendrie pass is intercepted and Andy Impey hares off down the right before sending over a deep cross which Steve Guppy knocks back into the middle for Muzzy Izzet to head the first goal from close range.

After George Boateng has headed narrowly wide from a Gareth Barry cross shortly after the own goal, Tony Cottee puts the game out of sight at 3-0 in typical poacher's style, scoring from the rebound after Enckelman has kept out a close-range header from Frank Sinclair.

With the rain now pouring down, the skies are weeping for a Villa team simply not on the same page as their opponents, yet they come close to making Leicester sweat over the points when Dion Dublin shoots home on the turn from a Barry cross after 73 minutes and Ugo Ehiogu heads just wide barely a minute later, following a Lee Hendrie free kick.

It's a period of sustained, if unconvincing pressure from Villa, but the Filberts remain menacing on the break and Enckelman has to save with his legs from Heskey, after Cottee pounces on a mix-up between Mark Delaney and Boateng, to set up his striking partner with another chance on goal.

One of Villa's most direct attacks of the game comes after the final whistle, when John Gregory blasts referee Jeff Winter's red card decision. "The sending off was totally unjustified. Otherwise, I thought we did quite well. Leicester worked hard to stop us from playing: we had a lot of possession but didn't use it as well as we could."

Fall guy Emile Heskey goes down and Gareth Southgate goes off

Saturday 2nd October 1999 • Villa Park • 3.00pm

ASTON VILLA 0   LIVERPOOL 0

Half-time 0-0 • Attendance 39,217

Referee Rob HARRIS (Oxford)

Referee's Assistants A. HOGG and W. TOMS

Claret and Blue Striped Shirts, Claret Shorts	Goals	Green Shirts with White and Navy Sash, Navy Shorts	Goals
39 Peter ENCKELMAN		1 Sander WESTERVELD	
4 Gareth SOUTHGATE (c)		2 Stephane HENCHOZ ❑	
5 Ugo EHIOGU		3 Rigobert SONG	
6 George BOATENG ❑ †		5 Steve STAUNTON ❑ ■31	
7 Ian TAYLOR		7 Vladimir SMICER †	
9 Dion DUBLIN		10 Michael OWEN #	
11 Alan THOMPSON ❑		11 Jamie REDKNAPP (c) ❑	
12 Julian JOACHIM		12 Sami HYYPIA ❑	
15 Gareth BARRY ❑		15 Patrik BERGER	
17 Lee HENDRIE ‡		16 Dietmar HAMANN ❑ ‡	
24 Mark DELANEY		18 Erik MEIJER ❑	

Substitutes

2 Steve WATSON		14 Vegard HEGGEM	
10 Paul MERSON †67		22 Titi CAMARA #81	
13 Michael OAKES (Gk)		23 Jamie CARRAGHER ‡76	
26 Steve STONE ‡80		26 Jorgen NIELSEN (Gk)	
34 Colin CALDERWOOD		28 Steven GERRARD †32	

BEFORE	P	W	D	L	F	A	pts	AFTER	P	W	D	L	F	A	pts
6 Villa	9	5	1	3	11	9	16	8 Villa	10	5	2	3	11	9	17
12 Liverpool	8	3	1	4	10	10	10	12 Liverpool	9	3	2	4	10	10	11

FACTFILE

Villa's fourth consecutive clean sheet at home... Villa's first goalless draw with Liverpool in 19 matches, the last being on 12th January 1991... Referee Rob Harris subsequently acknowledges he made an error with regard to Steve Staunton's second yellow card. The caution is rescinded.

Pool's 10 thwart Villa's full house

In what was meant to be a tough test of Aston Villa, it's football itself that goes under the microscope, after a game in which 10 bookings and a sending-off steal all the headlines.

15 years ago, that tally would have been indicative of a bloodbath. Now it is the gross product of a game that is spicy without ever threatening mayhem. John Gregory is not the only person to have noticed that a perusal of the Sunday papers these days shows too many games to revolve around reds and yellows rather than goals and skill.

Referees' officer Philip Don is at the game and it is disturbing to hear him breezily dismiss concerns over the stop-start nature of a game that left one man in the dressing-room after just half-an-hour and eight others walking on eggshells with a booking to their name.

"People keep asking for consistency and here we had it in the referee's decisions. I thought he had a good game and was utterly consistent in his application of the laws," says Don.

This, unfortunately, misses the point. "The law is an ass," said Mr Bumble in Dickens' 'Oliver Twist' and you suspect he might have come to the same conclusion were he around to watch Premiership football. Laws designed to control the game are being interpreted in such a way as to neuter it, and yet again the man in black will be the focal point of tomorrow's back pages.

If there is little in the way of dramatic action to compete with him, a game on a knife-edge between two evenly-matched sides has a certain absorbing tension about it, plus two minutes' light relief for the home fans when Steve Staunton gets his marching orders.

Booked for a foul on Boateng after six minutes, the ex-Villa defender is ruled to have encroached at an Alan Thompson free-kick, 26 minutes later, although replays show the decision to be wrong, a slight nudge of the ball into Thompson's path having preceded Staunton's rush towards it.

If Gareth Southgate thought an own goal compounded by a red card seven days earlier was the ultimate footballing nightmare, he may now feel it's trumped by being sent off in front of your former fans, the majority of them none too enamoured of you in the first place, who greet your departure with the scornful hilarity normally reserved for the demise of a pantomime villain.

Liverpool could claim they have the last laugh, however. Vladimir Smicer, who has earlier seen his shot go narrowly wide, becomes the sacrificial lamb, replaced by Steven Gerrard who fills Staunton's position as the visitors dig in.

For the hour which follows, an edge in speed of reaction keeps their defence a step ahead of their opponents, although Villa do find the net after 71 minutes, when Ugo Ehiogu nods down a free kick from the right for Dublin to poke the ball home, only for an offside flag to deny them.

Otherwise, honours are even in front of goal, Jamie Redknapp bringing a good save out of Enckelman with a 30-yard free kick in the 67th minute, but sadly they remain secondary to the referee's copious secretarial work.

Ugo and Michael Owen – all eyes on the ball

Wednesday 14th October 1999 • Villa Park • 7.45pm

ASTON VILLA 3 MANCHESTER UNITED 0

Half-time 1-0 • *Attendance* 33,815

Referee Mike RILEY (Leeds)

Referee's Assistants D.S. BRYAN and G.A. HALL

Claret and Blue Striped Shirts, Claret Shorts		Goals	Navy Blue Shirts, White Shorts		Goals
39	Peter ENCKELMAN		1	Mark BOSNICH (c)	
5	Ugo EHIOGU (c) †		13	John CURTIS ❑	
6	George BOATENG ❑		14	Jordi CRUYFF	
7	Ian TAYLOR	49	20	Ole Gunnar SOLSKJAER	
9	Dion DUBLIN ❑		23	Michael CLEGG	
11	Alan THOMPSON #		28	Danny HIGGINBOTTOM †	
12	Julian JOACHIM ‡	18	30	Ronnie WALLWORK	
15	Gareth BARRY		34	Jonathan GREENING	
17	Lee HENDRIE ❑		37	John O'SHEA	
24	Mark DELANEY		39	Luke CHADWICK	
34	Colin CALDERWOOD		42	Michael TWISS ‡	
	Substitutes			*Substitutes*	
2	Steve WATSON †45		29	Alex NOTMAN	
10	Paul MERSON		31	Nick CULKIN (Gk)	
13	Michael OAKES (Gk)		38	David HEALY †66	
22	Darius VASSELL ‡57		40	Lee ROCHE	
26	Steve STONE #75	90	41	Rick WELLENS ‡73	

FACTFILE

Villa advance to the Fourth Round of this competition for the first time in three years... Their cup aggregate this season now reads nine goals for and none against... Ian Taylor has scored in both rounds... Steve Stone is Villa's first substitute to score this term and the first since Gareth Barry against Nottingham Forest on 24th April 1999.

Steve Stone – first goal for Villa

Hollow victory, but we're through

There are bigger issues at stake than a stroll to Round Four on what is a grim night for football. Only 24 hours later, when you meet James, does the extent of United's disservice to the game hit home.

James is eight, a United fan and was taken to Villa Park by his dad as a birthday treat. Mark Bosnich he recognised, but the 10 men alongside him were complete strangers.

You can tell from his face, James isn't sure what's going on. How do you explain cynicism to an eight-year-old?

Given that the Worthington Cup has long ceased to merit a mention in the Old Trafford mission statement, no one really expected a full-strength Manchester team firing on all cylinders, but with no 50% cut in admission prices to mirror the depleted fare on offer, the paying customer is insultingly short-changed by the visitors' assortment of kids and reserves.

Villa's players make all the right diplomatic noises afterwards, but they too are entitled to feel offended by the snub and it's much to their credit that they dispose of the opposition in a professional manner.

It takes them just 18 minutes to open their account. Having picked holes in the visitors' defence with ease, they set up Julian Joachim, who shrugs off his marker with a quick turn before stroking the ball home with the outside of his boot.

The improving confidence and adventure of the visitors means Villa must wait until four minutes into the second half for number two, when a long throw from Mark Delaney appears to mesmerise United's defensive line, leaving a grateful Ian Taylor to stab the ball home.

With United's body language largely indifferent at both setbacks, 2-0 looks enough, but

there's a late bonus for Steve Stone, who's done far more bench-warming than he anticipated when arriving from Nottingham Forest last season. He has the consolation of scoring his first goal for Villa in the shadow of the Holte End, albeit with a little help from a deflection off a defender, as he cuts in from the right before shooting.

While it is a long way from being United's finest hour, their goalkeeper at least warrants an honourable mention.

The rancour reserved for Steve Staunton four days earlier was merely a warm-up for the hostility Mark Bosnich faces this evening and one has to admire the Australian's *chutzpah* in emerging alone before the second half to warm up. His slow, unflinching walk towards a Holte End that's doing a passable impression of a lynch mob, is one of the most enduring images of the season so far.

But for his heroics, United would have had the caning they deserved, but Bosnich bounces back from a Dion Dublin shoulder charge, straight out of the Pongo Waring era, to save well from an Ian Taylor header at a corner and then tips a Lee Hendrie shot onto the bar in the second half.

Five or six more players of his calibre and Villa would have had a game on their hands. And young James a birthday to remember.

So near yet so far for Darius Vassell

Monday 18th October 1999 • Stadium of Light • 8.00pm

SUNDERLAND 2 ASTON VILLA 1

Half-time 0-0 • *Attendance* 41,045

Referee David ELLERAY (Harrow-on-the-Hill)
Referee's Assistants I. BLANCHARD and J. DIVINE

Red and White Striped Shirts, Black Shorts		Goals	Turquoise Shirts with Black Trim, White Shorts		Goals
1	Thomas SORENSEN		1	David JAMES	
2	Chris MAKIN		4	Gareth SOUTHGATE (c)	
3	Michael GRAY		6	George BOATENG ‡	
5	Steve BOULD (c)		7	Ian TAYLOR ❑	
6	Paul BUTLER		9	Dion DUBLIN	47
7	Mike SUMMERBEE ‡		11	Alan THOMPSON ❑	
9	Niall QUINN		15	Gareth BARRY	
10	Kevin PHILLIPS	60pen,82	17	Lee HENDRIE	
16	Alex RAE †		22	Darius VASSELL †	
20	Stefan SCHWARZ ❑		24	Mark DELANEY ❑	
21	Gavin McCANN #		34	Colin CALDERWOOD	

Substitutes			*Substitutes*	
4	Kevin BALL #82		2	Steve WATSON
12	Daniel DICHIO		3	Alan WRIGHT
13	Andy MARRIOT (Gk)		10	Paul MERSON †56
29	Eric ROY †75		26	Steve STONE ‡83
31	Michael REDDY ‡80		39	Peter ENCKELMAN (Gk)

BEFORE		P	W	D	L	F	A	pts	AFTER		P	W	D	L	F	A	pts
3	Sunderland	10	6	2	2	18	8	20	3	Sunderland	11	7	2	2	20	9	23
6	Villa	10	5	2	3	11	9	17	9	Villa	11	5	2	4	12	11	17

FACTFILE

Villa's first-ever game at the Stadium of Light and their first at Sunderland in three years... Second time this season they have lost after scoring first... Ugo Ehiogu and Julian Joachim both miss the game with injuries but David James returns from his shoulder injury, after six games out.

Battling Villa have no luck

Most Villa fans have Mark Delaney down as a fast, skilful player but if David Elleray is to be believed, we're underestimating the Welshman's talents.

Ahead by one goal to nil, thanks to Dion Dublin, Villa look well on course for a morale-boosting win at the Stadium of Light when the ball is swung into their penalty box on the hour mark. As big Niall Quinn challenges for the ball, Delaney isn't quite on the same page. He has his back to the play when the ball appears to strike his left shoulder blade, yet in referee Elleray's opinion, the young defender has just executed a deliberate and inch-perfect handball to thwart Sunderland's bid for an equaliser.

In defence of the official, replays from a camera angle behind him show the ball to take a definite deflection as it strikes Delaney in the region of his upper arm, but with players obscuring the referee's view there seems ample scope for the wing-back to receive the benefit of the doubt.

The fact that he was facing the other way would persuade most people of his innocence and there is also the prior matter of an apparent handball by Quinn himself as he tried to prevent the ball from getting as far as Delaney. It is all to no avail. For the second time this term, Elleray has driven a stake through Villa's heart, yet this decision is infinitely more controversial than the free kick he awarded Arsenal deep into the Villa penalty area five weeks ago.

From the minute Kevin Phillips tucks the spot kick to one side of a wrong-footed David James, you suspect the visitors will do well to emerge with a point, as a 42,000 mausoleum becomes a cauldron once more.

Villa's frustration cannot be over-estimated. For an hour, they have foiled a side on the up

in front some of the most impassioned fans in the country, and when Dublin climbs unattended to head home Alan Thompson's quickly-taken free kick, 73 seconds into the second half, they look set to take control.

Ironically, it was Dublin's striking partner, Darius Vassell, who caused the main problems in a ragged first half. His pace repeatedly burns the home team's defence and a fine turn that shrugs off Michael Gray after 15 minutes leaves just Thomas Sorensen between Vassell and his first Premiership goal, only for the keeper to spread himself well and force the ball out of play.

Nine minutes later, it's the turn of Sunderland's groundsman to save them. So borderline is Chris Makin's foul on Vassell that another centimetre of white paint might have given Villa first use of the penalty spot.

Not so, however, and Sunderland, whose main thrust of the first half was a Quinn header that went wide, are a team revitalised after their equaliser. There is something grimly inevitable about the *denouement*, when Stefan Schwarz' ability to land his cross in a sliver of space between defenders, allows Phillips to nip in and put a header past James, eight minutes from time.

It's Sunderland's best winning sequence for 63 years and a long, long ride home for their dejected opponents.

Alan Thompson's quick thinking helped Dion Dublin put Villa into the lead

Saturday 23rd October 1999 • Villa Park • 3.00pm

ASTON VILLA 1 WIMBLEDON 1

Half-time 1-1 • *Attendance 27,160*

Referee Uriah RENNIE (Sheffield)

Referee's Assistants I. BLANCHARD and S. BRAND

Claret and Blue Striped Shirts, Claret Shorts	Goals	White Shirts, White Shorts	Goals
1 David JAMES		1 Neil SULLIVAN	
4 Gareth SOUTHGATE (c)		2 Kenny CUNNINGHAM	
6 George BOATENG †		3 Alan KIMBLE	
7 Ian TAYLOR		6 Ben THATCHER	
9 Dion DUBLIN	35	7 Carl CORT	
11 Alan THOMPSON ‡		8 Robbie EARLE (c)	27
15 Gareth BARRY ❏		9 John HARTSON †	
17 Lee HENDRIE		10 Jason EUELL	
18 Benito CARBONE		11 Marcus GAYLE ‡	
24 Mark DELANEY		29 Trond ANDERSEN	
34 Colin CALDERWOOD		30 Hermann HREIDARSSON	
Substitutes		*Substitutes*	
2 Steve WATSON		4 Andy ROBERTS	
3 Alan WRIGHT		15 Carl LEABURN ‡83	
10 Paul MERSON †74		20 Martin ANDRESEN †63	
20 Najwan GHRAYIB ‡78		22 Chris WILLMOTT	
39 Peter ENCKELMAN (Gk)		23 Kelvin DAVIS (Gk)	

BEFORE		P	W	D	L	F	A	pts
9	Villa	11	5	2	4	12	11	17
15	Wimbledon	11	2	5	4	17	25	11

AFTER		P	W	D	L	F	A	pts
9	Villa	12	5	3	4	13	12	18
15	Wimbledon	12	2	6	4	18	26	12

Benito Carbone signs for Villa on 20th October for a nominal fee and a sum to be based on appearances. His contract is to the end of the season ... Next day, FIFA's inspection team visit Villa Park as part of a tour of English stadia, to assess England's facilities in support of their application to host the 2006 World Cup.

Dazzling debut from new Italian

It may be a new era at Wimbledon but some things remain the same. Who better to ignore the script, as a new saviour and his adoring public wait to celebrate their acquaintance, than the Premiership's leading party-poopers?

Egil Olsen's dogged Dons withstand a *tour de force* from Villa striker Benito Carbone, who does everything but score in the first game since his arrival from Sheffield Wednesday in mid-week. His new chairman calls it the best curtain-raiser by a Villa player that he has ever seen.

With more twists and turns than a mountain road, the Italian not only threatens to reduce Wimbledon to an irrelevance, but also pushes his team into a noticeably higher gear, in particular striking up an immediate understanding with Dion Dublin.

With George Boateng heading just wide from a Carbone cross after six minutes and Benito himself having a diving header touched wide following a superb Mark Delaney cross, two disregarded penalty appeals by the home team in the first 20 minutes seem almost superfluous, until the Dons momentarily turn the tide with a goal that reduces Villa Park to near silence.

26 minutes have elapsed when Villa are Cort in the act, Wimbledon striker Carl Cort finding time to turn in the penalty area and chip the ball over Villa's defensive line. Robbie Earle is in so much space as he heads the ball past David James that all eyes turn to the touchline hoping for a flag that doesn't appear.

It is completely against the run of play and Villa make

Lee Hendrie has Trond Andersen back pedalling

amends in just 10 minutes, when Carbone drags Dons full-back Kenny Cunningham every which way on the left before chipping a cross to the far post, where Dublin executes a textbook downward header that beats keeper Neil Sullivan from a narrow angle.

The stage seems set for the job to be finished in some style after the interval, particularly as Wimbledon, seemingly resigned to Carbone's dominance, play with the dispirited air of a team four goals down. They can be thankful that their listlessness doesn't extend to Sullivan, who is the difference between the teams with a string of second-half saves. He pulls off a reflex save to tip a Dublin volley over the bar from point-blank range, just a minute after the restart and later parries a shot from Hendrie before Dublin fires the rebound over the bar.

Earlier, Carbone had seemed set for the crowning glory when Dublin back-heeled the ball into his path from the edge of the penalty area, as his team-mate came charging into the box. Expectation is crushed, however, when the Italian's shot goes wide.

The game's closing stages see the visitors' box peppered with crosses, but Villa cannot break the deadlock.

Ugo Ehiogu does not see that being an ongoing problem now that Carbone is on board, however. "He seems to be the missing link in the last third of the pitch," enthuses the Villa defender after the game. "What's most encouraging is that there still seems to be a lot to come from him because he wasn't really match-fit."

At any other time, two points dropped at home to Wimbledon would leave Villa Park in sombre mood, but today the result takes second place to the level of performance.

Saturday 30th October 1999 • Old Trafford • 3.00pm

MANCHESTER UNITED 3 ASTON VILLA 0

Half-time 2-0 • Attendance 55,211

Referee Alan WILKIE (Chester-le-Street)

Referee's Assistants A. BUTLER and P. NORMAN

Red Shirts, White Shorts		Goals	White Shirts with Claret and Blue Sash, Claret Shorts		Goals
1	Mark BOSNICH		1	David JAMES	
3	Denis IRWIN		4	Gareth SOUTHGATE (c)	
6	Jaap STAM		6	George BOATENG †	
7	David BECKHAM		7	Ian TAYLOR	
9	Andy COLE #	45	9	Dion DUBLIN	
11	Ryan GIGGS ‡		11	Alan THOMPSON ‡	
12	Phil NEVILLE		15	Gareth BARRY ❑	
16	Roy KEANE (c)	65	17	Lee HENDRIE	
18	Paul SCHOLES	30	18	Benito CARBONE #	
19	Dwight YORKE †		24	Mark DELANEY	
27	Mikael SILVESTRE		34	Colin CALDERWOOD	
Substitutes			*Substitutes*		
14	Jordi CRUYFF ‡79		2	Steve WATSON	
17	Raimond VAN DER GOUW (Gk)		3	Alan WRIGHT ‡72	
20	Ole Gunnar SOLSKJAER †66		10	Paul MERSON #76	
21	Henning BERG		26	Steve STONE †55	
33	Mark WILSON #79		39	Peter ENCKELMAN (Gk)	

BEFORE		P	W	D	L	F	A	pts	AFTER		P	W	D	L	F	A	pts
4	United	12	7	3	2	28	19	24	2	United	13	8	3	2	31	19	27
10	Villa	12	5	3	4	13	12	18	11	Villa	13	5	3	5	13	15	18

Heaviest margin of defeat since losing to Chelsea by same score on 21st March this year... In the week before the game, John Gregory loses his appeal against a £2,000 FA fine for comments made to referee in Newcastle game in August... Michael Oakes completes a £500,000 transfer to Wolves on a five-year contract.

United hand out lesson in finishing

It's as if those United kids trounced by Villa in the Worthington Cup game two weeks ago had muttered "We'll get our brothers onto you," before they disappeared into the dressing room.

Big brother is waiting for John Gregory's men at Old Trafford, and if he looks no more intimidating than his opponent, his knockout punch is in a different league.

In a game controlled by Villa for lengthy periods, United illustrate Brian Clough's adage that it only takes one kick to score a goal, ruthlessly cashing in a handful of chances to extend Villa's lamentable record at Old Trafford, which now stands at one win in 36 attempts.

After a brisk Villa start, Paul Scholes reminds them exactly what they are up against, when he arrives at the near post in the 30th minute, to flick a David Beckham cross sublimely over David James' outstretched arm and into the far corner of the goal.

With the first half into injury time, Villa sights are lowered to a draw, as Andy Cole slots home a pull-back by Beckham, and it falls to Roy Keane to secure the points in the 61st minute, with a thundering 25-yard shot into the corner.

That this clincher should come in what is only the hosts' second attack of the second half merely highlights Villa's ability to make so little of so much.

In contrast to their opponents, they drum up an assortment of openings, but putting any of them away is the one area in which they are distinctly second-best.

Time and again the hosts' defence is caught flat by Villa's enterprise.

With room to compose himself, Dion Dublin has the goal loom large in front of him after just 19 minutes of the first half but shoots wide, and Benito Carbone can't find a wide-open Lee Hendrie to his right when the duo leave United's offside trap in tatters just before the hour mark.

It's hard luck on Villa's defence, which despite the scoreline, works well in generally giving Andy Cole and Dwight Yorke short shrift up the middle, with Gareth Southgate outstanding in repeatedly shepherding his former team-mate back into midfield.

On the flanks, however, Manchester are more menacing, with Denis Irwin and Ryan Giggs maintaining a bombardment from the left wing, while David Beckham has a field day on the right, with a hand in all three goals.

Villa, on the other hand, have a meagre ration of crosses to work with and their chances of getting back into the game are not helped by Benito Carbone being unable to find an encore to his performance against Wimbledon.

He sends an overhead shot above the bar from a Lee Hendrie cross early in the second half and is twice set free later on, only for Mark Bosnich to block his shot on goal, but it is his failure to find Hendrie with the goal at his mercy in the 57th minute which costs Villa dear.

A goal at that point would have halved United's lead and given Villa fresh hope.

"Clinical finishing was the difference," says John Gregory afterwards. "I don't think we'll ever have more chances to score here than we did today. United had three, and they took them all."

David James

Saturday 6th November 1999 • Villa Park • 3.00pm

ASTON VILLA 0 SOUTHAMPTON 1

Half-time 0-0 • Attendance 26,474

Referee Andy D'URSO (Billericay)

Referee's Assistants R. BONE and K. PIKE

Claret and Blue Striped Shirts, Claret Shorts		Goals	Red and White Striped Shirts, Black Shorts		Goals
1	David JAMES		1	Paul JONES	
3	Alan WRIGHT		2	Jason DODD (c)	
4	Gareth SOUTHGATE (c)		5	Claus LUNDEKVAM	
9	Dion DUBLIN		6	Dean RICHARDS ❑	83
10	Paul MERSON †		8	Matthew OAKLEY	
11	Alan THOMPSON ❑ ‡		9	Mark HUGHES	
15	Gareth BARRY		14	Stuart RIPLEY †	
18	Benito CARBONE		17	Marian PAHARS	
24	Mark DELANEY		24	Patrick COLLETER ❑	
26	Steve STONE		30	Hassan KACHLOUL ❑	
34	Colin CALDERWOOD		32	Trond SOLTVEDT ‡	
Substitutes			*Substitutes*		
2	Steve WATSON		7	Matthew LE TISSIER	
6	George BOATENG †80		13	Neil MOSS (Gk)	
8	Mark DRAPER		15	Francis BENALI	
20	Najwan GHRAYIB ‡80		16	James BEATTIE ‡85	
39	Peter ENCKELMAN (Gk)		35	Luis BOA MORTE †74	

BEFORE		P	W	D	L	F	A	pts	AFTER		P	W	D	L	F	A	pts
11	Villa	13	5	3	5	13	15	18	12	Villa	14	5	3	6	13	16	18
14	Saints	12	3	4	5	19	23	13	14	Saints	13	4	4	5	20	23	16

FACTFILE *Steve Stone makes his first start of the season... Lee Hendrie misses his first game of the season with a calf strain... Villa's first home defeat of the season... They are goalless at home for only the second time in 12 games, both occasions coming in the last three games.*

Wolves at door as Dean strikes

Southampton's visit represents a perfect chance to break a Villa winless streak in the Premiership that now stretches embarrassingly back to mid-September.

The flip-side of a potentially easy kill, however, is the plague that descends on your house if you contrive to blow it, and Villa are left in no doubt about the fading patience of their supporters as they leave the field at full time, seven minutes after ex-Wolves defender Dean Richards has headed the game's only goal to earn Southampton the points.

A corner from the left in front of the visiting fans is flicked on by Claus Lundekvam at the near post and Richards is irresistible as he hurtles in at the back post to head home from close range.

There can be no complaints from a Villa side that has again subsided disturbingly once their early brightness fails to breach Saints' defences. A first half that degenerates into a comedy of errors is to Southampton's advantage and their increasing prominence in its closing stages - Patrick Colleter and Hassan Kachloul intercepting passes to test David James in the Villa goal - earns a chorus of boos for the hosts as they head for the dressing-room.

Once James has got down well to keep out a Richards header from a corner, three minutes after the restart, the best chances of the second half fall to Villa. A cross from the right is volleyed just over by Dion Dublin in the 51st minute and the big striker, who plundered the Southampton defence for four goals in Villa colours last term, flicks a header just wide of the far post from a Benito Carbone cross 17 minutes later.

The Italian will himself be denied in the 68th minute, when a fine run down the right by Paul Merson results in the ball being pulled back to Carbone, only for a stretching Paul Jones to tip the ball to safety.

It is an echo of the game's early stages, when Villa looked poised to take control after Alan Thompson slammed a free kick from an acute angle against the crossbar.

Villa do not look to be missing the suspended Ian Taylor, with Gareth Barry moved into a midfield role you suspect he savours, while Steve Stone and Merson are drafted into the starting line-up.

Linking nicely with Thompson, Merson starts well, but is largely anonymous by the time the second half arrives, and it is the visitors' personnel that catches the eye as the game progresses.

Even his biggest fan would have to concede that Matthew Le Tissier's days as the essence of Southampton appear to be over. The Channel Islander will spend the afternoon on the bench, such is the menacing fervour with which Kachloul goes about his work in midfield. Constantly prompting his side, the Moroccan's supply line is constantly seized upon by the dangerous combination of Stuart Ripley, Marian Pahars and Mark Hughes.

"We thought we'd take it to Villa; we wanted to have a go at them," says their manager Dave Jones afterwards.

Gareth Southgate clears his lines

Monday 22nd November 1999 • Highfield Road • 8.00pm

COVENTRY CITY 2 ASTON VILLA 1

Half-time 1-1 • *Attendance 20,184*

Referee Graham BARBER (Tring)
Referee's Assistants G. ATKINS and J. ROSS

Sky Blue Shirts with Navy Trim, Sky Blue Shorts		Goals	White Shirts with Claret and Blue Sash, White Shorts		Goals
1	Magnus HEDMAN		1	David JAMES	
4	Paul WILLIAMS		3	Alan WRIGHT	
7	Robbie KEANE	65	4	Gareth SOUTHGATE (c)	
10	Gary McALLISTER (c)		6	George BOATENG ❏	
11	Moustapha HADJI		7	Ian TAYLOR ❏	
12	Paul TELFER ❏		9	Dion DUBLIN	41
14	Carlton PALMER		12	Julian JOACHIM ‡	
17	Gary BREEN		17	Lee HENDRIE ❏	
18	Youssef CHIPPO ‡		24	Mark DELANEY †	
19	Marcus HALL		26	Steve STONE	
31	Cedric ROUSSEL †	8	34	Colin CALDERWOOD	
	Substitutes			*Substitutes*	
3	David BURROWS ‡90		2	Steve WATSON †75	
6	Muhamed KONJIC		10	Paul MERSON	
8	Noel WHELAN †88		18	Benito CARBONE	
24	John EUSTACE		22	Darius VASSELL ‡75	
26	Steve OGRIZOVIC (Gk)		39	Peter ENCKELMAN (Gk)	

BEFORE		P	W	D	L	F	A	pts	AFTER		P	W	D	L	F	A	pts
12	Villa	14	5	3	6	13	16	18	11	Coventry	15	5	5	5	23	17	20
13	Coventry	14	4	5	5	21	16	17	12	Villa	15	5	3	7	14	18	18

FACTFILE

City break a run of six straight defeats by Villa at Highfield Road... Steve Watson's introduction from the bench is his first Premiership appearance since the defeat at Leicester... Julian Joachim returns from injury in place of Benito Carbone, who is relegated to the bench for the first time since joining the club.

Irish ace inspires Sky Blues' win

If John Gregory was to draw up a list of things he could do without in Villa's current slump, having his forays into the transfer market come back to haunt him would be fairly close to the top.

However satisfied the manager might be with his decision not to pursue Wolverhampton Wanderers' young Irish striker, Robbie Keane, earlier this season, there can be little pleasure in watching the 19-year-old take centre stage as the club which did buy him claim a second straight win against their local rivals, to the mocking delight of the Highfield Road patrons.

Long used to being Villa's doormat on the way to three points, Coventry revel in their rivals' discomfiture, yet the visitors will rue a 1-of-9 statistic in the 'shots on goal' category, which stopped them making the most of a wounding equaliser shortly before half-time.

The TV replays suggest that Julian Joachim body-checked his 'shadow' Paul Williams as the ball rolls out for a Villa corner in the 41st minute. Having had a vociferous claim for a penalty rejected when Joachim locked horns with Williams in the area just four minutes into the match, however, Villa see it as sauce for the gander, and unrestrained jubilation follows when Steve Stone's accurate corner-kick allows an unguarded Dion Dublin to head home against his old club.

City are visibly rocked by this setback to their evening. Bright and breezy throughout the first half, they had been given the perfect start when Keane wriggled past Mark Delaney with a burst of speed on the left flank, before passing to the near post, where Cedric Roussel thumped an unstoppable header past David James.

It erased a promising start by City's opponents and there's a spring in Coventry's step as they begin to enjoy themselves. James is at full stretch to slap away a long shot from Moroccan Youssef Chippo in the 24th minute and Villa then have possibly the escape of their season when Keane pounces on an under-hit back-pass by Boateng in the 36th minute and tries to chip the advancing James. A slight deflection from the big goalie's shoulder sends the ball against a post, however, after which it rolls along the goalline without ever crossing it, before Alan Wright hoofs it clear.

Villa's equaliser makes the most of this good fortune and as the pace hots up after the interval, Coventry are firmly in reverse gear, only for Villa's lack of a clinical finish in front of goal to allow their hosts sufficient time to clear their heads. As the cliche goes, you only get one chance at this level, and Villa's departs when the man many fans hoped might be scoring goals for the claret and blues this season, strikes one for the Sky Blues instead. City break in the 65th minute and Chippo flicks the ball through Villa's flat back line for Keane to stroke the ball under James' body for the winner.

"I've got a thick skin," says Gregory showing a wry smile afterwards, when asked just how dark a shadow Keane has cast over his evening. At least it'll be another three months before he has to face Juninho.

Steve Stone

Saturday 27th November 1999 • Goodison Park • 3.00pm

EVERTON 0 ASTON VILLA 0

Half-time 0-0 • *Attendance 34,750*
Referee Peter JONES (Loughborough)
Referee's Assistants M. WILLIAMS and M. SHORT

Blue Shirts, White Shorts	Goals	Claret and Blue Striped Shirts, Claret Shorts	Goals
13 Paul GERRARD		1 David JAMES	
4 Richard GOUGH		2 Steve WATSON ❑	
6 David UNSWORTH		3 Alan WRIGHT ❑	
7 John COLLINS		4 Gareth SOUTHGATE (c)	
8 Nick BARMBY †		6 George BOATENG	
9 Kevin CAMPBELL		7 Ian TAYLOR ❑	
10 Don HUTCHISON (c) ❑		9 Dion DUBLIN	
12 Mark PEMBRIDGE		12 Julian JOACHIM †	
14 David WEIR		15 Gareth BARRY	
15 Richard DUNNE		17 Lee HENDRIE	
17 Francis JEFFERS		34 Colin CALDERWOOD ❑	
Substitutes		*Substitutes*	
2 Alex CLELAND		10 Paul MERSON	
3 Michael BALL		18 Benito CARBONE †66	
19 Abel XAVIER		20 Najwan GHRAYIB	
24 Tony GRANT †77		26 Steve STONE	
35 Steve SIMONSEN (Gk)		39 Peter ENCKELMAN (Gk)	

BEFORE		P	W	D	L	F	A	pts	AFTER		P	W	D	L	F	A	pts
12	Everton	15	5	5	5	24	22	20	11	Everton	16	5	6	5	24	22	21
13	Villa	15	5	3	7	14	18	18	13	Villa	16	5	4	7	14	18	19

FACTFILE

Villa break a five-game losing streak away from home in the Premiership...
They have now been held scoreless three times in their last four games...
The result means Everton and Villa have duplicated their results from last season,
when Villa won 3-0 at home while the return fixture was a goalless draw.

Carbone rues late opportunity

Three months after testing Danny Wilson's self-control, Benito Carbone does it again. It is no secret that love and harmony were conspicuously absent from the latter days of the duo's working relationship at Sheffield Wednesday, so if Wilson is able to resist a guffaw after 89 minutes of his scouting visit to Goodison Park this afternoon, he is a better man than many.

Before him, his former striker is flat out on the turf, holding his head, after seizing upon a woeful attempt at a back pass by Richard Dunne, to find himself with only the keeper to beat. Carbone's shot beats the outstretched Paul Gerrard but not the far post, however, the ball bouncing out to safety from the woodwork.

In retrospect, Villa may have rather the opportunity had not presented itself, for it transforms perfectly justifiable satisfaction with a hard-earned point into forlorn yearning for what might have been.

If Carbone needs to cheer himself up afterwards, however, he need look no further than his opposite number, Francis Jeffers. The teenager's effective partnership with Kevin Campbell sets Villa's defenders a stringent examination all afternoon, but he is momentarily reduced to the level of hapless pub footballer after 71 minutes when the ball is crossed back into the box after a save by David James, only for Jeffers to spoon his shot over the bar from six yards out with an open goal beckoning.

If we are left with no goals, we at least get rather more excitement than seemed likely after an unremarkable first half, in which Everton - no home win since September - and Villa - no league win of either ilk since roughly the same point, pawed at each other like two old boxers whose instinct for survival had begun to outweigh their thirst for glory.

While the impatience of the home crowd pushes their team up a gear after the interval, Villa's inability to find their men when clearing their own lines, means that most of the action takes place in their half of the field.

Reverting to a 3-5-2 formation for increased solidity in defence, the visitors battle away diligently and while they are occasionally vulnerable to Campbell's pace on the counter-attack, they deserve the breaks that come their way, when Jeffers gets the ball in the net in the first half, only to be ruled offside, and then has a penalty appeal in front of the home fans waved off in the 51st minute, James timing to perfection his interception at the youngster's feet.

For their part, Villa had looked set to have a bigger say in the game once they had seen off the Toffees' early surge at the start of the game, and begun to capitalise on some of the holes appearing in Everton's midfield.

Dion Dublin eludes his marker in the Everton box after 26 minutes and sends over a cross which Julian Joachim can't get enough power behind, leaving a comfortable save for Gerrard.

Dublin himself can't find the necessary clout when he tries a shot on the turn from 25 yards in the 41st minute, and Gerrard is again left with a routine stop.

Both efforts are at least on target, a quality for which Benito Carbone would have paid handsomely before the day is out.

Gareth Barry gets the better of Kevin Campbell

Wednesday 1st December 1999 • Villa Park • 7.45pm

ASTON VILLA 4 SOUTHAMPTON 0

Half-time 1-0 • *Attendance 17,608*

Referee Barry KNIGHT (Orpington)

Referee's Assistants D.P. MORRISON and B. BELLO

Claret and Blue Striped Shirts, Claret Shorts		Goals	Red and White Striped Shirts, Black Shorts		Goals
1	David JAMES		1	Paul JONES	
2	Steve WATSON	22	5	Claus LUNDEKVAM	
3	Alan WRIGHT		6	Dean RICHARDS	
4	Gareth SOUTHGATE (c)		8	Matthew OAKLEY ❑	
6	George BOATENG ❑		9	Mark HUGHES (c)	
7	Ian TAYLOR †		14	Stuart RIPLEY ‡	
9	Dion DUBLIN	72,90	17	Marian PAHARS	
12	Julian JOACHIM ❑ ‡	67	21	Jo TESSEM	
15	Gareth BARRY		24	Patrick COLLETER	
17	Lee HENDRIE #		30	Hassan KACHLOUL #	
34	Colin CALDERWOOD		32	Trond SOLTVEDT †	
Substitutes			*Substitutes*		
10	Paul MERSON ‡75		2	Jason DODD ‡83	
11	Alan THOMPSON #79		7	Matthew LE TISSIER †45	
20	Najwan GHRAYIB		13	Neil MOSS (Gk)	
26	Steve STONE †74		16	James BEATTIE	
39	Peter ENCKELMAN (Gk)		35	Luis BOA MORTE #83	

FACTFILE

Without the services of cup-tied Benito Carbone, Villa reach the quarter-finals of this competition for the first time since 1995-96, when they went on to win the trophy... Steve Watson scores his first goal for the club... Dion Dublin has now matched his haul for the whole of last season, with 11 goals from 19 games so far this season... Thirteen years after their only previous meeting in cup football, Villa avenge the 2-1 defeat to Southampton at The Dell in this competition back in 1986.

Saints reshuffle helps Villa

Whatever their problems in the league, Villa continue to be a different side in cup competition, as the team which deepened their woes in the last game played here is swept aside once Villa discover that they too can still play a bit.

It needs a speculative goal from Steve Watson and a Southampton defensive howler to allow the hosts to breathe easily, but once they do, they end the game playing the type of confident football which bodes well for the future.

Equally helpful to their cause is an enforced Southampton reorganisation which follows an injury to Trond Soltvedt. The Norwegian has to leave the game after colliding with David James in pursuit of a rebound on the stroke of half-time, forcing Mark Hughes out of the forward line and into midfield. The visitors' attack loses most of its teeth as a result.

Southampton start in the same confident manner in which they finished their last outing at Villa Park, with Hassan Kachloul and Marian Pahars having shots blocked as the home defence comes under pressure.

It needs a goal somewhat against the run of play to steady Villa's ship in the 22nd minute. An Alan Wright cross is too deep for Dion Dublin but drops nicely on the head of Steve Watson behind him. The wing-back's looping header looks to be part-hope, part-intent but it arcs perfectly over Paul Jones in the Southampton goal to break the deadlock.

Sparked into life, Villa begin to threaten the Saints' goal more regularly and Joachim is twice released behind the Saints' defence, only to be denied by crucial tackles from Jones and Claus Lundekvam.

The loss of Soltvedt breaks the visitors' spell. Up against some tight marking, Pahars poses much less menace than usual and the lack of height in the forward line is compounded by Southampton's insistence on taking the aerial route when attempting to launch an attack.

Villa open up the game in the 67th minute, when Joachim is on the case after Patrick Colleter fluffs an attempted header back to his goalkeeper. Jones creditably tries to impede Joachim's progress by fair means but the striker is able to take the ball around him and stroke it into an empty net.

It's now just an exhibition game for Villa. Released from the tension which has hampered so many games of late, they need just five more minutes to increase their lead. Centre-back Colin Calderwood sets Watson away down the right and the Geordie's cross finds Dublin, who recovers from a poor first touch to shoot the ball high into the net.

He picks the last meat from the Saints' bones in the last minute, rising high above Dean Richards to head a Wright cross past Jones.

Southampton squander several chances to save a little face as the game enters its closing stages, but these are minor aberrations for the hosts, who have put together a more than competent performance that is a world away from their diffident showing in the last meeting of these teams.

The Worthington Cup is not without its detractors but it continues to keep Aston Villa's season alive.

Colin Calderwood benefits as Saints' striker Marian Pahars overruns the ball

Saturday 4th December 1999 • Villa Park • 3.00pm

ASTON VILLA 0 NEWCASTLE UNITED 1

Half-time 0-0 • *Attendance* 34,531

Referee Mike RILEY (Leeds)

Referee's Assistants A. GREEN and A. BUTLER

Claret and Blue Striped Shirts, Claret Shorts	Goals	Black and White Striped Shirts, Black Shorts	Goals
1 David JAMES		13 Steve HARPER	
3 Alan WRIGHT ❑		8 Franck DUMAS	
4 Gareth SOUTHGATE (c)		9 Alan SHEARER (c)	
6 George BOATENG ❑		10 Silvio MARIC †	
7 Ian TAYLOR		11 Gary SPEED ❑	
9 Dion DUBLIN ‡		14 Temuri KETSBAIA ‡	
12 Julian JOACHIM		15 Nolberto SOLANO #	
15 Gareth BARRY		34 Nikolaos DABIZAS ❑	
17 Lee HENDRIE †		36 Alessandro PISTONE ❑	
24 Mark DELANEY ❑		37 Robert LEE	
34 Colin CALDERWOOD		39 HELDER	
Substitutes		*Substitutes*	
10 Paul MERSON #73		1 Shay GIVEN (Gk)	
11 Alan THOMPSON †9 #		2 Warren BARTON #86	
18 Benito CARBONE ‡51		17 Stephen GLASS	
26 Steve STONE		18 Aaron HUGHES ‡84	
39 Peter ENCKELMAN (Gk)		20 Duncan FERGUSON †58 66	

BEFORE		P	W	D	L	F	A	pts	AFTER		P	W	D	L	F	A	pts
13	Villa	16	5	4	7	14	18	19	14	Newcastle	17	5	4	8	28	30	19
15	Newcastle	16	4	4	8	27	30	16	15	Villa	17	5	4	8	14	19	19

FACTFILE

Villa lose consecutive league games at home for the first time since 21st March 1999... They and Newcastle have not shared a goalless draw since 1924... Steve Watson is ruled out of the game with his old club by a hamstring injury... Villa Park has witnessed just one Villa goal in the league in four games.

Comeback kid breaks Villa hearts

Sixteen months have elapsed since Aston Villa last faced Duncan Ferguson.

In that time, the 6' 3" Scot has changed his club and seen far more of the treatment room than he would have wished, but in the 32 minutes he plays this afternoon, it is just as it was when he lined up for Everton against Villa at Goodison Park on the opening day of last season. Utter torment.

A rare fusion of grace and power for one so tall, Ferguson drove Villa to distraction on that hot summer's day, without managing to score. Now in the famous black and white stripes, he emerges from a year of injury problems to decide the issue on a much colder afternoon, illustrating as he does so why a good big 'un is reckoned to have the better of a good little 'un.

His substitution for Silvio Maric is only eight minutes old when Temuri Ketsbaia, by the Villa defence's own admission, is allowed too much time and space to send a cross over from the right. Like an anaconda, Ferguson flings himself in front of compatriot Colin Calderwood and heads the ball past David James for the game's only goal.

25 minutes remain, but Villa know they are staring up a mountain in more ways than one, the deficit compounded by the fact that their own target man, Dion Dublin, has had to limp out of the game seven minutes before Ferguson strode into it, with a knee injury.

It is a bitter blow for the hosts, who enjoy most of the possession against a Newcastle side which is well-organised, without creating much.

While Dublin's presence as a fulcrum in attack is sorely missed, his replacement Benito Carbone works feverishly to get his side back on terms and it needs a brilliant save by Steve Harper, throwing himself instinctively to his right, to deny the Italian five minutes from full-time, as he gets his head to an Alan Wright cross despite falling backwards while making contact.

Julian Joachim had the chance to give Villa the lead in only the sixth minute of the second half when Newcastle waited for an offside decision as Joachim latched onto a header out of midfield by Alan Thompson with Dion Dublin trotting back towards his own half and adjudged not to be interfering with play by referee Mike Riley.

Joachim takes the ball forward before hesitating and eventually finding Dublin after the latter has completed a U-turn back into the danger zone, but Dion shoots high over the bar.

In the first half, its latter stages played out beneath a downpour, Villa recover from the loss of Lee Hendrie with an ankle injury after just eight minutes, but fritter away much of their possession with a series of crosses too close to the Newcastle keeper.

Colin Calderwood has a sniff of his first goal in Villa colours when Alan Wright fires the ball back into Newcastle's area after a 15th-minute corner. The ball is quickly onto the Scot before he knows it, however, and his instinctive jab is off target.

He will receive an object lesson in the art of taking the half-chance before his day is done.

Benito Carbone has Steve Harper struggling

Saturday 11th December 1999 • Villa Park • 3.00pm

ASTON VILLA 2 DARLINGTON 1

Half-time 1-0 • *Attendance* 22,101

Referee Phil RICHARDS (Preston)

Referee's Assistants D. BABSKI and T. KETTLE

Claret and Blue Striped Shirts, Claret Shorts		Goals	White Shirts with Black Trim, Black Shorts		Goals
1	David JAMES		22	Mark SAMWAYS	
3	Alan WRIGHT		4	Craig LIDDLE	
4	Gareth SOUTHGATE (c)		5	Steve TUTILL (c)	
5	Ugo EHIOGU		6	Neil ASPIN	
7	Ian TAYLOR ❑		8	Martin GRAY ❑ #	
9	Dion DUBLIN	63	9	Peter DUFFIELD	
10	Paul MERSON		11	Brian ATKINSON ❑ †	
11	Alan THOMPSON †		12	Michael OLIVER	
15	Gareth BARRY		15	Paul HECKINGBOTTOM	71
18	Benito CARBONE ‡	43	24	Neil HEANEY	
24	Mark DELANEY		28	Lee NOGAN ‡	
	Substitutes			*Substitutes*	
12	Julian JOACHIM ‡82		2	Adam REED #90	
13	Neil CUTLER (Gk)		3	Phil BRUMWELL †65	
22	Darius VASSELL		17	Jesper HIORTH ‡69	
26	Steve STONE †80		21	John LEAH	
34	Colin CALDERWOOD		32	Keith FINCH (Gk)	

FACTFILE

Villa make history as the opponents of the first-ever 'wild card' in the FA Cup, Darlington having been controversially drawn from among the Second Round losers, to make up the numbers and Villa having been last out of the bag from 63 teams, with Manchester United excused from this season's competition because of the World Club Championship... To free up some space in the calendar for European commitments, the Third Round is moved forward from its traditional early-January date, with disastrous consequences for attendance figures around the country.

Villa survive second-half scare

On a day in the football calendar renowned for upsets, Villa v Darlington is a gilt-edged banana skin surrounded by flashing lights.

A club which is on the up faces a club beset by a crisis of confidence. A team that scored four goals the previous Saturday faces one which boasts two in its previous five league games. To Villa fans, there's a worrying look of the Fulhams about Darlington.

Credit to the hosts, then, for overcoming all this and a knee-knocking 20 minutes in the second half, when the County Durham side bring a contest that looked dead and buried back to its feet. 2-0 down, yet refusing to give up, the Quakers surge forward and some nice inter-passing results in Peter Duffield being tripped as he charges threateningly into the Villa area in the 71st minute.

Duffield's spot-kick is saved by James but Paul Heckingbottom - surely the sort of name that is made for Division Three - is first to the rebound and gleefully cuts Villa's lead to one.

Playing towards a jam-packed visiting fans' enclosure, Darlington proceed to throw everything at their wobbling opponents but Villa grit their teeth and weather the storm, ending the game with much the same control as they had enjoyed earlier, thanks to Benito Carbone and Dion Dublin. The little Italian, whose sparkling debut against Wimbledon has proved a hard act to follow, is delighted to break his scoring duck when he gets a flamboyant goal two minutes from the end of the first half.

Darlington manager David Hodgson will later be stung into a scathing attack on John Gregory when the Villa manager claims his men could have won the game at a canter, but a review of the first half shows that Villa have again lacked a knock-out punch to finish off numerous

chances, and there is relief around the stadium when Carbone gets a flick on by Dion Dublin and sends a looping 20-yard shot into the top corner in the 43rd minute.

It was a goal shortly before the interval that took the wind out of Hull City's sails in this round last season and Villa look to be following the same gameplan when Dublin makes it 2-0, 18 minutes into the second half.

An Alan Thompson corner appears to have gone beyond Dublin, yet he dexterously gets his head around the ball to send an angled header into the goal.

With Paul Merson and Mark Delaney in particular providing some menacing crosses, it has been a good afternoon for Villa in the air, Gareth Barry having a header cleared off the line in the 17th minute.

Darlington are worthy opponents, though. David James' hands are just a little too firm when he parries a 29th minute shot from Neil Heaney, but Duffield is unable to make use of the rebound. 15 minutes later, James is at full stretch to deny Duffield in the visitors' best move of the game, when the striker gets a full-blooded header to a Michael Oliver cross.

The addition of Jesper Hiorth shortly before their goal gives Darlington a cutting edge in attack, but marshalled superbly by Gareth Southgate, Villa hold out for a creditworthy win in difficult circumstances.

It's 'heads I win' for Dion Dublin

Wednesday 15th December 1999 • Upton Park • 7.55pm

WEST HAM UNITED 2 ASTON VILLA 2*

After extra time • Villa lose 5-4 on penalties
Half-time 0-1 • Attendance 23,974

Referee Stephen LODGE (Barnsley)
Referee's Assistants A.C. HARVEY and K.J. HAWKES

Claret and Blue Striped Shirts, White Shorts		Goals	White Shirts with Claret and Blue Sash, Blue Shorts		Goals
1	Shaka HISLOP		1	David JAMES	
6	Neil RUDDOCK		2	Steve WATSON	
7	Marc KELLER		3	Alan WRIGHT	
8	Trevor SINCLAIR		4	Gareth SOUTHGATE (c)	
10	Paolo DI CANIO ❑	90pen	5	Ugo EHIOGU	
11	Steve LOMAS (c) ❑		6	George BOATENG ❑	
12	Paulo WANCHOPE ❑ ‡		7	Ian TAYLOR ❑	4
15	Rio FERDINAND		9	Dion DUBLIN	90
18	Frank LAMPARD	72	10	Paul MERSON †	
26	Joe COLE †		12	Julian JOACHIM ‡	
30	Javier MARGAS ❑		15	Gareth BARRY	

Substitutes			*Substitutes*		
9	Paul KITSON †45		13	Neil CUTLER (Gk)	
13	Marc-Vivien FOE		22	Darius VASSELL ‡112	
20	Scott MINTO		26	Steve STONE †77	
22	Craig FORREST (Gk)		31	Jlloyd SAMUEL	
27	Emmanuel OMOYINMI ‡114		34	Colin CALDERWOOD	

PENALTY SHOOT-OUT				PENALTY SHOOT-OUT			
1	Frank LAMPARD	scored	1-0	1	Steve STONE	scored	1-1
2	Steve LOMAS	scored	2-1	2	Dion DUBLIN	scored	2-2
3	Paolo Di CANIO	scored	3-2	3	Gareth BARRY	scored	3-3
4	Trevor SINCLAIR	saved	3-3	4	Alan WRIGHT	hit bar	3-3
5	Neil RUDDOCK	scored	4-3	5	Ugo EHIOGU	scored	4-4
6	Marc KELLER	scored	5-4	6	Gareth SOUTHGATE	saved	5-4

FACTFILE

* This match was declared void when it was discovered that West Ham United had used an ineligible player, Omoyinmi having played previously in the competition when on loan at Gillingham (appearances/goalscorers not included in statistics). Restaged 11.1.2000.

Broken rule spares Southgate

"It's a very insular and unreal profession," was how ex-striker Lee Chapman once described his line of work. "They tell you when to sleep, when to eat, when to train, when you can drink. As a result most footballers are very irresponsible... they let you down and that is part and parcel of the way they are treated."

It's not the most flattering assessment, but it will survive for a while longer yet, after the unforgettable contribution to this season's Worthington Cup of Manny Omoyinmi.

You wouldn't think it was asking too much of a 22-year-old to familiarise himself with the cup-tied rule and make sure he doesn't play in a cup competition for two teams in the same season.

Apparently, this is beyond Omoyinmi, whose six minutes as a Hammers substitute are later revealed to be an inadvertent encore to the minutes he played when on loan earlier this season, a breach of the rule-book which will ultimately nullify an evening of amazing drama that sees West Ham twice come back from being a goal down, before winning on penalties.

If the Nigerian-born forward won't be getting many Christmas cards from West Ham fans, he might just find one from the Southgate family in his letterbox. Bravely stepping up to take a must-make spot kick after the first five penalties apiece left the teams tied at 4-4, Villa's captain discovers that lightning can indeed strike twice.

His attempt is struck confidently enough but Shaka Hislop is smartly across to his left to

gather the ball. Hammers are in the semi-finals, for the next 72 hours at least, and it's Euro 96 all over again for Southgate.

Villa's players admit later that it doesn't feel like a defeat, and with good reason. Ahead after just four minutes, when Ian Taylor converts a Paul Merson cross following sloppy work by West Ham defender Neil Ruddock, they look rather more convincing than their hosts and their passage to the semis appears booked when Dion Dublin negates Frank Lampard's 73rd minute equaliser, with a grandiose volley on the turn that slams Julian Joachim's last-minute cross into the roof of the net.

The visitors' jubilation is strangled at birth, however, as Paul Kitson goes bundling into the penalty area in the last attack of regulation time. The visitors' defence couldn't have handled plutonium with greater caution, yet still the Hammers man finds someone to bounce off and to Villa's disbelief the referee points to the spot as Kitson hits the turf.

Paolo di Canio converts the penalty with a coolness he will display once more, after a tame session of extra-time makes way for penalties.

Villa spy the first ray of hope as the shoot-out begins, when David James dives to save Trevor Sinclair's penalty, only for the West Ham player's former Blackpool team-mate, Alan Wright, to send the very next spot-kick thundering against the crossbar.

Marc Keller makes it 5-4 to the Hammers as the penalties become sudden death; then Gareth Southgate steps up for what you suspect may be his last penalty kick for some time.

Little do those cat-calling Hammers fans know, however, that the Clanger of the Night award has already been claimed.

Gareth Southgate

Saturday 18th December 1999 • Villa Park • 3.00pm

ASTON VILLA 2 SHEFFIELD WEDNESDAY 1

Half-time 0-1 • *Attendance* 23,885

Referee Steve BENNETT (Orpington)

Referee's Assistants J.A. SHEFFIELD and M.L. SHORT

Claret and Blue Striped Shirts, Claret Shorts		Goals	Blue and White Striped Shirts, Black Shorts		Goals
1	David JAMES		28	Pavel SRNICEK	
2	Steve WATSON		2	Peter ATHERTON (c)	
3	Alan WRIGHT †		4	Wim JONK ‡	
4	Gareth SOUTHGATE (c)		5	Emerson THOME	
5	Ugo EHIOGU		6	Des WALKER	
6	George BOATENG		7	Danny SONNER ❏	
7	Ian TAYLOR ❏	82	10	Andy BOOTH	
9	Dion DUBLIN #		16	Niclas ALEXANDERSSON	
10	Paul MERSON	69	17	Ian NOLAN	
15	Gareth BARRY		23	Gilles DE BILDE	20pen
18	Benito CARBONE ‡		33	Alan QUINN ❏ †	
Substitutes			*Substitutes*		
12	Julian JOACHIM †39		1	Kevin PRESSMAN (Gk)	
13	Neil CUTLER (Gk)		9	Gerald SIBON ‡84	
22	Darius VASSELL ‡81		12	Richard CRESSWELL	
26	Steve STONE		22	Stephen HASLAM †55	
34	Colin CALDERWOOD #85		38	Kevin NICOLSON	

BEFORE		P	W	D	L	F	A	pts	AFTER		P	W	D	L	F	A	pts
15	Villa	17	5	4	8	14	19	19	12	Villa	18	6	4	8	16	20	22
20	Sheff Wed	16	1	3	12	14	40	6	20	Sheff Wed	17	1	3	13	15	42	6

FACTFILE

Leaving the game after an accidental collision with Gerald Sibon, Dion Dublin receives extensive treatment on the touchline and undergoes an operation on Saturday evening to repair damaged vertebrae with bone taken from his hip. Had it been any worse, the injury could have left him in a wheelchair.

The end of the beginning?

On paper, it should take something a little more remarkable than a home win over the team stranded at the foot of the Premiership, to constitute a turning point in Villa's season. Such is the calamity from which they recover, however, that you suspect the inspiration they will take from this game could last for some time.

When a very ordinary Wednesday find themselves a goal up from the penalty spot despite having contributed to the opening 20 minutes like the punchbag contributes to a Lennox Lewis workout, it could easily be the cue for wavering Villa hearts to decide that this really isn't their year and switch to auto-pilot.

Danny Sonner takes a tumble on his way into the penalty area and in the altercation that follows with Ian Taylor, the thought occurs that the Villa midfielder is raging as much at the season as he is at Sonner's creativity in response to a challenge.

Gilles de Bilde scores from the spot, making a mockery of a strong Villa start that saw shots from Gareth Barry, Ugo Ehiogu and Benito Carbone, facing his old club for the first time since joining Villa, peppering the Owls' goal.

Dion Dublin heads against the bar from a Paul Merson free-kick two minutes later, and the furrows on Villa brows only deepen when they have their own chance to get on the scoresheet via a penalty, Alan Quinn handling the ball as the hosts attack down the left in the 33rd minute.

This will be an heroic afternoon for Pavel Srnicek, however, and the big Czech keeper saves well to his left from Dion Dublin's effort.

The signs are no better when the teams swap ends. Villa's passing is ragged, their crossing lacks precision and for once Dublin doesn't enjoy his usual command of the air, with Des

Walker and Emerson Thome defending doggedly at the heart of Wednesday's defence.

Just when it appears that the routine will not suffice against a desperate side with its back to the wall, Paul Merson delivers something from his special reserve that we must hope boosts him as much as his team.

Becalmed in a sporadic season, the midfielder does his hopes of a long-term escape from the subs' bench no harm when he collects a knock-on from Julian Joachim after 68 minutes and curls a shot around Srnicek from the edge of the area with all the aplomb of someone whose side is 4-0 up.

For game-breaking moments such as this, Villa paid Middlesbrough £6.75m, but not even an inspired Merson can escape the clutches of an afternoon of torment. Three minutes later, he has the chance to restore normal service from the penalty spot after Thome is caught doing press-ups on Dublin's shoulders, only for Srnicek to save a firmly struck shot to his right.

Merson's goal has dislodged the notion that doom is pre-ordained for Villa this afternoon, however, and when an unmarked Ian Taylor dives to head home his 82nd minute cross, the mood around Villa Park is more 'que sera' than 'get out of jail'.

Dublin comes under pressure from Thome

Sunday 26th December 1999 • Pride Park • 3.00pm

DERBY COUNTY 0 ASTON VILLA 2

Half-time 0-0 • Attendance 33,222

Referee Alan WILKIE (Chester-le-Street)
Referee's Assistants J. ROSS and R. BONE

White Shirts, Black Shorts		Goals	Claret and Blue Striped Shirts, Claret Shorts		Goals
21	Mart POOM		1	David JAMES	
4	Darryl POWELL (c)		2	Steve WATSON	
5	Tony DORIGO †		3	Alan WRIGHT	
7	Seth JOHNSON		4	Gareth SOUTHGATE (c)	
9	Deon BURTON #		5	Ugo EHIOGU	
14	Lars BOHINEN ‡		6	George BOATENG	69
16	Jacob LAURSEN		7	Ian TAYLOR	78
17	Spencer PRIOR ❏		10	Paul MERSON ‡	
19	Steve ELLIOTT		12	Julian JOACHIM	
33	Craig BURLEY		15	Gareth BARRY	
35	Branko STRUPAR ❏		18	Benito CARBONE †	

Substitutes			Substitutes		
1	Russell HOULT (Gk)		13	Neil CUTLER (Gk)	
2	Horacio CARBONARI		20	Najwan GHRAYIB	
3	Stefan SCHNOOR †45		22	Darius VASSELL †57	
12	Malcolm CHRISTIE ‡66		26	Steve STONE ‡76 ❏	
26	Marvin ROBINSON #76		34	Colin CALDERWOOD	

BEFORE		P	W	D	L	F	A	pts	AFTER		P	W	D	L	F	A	pts
12	Villa	18	6	4	8	16	20	22	12	Villa	19	7	4	8	18	20	25
18	Derby	18	4	3	11	16	29	15	18	Derby	19	4	3	12	16	31	15

FACTFILE

Villa's first clean sheet in four games... Ian Taylor has goals in back-to-back games for the first time since 17th March 1998... Dion Dublin misses his first game since the Worthington Cup visit to Chester... Villa win three straight games (all competitions) for the first time since 21st September.

Supersub striker turns provider

All that stuff about travelling hopefully being better than arriving wears thin when you're four months without a league win on the road, so while the opposition is admittedly a struggling side in woeful form at home, Villa's joy is nevertheless unconfined as they take maximum points from a second consecutive game.

If it's Ian Taylor and George Boateng who continue the midfield's run of goal-getting form, however, it's substitute striker Darius Vassell who tees up both goals within a nine minute stretch of the second half.

The young forward is aching to add some fresh press cuttings to his scrapbook after his match-winning performance against Strømsgodset last season, but he does his burgeoning reputation no harm at all with a confident display, after replacing Benito Carbone in the 56th minute.

A mediocre first half by the visitors is forgotten the moment Vassell surges towards County goal in the 69th minute, threading the ball through to Boateng, who hits Premiership goal number one for his latest club with a left-foot drive past Mart Poom in the Derby goal.

Nine minutes later, it's game set and match for Villa, when Vassell shows he has patience to go with his exuberance, as he bides his time in search of an opening, before sending in a cross from the left which Taylor heads home, diving in front of Derby's Seth Johnson.

When you're missing Giorgi Kinkladze and Rory Delap, and staring home defeat number 10 in the face, your chances of tearing the stuffing out of that kind of cushion are nil, and Derby can only tread water as Gareth Southgate and Ugo Ehiogu seal off all valves at the back.

The hosts' best chance had been before the break, when Carbone and Julian Joachim were the ones hammering in vain at a solid defence. County skipper Darryl Powell saw two shots deflected to safety and Spencer Prior was left kicking himself when unable so much as to hit the target when gifted a free header from a 22nd minute corner kick.

After the interval, Villa serve early notice of a swing in the game's momentum when Carbone shoots wide and Poom pushes away a Joachim effort while at full stretch.

The Estonian keeper gives his side further hope with a superb double save, deflecting a Joachim shot onto the post and scrambling to his feet in time to deny Alan Wright after Carbone set up the defender from the rebound.

Then comes the hassle from Vassell that finally makes the home side wilt, although once again, no one can accuse manager, John Gregory of allowing his players to get too full of themselves.

"We know he has a lot of ability. It's just a question of whether or not he can produce it consistently and do it for 90 minutes," says the manager afterwards, when quizzed on Vassell's chances of a starting role against Spurs in three days' time. "He switched off for the last 10 minutes today and thought the game was over. He's very wet behind the ears, but we feel we can get more out of him." What they got this afternoon was more than enough.

Supersub – Darius Vassell

Wednesday 29th December 1999 • Villa Park • 7.45pm

ASTON VILLA 1 TOTTENHAM HOTSPUR 1

Half-time 0-1 • *Attendance* 39,217

Referee Graham BARBER (Tring)

Referee's Assistants C. BASSINDALE and D. DRYSDALE

Claret and Blue Striped Shirts, Claret Shorts		Goals	White Shirts, Navy Blue Shorts		Goals
1	David JAMES		1	Ian WALKER	
2	Steve WATSON		2	Stephen CARR	
3	Alan WRIGHT ‡		3	Mauricio TARICCO	
4	Gareth SOUTHGATE (c)		5	Sol CAMPBELL (c)	
5	Ugo EHIOGU		6	Chris PERRY	
6	George BOATENG		8	Tim SHERWOOD	44
7	Ian TAYLOR ❏	75	10	Steffen IVERSEN ❏	
10	Paul MERSON		14	David GINOLA	
12	Julian JOACHIM		16	Chris ARMSTRONG	
15	Gareth BARRY		22	Allan NIELSEN †	
18	Benito CARBONE †		25	Stephen CLEMENCE	
	Substitutes			*Substitutes*	
8	Mark DRAPER		13	Espen BAARDSEN (Gk)	
13	Neil CUTLER (Gk)		15	Ramon VEGA	
22	Darius VASSELL †65		20	Jose DOMINGUEZ	
26	Steve STONE ‡73		21	Luke YOUNG †83	
34	Colin CALDERWOOD		27	Mark GOWER	

BEFORE		P	W	D	L	F	A	pts	AFTER		P	W	D	L	F	A	pts
6	Spurs	18	9	3	6	30	22	30	6	Spurs	19	9	4	6	31	23	31
12	Villa	19	7	4	8	18	20	25	12	Villa	20	7	5	8	19	21	26

FACTFILE

Ian Taylor scores his third goal in as many games... Villa concede no more than one goal for the seventh successive game... Spurs still waiting for their first league win at Villa Park since 1986-87.

Villa hardly make their point

Only the Sheriff of Nottingham can have disliked Sherwood more than Aston Villa do.

Consider the exploits of a certain midfielder on the last three occasions he has had Villa in his cross-hairs: 17th January 1998 - Blackburn Rovers 5 Aston Villa 0. Tim Sherwood opens the scoring for Rovers after 21 minutes. 26th December 1998 - Blackburn Rovers 2 Aston Villa 1. Tim Sherwood scores the winner with two minutes left. 13th March 1999 - Tottenham Hotspur 1 Aston Villa 0. Tim Sherwood scores the winner with one minute left.

Given the recurrent theme, Villa could be said to have partly stopped the rot in the latest chapter, earning a point in spite of Sherwood's first-half goal. The statistics offer just a fragment of the story, however, for so dominant are the hosts in their final game of the 20th century that a solitary point feels as unpalatable as the wrong end of a hammering.

The kind of bumper crowd that has been in danger of becoming a distant memory at Villa Park this season is rewarded with a dazzling performance by Villa, who could have easily gone into half-time with a 2-0 lead, but for superb work by Spurs' goalkeeper Ian Walker and full-back Stephen Carr.

Instead, the hosts are left fuming, as that man Sherwood puts the Londoners in front with a goal out of nothing on the stroke of half-time. Collecting a square pass from David Ginola just inside Villa territory, his opportunistic shot from a full 35 yards arrives in the net via the underside of the crossbar.

The home side understandably take a while to recover their momentum after the interval, as Ginola begins to exert an influence and the game opens up. Villa are indebted to David James for keeping them in a game that they

eventually tie-up after 74 minutes, when Ian Taylor gets the drop on Chris Perry and is first to a Paul Merson cross, which he sidefoots home from close range.

The Villa midfielder was owed one, after he looked poised to reap the rewards of his team's first half barrage. Julian Joachim has already made a thorough nuisance of himself in the Tottenham penalty area when his 17th minute shot is parried by Walker to Taylor's feet. The goal yawns sumptuously in front of the Villa midfielder but Carr hurls himself into a last-ditch tackle which is just enough to block what had looked a certain goal.

Five minutes before the interval, it is Walker's turn to earn the applause of the visiting supporters. Filling in admirably as an aerial target man in the absence of Dion Dublin, Taylor meets a Merson free-kick which he heads across the face of goal. Joachim's own header is textbook, downwards and towards the corner, but there are shades of Gordon Banks' legendary save from Pele in the way Walker plummets to his right to claw the ball away, with Ugo Ehiogu unable to get to the rebound.

And so Villa must make do with a measly point, 100 years after they finished the 19th century with a 4-2 win over Sunderland.

Sunderland, of course, didn't have one Tim Sherwood playing for them.

Carbone gets the elbow

Monday 3rd January 2000 • Elland Road • 3.00pm

LEEDS UNITED 1 ASTON VILLA 2

Half-time 0-1 • Attendance 40,027

Referee Uriah RENNIE (Sheffield)

Referee's Assistants M.A. COOPER and S.R. BRAND

White Shirts, White Shorts		Goals	Claret and Blue Striped Shirts, Claret Shorts		Goals
1	Nigel MARTYN		1	David JAMES	
2	Gary KELLY (c)		2	Steve WATSON ❑	
3	Ian HARTE ❑		3	Alan WRIGHT	
4	Alf Inge HAALAND		4	Gareth SOUTHGATE (c)	18,62
6	Jonathan WOODGATE		5	Ugo EHIOGU	
8	Michael BRIDGES		6	George BOATENG ❑	
10	Harry KEWELL	46	10	Paul MERSON ❑	
17	Alan SMITH ‡		12	Julian JOACHIM	
19	Eirik BAKKE		15	Gareth BARRY	
20	Matthew JONES †		18	Benito CARBONE ❑ †	
22	Michael DUBERRY ❑		26	Steve STONE	
Substitutes			*Substitutes*		
12	Darren HUCKERBY ‡76		8	Mark DRAPER	
13	Paul ROBINSON (Gk)		13	Neil CUTLER (Gk)	
16	Jason WILCOX †76		20	Najwan GHRAYIB	
18	Danny MILLS		22	Darius VASSELL †80 ❑	
21	Martin HIDEN		34	Colin CALDERWOOD	

BEFORE		P	W	D	L	F	A	pts	AFTER		P	W	D	L	F	A	pts
1	Leeds	20	14	2	4	34	22	44	1	Leeds	21	14	2	5	35	24	44
12	Villa	20	7	5	8	19	21	26	10	Villa	21	8	5	8	21	22	29

FACTFILE

Unbeaten run at Elland Road extends to five games... They record back-to-back league wins away from home for the first time since 2nd May 1998... Gareth Southgate increases his Villa career goal count by 50%, scoring for the first time since his goal against Sheffield Wednesday on 28th December 1998.

Southgate strikes to stun United

It's hard to know which is more sensational, three points at the home of the Premiership's young pretenders or two goals that transform Gareth Southgate from penalty-spot pauper to the emperor of open play.

Disconsolate after his missed penalty kick seemed to have consigned Villa to the League Cup dustbin just three weeks earlier, the Villa defender twice pops up in the Leeds box to bang in a brace of goals that reduce a fabulous 30-yard score by Leeds' Australian striker Harry Kewell to a sideshow, and confirm that there is nothing illusory about Villa's revival.

With both sides missing key players, it is Villa who adapt the better, George Boateng, Paul Merson and Steve Stone swallowing up the midfield gap left by Ian Taylor's absence through suspension and never allowing their hosts to settle.

Villa go ahead after 18 minutes, when South-gate collects the ball from a Merson corner and mishits a shot that dribbles over the goalline.

If his first goal in 12 months is important as a nerve-settler, his second, 44 minutes later, is invaluable, as it snuffs out a Leeds revival that had begun almost contemporaneously with the second half.

If Leeds are missing Lee Bowyer, David Hopkin, Lucas Radebe and David Batty, they still have Harry Kewell, who adds another coat of gloss to his penchant for panache when he intercepts a Boateng pass and blasts a 30-yard shot past David James with the second half just 14 seconds old.

Just as he did against Spurs five days earlier, James then plays a vital role in ensuring that a shift of momentum to the opposition doesn't become an avalanche. The Villa keeper saves from Alan Smith five minutes after Kewell's goal, when the young Englishman looks certain to score and it draws the Yorkshire club's sting.

In the 62nd minute, Paul Merson sends a free kick towards the United goal and Southgate emerges from the throng once more to put an angled header just inside the far post.

"They were the two worst goals you could wish to see," the Villa captain says later, "but I was pleased to get away from my marker on both occasions, and the way Nigel Martyn is playing, it needed a couple of mishits to get past him!"

At his usual end of the field, Southgate is no less effective, as he, Ugo Ehiogu and Gareth Barry restrict Leeds to just a handful of chances, while the visitors dominate the first half.

Benito Carbone has a 25-yard effort saved by Martyn, who will spare his side further blushes after the interval when he tips away Merson's header from a Watson cross, before recovering quickly to deflect a Boateng shot for a corner.

The damage is done with Southgate's second goal, though. Leeds show no signs of being able to redeem the situation a second time and must now hope their season is not about to embark on the kind of second-half stutter that afflicted their opponents 12 months ago.

No such worries for Villa, this year, however. A team transformed, they can face mid-winter with relish this time around, none more so than their captain.

**George Boateng –
strong in midfield**

Saturday 8th January 2000 • Villa Park • 3.00pm

ASTON VILLA 1 SOUTHAMPTON 0

Half-time 1-0 • *Attendance* 25,487

Referee Neale BARRY (Scunthorpe)
Referee's Assistants D. DRYSDALE and A.S. HOGG

Claret and Blue Striped Shirts, Claret Shorts	Goals	Red and White Striped Shirts, Black Shorts	Goals
1 David JAMES		1 Paul JONES	
2 Steve WATSON †		2 Jason DODD (c) ‡	
3 Alan WRIGHT		4 Chris MARSDEN †	
4 Gareth SOUTHGATE (c) 19		5 Claus LUNDEKVAM ❏	
5 Ugo EHIOGU		10 Kevin DAVIES ❏	
6 George BOATENG		14 Stuart RIPLEY	
7 Ian TAYLOR		15 Francis BENALI	
10 Paul MERSON ‡		17 Marian PAHARS #	
12 Julian JOACHIM #		18 Wayne BRIDGE	
15 Gareth BARRY		21 Jo TESSEM	
18 Benito CARBONE ❏		35 Luis BOA MORTE	
Substitutes		*Substitutes*	
13 Neil CUTLER (Gk)		9 Mark HUGHES #71	
17 Lee HENDRIE ‡71		13 Neil MOSS (Gk)	
20 Najwan GHRAYIB		24 Patrick COLLETER	
22 Darius VASSELL #80		30 Hassan KACHLOUL ‡66 ❏	
26 Steve STONE †68		32 Trond SOLTVEDT †45	

FACTFILE

Villa's remarkable FA Cup sequence goes on. Since 1989, they have reached the Fifth Round in 'even' years, while they have never done so in 'odd' years... Villa's fifth clean sheet in six cup-ties this season... Gareth Southgate now has his best-ever haul of goals for Villa, beating the two he scored in his first season at Villa Park.

**Gareth
Southgate**

Saints flattered by scoreline

For the second home game in a row, Villa leave the field wondering what happened to all the other goals they might have scored.

This time, victory notwithstanding, the query is all the more pointed. While Spurs offered flashes of skill to keep Villa on their toes, a Southampton team bereft of enterprise is little more than a punchbag and could have had no complaints if the game produced the same 4-0 scoreline as when these teams last met.

Their one plus point is a dogged defensive organisation, particularly in the first half, which soaks up punishment like a gnarled old sparring partner. Unfortunately for the Saints, they have no answer to the goal machine that is Gareth Southgate.

The captain had just four goals to his name for Villa six days ago yet suddenly he is the club's leading scorer for the millennium. No wonder the Holte End starts chanting 'shoot, shoot' every time he gets possession, even when in his own half.

This afternoon's contribution, as he acknowledges later, is something of a 'belt and braces' job, as he applies the finishing touch to a header from Ian Taylor that appears to be on its way into the net already. "You know what we poachers are like...," says a tongue-in-cheek Southgate after the game.

The goal comes after 19 minutes of largely one-way traffic that sees Taylor, Julian Joachim and Benito Carbone go close, while Alan Wright spurns a glorious chance when the ball breaks to him in the Southampton penalty box.

An unnecessary free kick is conceded by Claus Lundekvam on the left and is punished by a Paul Merson free kick that picks out Taylor at the far post, from which Southgate puts the hosts in front.

Southampton would kill for just a sniff of such moments in front of goal. Still recovering from flu, Marian Pahars is a shadow of his normal self and Kevin Davies, back at The Dell after his goal famine for Blackburn Rovers, is prominent only via a series of crunching tackles when dropping back to help out with his side's formidable rearguard action.

It cannot be be a terribly invigorating existence, toiling to stop goals when your own chances of scoring them are non-existent, but Saints set about it with some relish, Lundekvam diving in to stop Gareth Barry's shot at an open goal after Joachim beats Jones to a loose ball shortly before half-time.

Lundekvam is an accomplished defender and central to Saints' continued diligence after the break, as Villa struggle to find the rhythm their dominance would normally guarantee.

Either side of Taylor slamming a powerful header against the bar in the 57th minute from Merson's cross, Paul Jones saves from Joachim, who has broken behind the defence, and then tips a 25-yard effort from Carbone over the bar.

Joachim has another good chance in the 73rd minute when Francis Benali makes a pig's ear of a simple back-pass, but the Villa man's shot slips wide of the far post.

This makes it five games since a Villa striker scored, but with the team's unbeaten record now standing at six games, only the hardened sceptics are complaining.

Pick that one out!!

Tuesday 11th January 2000 • Upton Park • 7.45pm

WEST HAM UNITED 1 ASTON VILLA 3

After extra time
Half-time 0-0 • Full time 1-1 • Attendance 25,592
Referee Jeff WINTER (Stockton-on-Tees)
Referee's Assistants S.R. GAGEN and T.J. POLLARD

Claret and Blue Shirts, White Shorts	Goals	Turquoise Shirts with Black Trim, Black Shorts	Goals
1 Shaka HISLOP		1 David JAMES ❑	
4 Steve POTTS †		2 Steve WATSON ‡	
5 Igor STIMAC ❑		3 Alan WRIGHT	
8 Trevor SINCLAIR ‡		4 Gareth SOUTHGATE (c)	
10 Paolo DI CANIO ❑		5 Ugo EHIOGU	
11 Steve LOMAS (c)		6 George BOATENG #	
13 Marc-Vivien FOE		7 Ian TAYLOR ❑	80,118
15 Rio FERDINAND		10 Paul MERSON †	
18 Frank LAMPARD	47	12 Julian JOACHIM	94
20 Scott MINTO		15 Gareth BARRY	
26 Joe COLE		26 Steve STONE	
Substitutes		*Substitutes*	
6 Neil RUDDOCK †91		11 Alan THOMPSON ‡68	
7 Marc KELLER ‡108		13 Neil CUTLER (Gk)	
21 Michael CARRICK		22 Darius VASSELL †55	
30 Javier MARGAS		24 Mark DELANEY	
32 Stephen BYWATER (Gk)		34 Colin CALDERWOOD #102	

FACTFILE

Villa reach the semi-finals of this competition for the first time in four years... Julian Joachim's goal is the first scored by a Villa striker in six games... Villa's last five games with West Ham have ended all square after 90 minutes.

Two goal Ian Taylor

Hammers curse a sub too Manny

Football's glossary will need to come up with the antithesis of 'supersub', after West Ham pay the full price for Manny Omoyinmi's fateful introduction late in the first edition of this restaged quarter-final tie.

How many thousands of pounds were lost as a result of the cup-tied forward's appearance is something those in charge of the London club would rather not contemplate, as they watch two goals from Ian Taylor condemn them to an exit from the competition.

Up until the 80th minute of this game, it seemed Omoyinmi might be able to return to the East End of London without the need for a false beard and dark glasses after all, as Frank Lampard's goal two minutes into the second half looks set to be the difference between the equally matched teams.

An inch-perfect pass from Steve Lomas in midfield, sent Lampard running clear of the Villa defence down the inside-right channel and as David James advanced to the edge of his area in an attempt to intercept, Lampard coolly chipped the ball over the oncoming keeper and into the far corner of the net.

Villa are far from convincing in their return to Upton Park. Initially packing their midfield with six bodies in a fruitless attempt to shackle the industrious Lampard and Joe Cole, they leave Julian Joachim on his own up front and it is ultimately down to a midfielder to transform the game and perpetuate Villa's mid-season purple patch.

Having laid on his captain's goal against Southampton in the previous game, Taylor finds the compliment being returned in this one, as Gareth Southgate gets his head to an Alan Thompson corner and feeds Taylor, who volleys the equaliser 10 minutes from time.

Villa have suddenly become a different team. With extra time looming, Thompson just fails to preclude it when his rasping 20 yard shot is tipped narrowly over by Hammers' goalkeeper Shaka Hislop.

The hosts' reprieve lasts just four minutes, however. In the first period of extra time, Julian Joachim puts Villa in front from another set-piece, as Ugo Ehiogu nods Gareth Barry's free-kick towards the unmarked striker, who is in prime position in front of the Hammers' goal, to head firmly past Hislop from six yards.

Even now, this four-hour saga refuses to go quietly. Paolo Di Canio gets some long and meaningful looks from David James when he tumbles to the floor after the Villa keeper dives at his feet in the penalty area. If James feels a victim of the performing arts, he gains instant retribution at the resultant spot-kick, diving to his right to deny Di Canio, who claims later that it is the first penalty kick he has ever missed.

The life has finally gone from Harry Redknapp's men and there is an element of formality in the game's final goal, when Taylor doubles his tally for the night, after being put through in the West Ham area by Joachim, two minutes from the final whistle.

"We just kept going," Taylor admits afterwards. "I think we were on our last reserves, I know I was, but the lads showed a never-say-die attitude."

Villa opt for a 3-5-2 formation in the second half, with Merson partnering Joachim in attack, yet the visitors are still adjusting to their new shape when Frank Lampard finds the net.

It is one of the few occasions Hammers find the finish to go with their approach and when the going gets tough, it is the Londoners who blink first.

"It looks like our name could well be on the cup because of the luck we're having," is Ian Taylor's view; an opinion it's hard to argue with.

Saturday 15th January 2000 • Upton Park • 3.00pm

WEST HAM UNITED 1 ASTON VILLA 1

Half-time 0-1 • *Attendance* 24,237
Referee Graham POLL (Tring)
Referee's Assistants G. BEALE and L. CABLE

Claret and Blue Striped Shirts, Claret Shorts		Goals	Turquoise Shirts with Black Trim, Black Shorts		Goals
1	Shaka HISLOP		1	David JAMES	
5	Igor STIMAC ❑		3	Alan WRIGHT	
7	Marc KELLER		4	Gareth SOUTHGATE (c)	
8	Trevor SINCLAIR		5	Ugo EHIOGU	
10	Paolo DI CANIO	78	6	George BOATENG ‡	
11	Steve LOMAS (c)		7	Ian TAYLOR	24
12	Paulo WANCHOPE		10	Paul MERSON	
15	Rio FERDINAND		12	Julian JOACHIM	
18	Frank LAMPARD		15	Gareth BARRY	
26	Joe COLE		18	Benito CARBONE †	
30	Javier MARGAS		26	Steve STONE	
	Substitutes			*Substitutes*	
2	Gary CHARLES		11	Alan THOMPSON	
6	Neil RUDDOCK		13	Neil CUTLER (Gk)	
20	Scott MINTO		22	Darius VASSELL †80	
21	Michael CARRICK		24	Mark DELANEY	
22	Craig FORREST (Gk)		34	Colin CALDERWOOD ‡80	

BEFORE		P	W	D	L	F	A	pts	AFTER		P	W	D	L	F	A	pts
10	Villa	21	8	5	8	21	22	29	10	Villa	22	8	6	8	22	23	30
11	West Ham	20	7	7	6	24	23	28	11	West Ham	21	7	8	6	25	24	29

FACTFILE

Villa's unbeaten run stretches to eight games... Ian Taylor's goal gives him nine for the season to date, equalling his season-high as a Villa player, set in 1997-98... Villa are quoted by William Hills as 6-4 favourites to win the Worthington Cup.

Revenge of sorts for Hammers

Faced with the flak David James took at Anfield, it's not hard to imagine most keepers being reduced to goalline-bound shrinking violets for the rest of their careers.

One of the most impressive features of James' performances since becoming Villa's number one in the summer, however, has been his refusal to be entombed by the past.

The big keeper's confidence in commanding his area and attacking crosses has been positively inspirational this season, but today he learns the truth of the adage about those who live by the sword.

The law of averages decree that the more you go to the well, the greater the chance that you will one day find it empty and those averages balance to telling effect out this afternoon, as James finds three deliveries from the flanks slipping out of his grasp.

The first two are cleared by his defenders but the third falls to a West Ham forward, who hooks the ball home from 12 yards to cancel out Ian Taylor's 24th-minute goal with just 13 minutes left on the clock.

Of all people, that forward had to be Paolo Di Canio.

After the Italian won a penalty against James in controversial circumstances just four days earlier, there is history between these two, and it erupts at the final whistle, when James' despondency is not improved by the sight of Di Canio offering to shake his hand.

The offer is declined, which is the Italian's cue to switch from bonhomie to belligerence and only the intervention of Colin Calderwood prevents an ugly ending to the game.

For Villa, it is bad enough as it is. They had swept to a half-time lead with some confident, purposeful football that saw Taylor put them

ahead with a close-range shot, after Julian Joachim and Benito Carbone had worked the ball across from the right.

The interval takes the wind from their sails for some reason and they are on the defensive for much of the second half, with Steve Stone slotting in at right wingback, while his fellow Geordie Steve Watson is rested.

After Di Canio has given the hosts fresh hope, Marc Keller brings a good save out of James with a fierce shot and Steve Lomas shoots narrowly over late in the game.

In between, Paolo Wanchope completes a wretched afternoon, heading against the woodwork, having missed one of the sitters of the season in the first half, when he somehow contrived to turn a cross over the bar when it looked easier to score.

"It's a sign of how far Aston Villa have come in the last month that we're all disappointed to have to settle for a point", reflected John Gregory after the game.

"That's the standard we have set ourselves in this last few weeks and there were a lot of very dejected players in our dressing room after the game.

"As for David James, he has played almost 30 games since he joined us and has been truly outstanding. If he only has one bad game in every 30, I'll be perfectly happy."

Benito Carbone – set up Dion Dublin's goal

Saturday 22nd January 2000 • Villa Park • 3.00pm

ASTON VILLA 0 CHELSEA 0

Half-time 0-0 • *Attendance* 33,704

Referee Alan WILKIE (Chester-le-Street)
Referee's Assistants J. ROSS and A. BUTLER

Claret and Blue Striped Shirts, Claret Shorts	Goals	White Shirts with Blue Trim, White Shorts	Goals
1 David JAMES		1 Ed DE GOEY	
2 Steve WATSON ‡		5 Frank LEBOEUF †	
3 Alan WRIGHT		7 Didier DESCHAMPS	
4 Gareth SOUTHGATE (c)		8 Gustavo POYET ‡	
5 Ugo EHIOGU		9 Chris SUTTON #	
6 George BOATENG		11 Dennis WISE (c)	
7 Ian TAYLOR		20 Jody MORRIS	
10 Paul MERSON		21 Bernard LAMBOURDE	
12 Julian JOACHIM †		30 Emerson THOME	
15 Gareth BARRY		31 George WEAH	
18 Benito CARBONE		34 Jon HARLEY	

Substitutes		*Substitutes*	
11 Alan THOMPSON		4 Jes HOGH †53	
13 Neil CUTLER (Gk)		18 Gabriele AMBROSETTI	
22 Darius VASSELL †45 #		19 Tore Andre FLO ‡74	
24 Mark DELANEY ‡59		23 Carlo CUDICINI (Gk)	
26 Steve STONE #63		25 Gianfranco ZOLA #74	

BEFORE		P	W	D	L	F	A	pts	AFTER		P	W	D	L	F	A	pts
6	Chelsea	22	10	6	6	31	22	36	6	Chelsea	23	10	7	6	31	22	37
10	Villa	22	8	6	8	22	23	30	9	Villa	23	8	7	8	22	23	31

Villa's first goalless draw since their game at Everton in November and their first at home since Liverpool visited in October... They are winless v Chelsea in their last four games... It's goodbye to Mark Draper, who goes on loan to Spanish side Rayo Vallecano until the end of the season, with a view to a permanent move.

Blues lucky to take a point

Beaten by 9-2 on aggregate over their three meetings with Chelsea in 1998-99, Villa can take much heart from reducing their nemesis of a year ago to the level of mere mortals, even if they must again settle for a single point.

In one respect, though, the Blues steal the limelight once more, unveiling recent signing George Weah before the Villa Park crowd, just weeks after his arrival from *Serie A* giants, AC Milan. Like a typical game in the Italian league, Weah is quiet for long periods before bursting into life and almost finding the winner.

Twice in the last three minutes, the Liberian has his moment, flicking a header from a Didier Deschamps cross towards the top corner and then breaking behind the Villa defence to find himself with just the goalkeeper to beat.

That goalkeeper, however, is David James, who makes amends with interest for his lapse at Upton Park a week earlier. He flings himself to his right to tip Weah's header over the bar and then charges out to smother the striker's one-on-one, before Alan Wright clears the danger.

Weah had started as he finished, jinking past George Boateng in the 5th minute with an agility surprising for such a big man, before screwing his shot wide of the near post from an acute angle.

Fourteen minutes later, he is round Ugo Ehiogu and stroking the ball just past James' far post. It's a busy spell for the Villa keeper, who is almost lobbed by Jon Harley a minute later from all of 30 yards.

Villa, too, have their chances, one of them almost gifted by Chelsea goalkeeper Ed de Goey, who comes within centimetres of dragging a backpass from Emerson Thome over his own goalline just 17 minutes into the game, before booting the ball to safety.

Villa's central defensive unit threatens to maintain its current run of contributions to the scoresheet in the first half, when both Gareth Southgate and Ugo Ehiogu have shots blocked. The visitors intervene once again to block a Merson shot following De Goey's poorly-punched clearance. This time, however, the ball deflects to Benito Carbone, who is close to goal but at an acute angle and can only send his shot wide of the far post.

It's a far from convincing performance in their own area by Chelsea and de Goey is lucky to have no Villa players in close attendance when he can only swat a Merson free kick in front of him 12 minutes before half-time.

If it's hard going on the ground, it's considerably easier in the air for Chelsea, with Leboeuf and Thome dominant as the lack of height in the hosts' attack begins to tell after the break.

The Frenchman leaves the game with an injury after he is accidentally caught by Villa sub Darius Vassell, who departs himself soon afterwards, after injuring an ankle while attempting to keep the ball in play.

Despite his departure, Villa continue to keep their opponents in reverse gear but are left with nothing to show from a succession of crosses, Ugo Ehiogu missing a golden chance to head Villa in front from a Merson free kick and Southgate being just inches away from an Alan Wright daisycutter.

Dennis Wise is in the way as George Boateng chases the ball

Tuesday 25th January 2000 • Villa Park • 7.45pm

ASTON VILLA 0 LEICESTER CITY 0

Half-time 0-0 • *Attendance* 28,037

Referee Terry HEILBRON (County Durham)

Referee's Assistants P.V. NORMAN and G.A. HALL

Claret and Blue Striped Shirts, Claret Shorts	Goals	Yellow Shirts with Blue Trim, Blue Shorts	Goals
1 David JAMES		1 Tim FLOWERS	
2 Steve WATSON ‡		3 Frank SINCLAIR	
3 Alan WRIGHT		4 Gerry TAGGART	
4 Gareth SOUTHGATE (c)		6 Muzzy IZZET ‡	
5 Ugo EHIOGU		9 Emile HESKEY ❏	
6 George BOATENG		11 Steve GUPPY †	
7 Ian TAYLOR		14 Robbie SAVAGE	
10 Paul MERSON		15 Phil GILCHRIST	
12 Julian JOACHIM		18 Matt ELLIOTT (c)	
15 Gareth BARRY		24 Andrew IMPEY #	
26 Steve STONE †		29 Stefan OAKES	

Substitutes		*Substitutes*	
11 Alan THOMPSON		5 Steve WALSH ‡74	
13 Neil CUTLER (Gk)		16 Stuart CAMPBELL #83	
19 Richard WALKER †57		21 Graham FENTON	
24 Mark DELANEY ‡57		22 Pegguy ARPHEXAD (Gk)	
34 Colin CALDERWOOD		37 Theo ZAGORAKIS †65	

Villa involved in two straight goalless draws for the first time since 26th October 1998 (Athletic Bilbao and Arsenal)... Richard Walker's first senior appearance since 28th December 1997, versus Leeds... Villa announce a £26m partnership with cable TV giants NTL.

FACTFILE

Richard Walker – a rare senior appearance

Aston Villa Review 2000

Advantage Foxes as Villa thwarted

A leg-break and deep extra cover combine to dash Villa hopes, as Leicester negotiate the away leg of this local showdown to boost their chances of a third League Cup Final in four seasons.

Villa dominance in the face of a blanket City defence looks to have finally paid off when Ian Taylor flings himself into a low-level flight-path to get a glancing header to a 62nd minute cross from Paul Merson.

With goalkeeper Tim Flowers beaten, the ball seems destined to find the far corner of the goal, only to take a wicked bounce and sneak by on the wrong side of the post.

Villa's fears that the Leicester jinx remains are confirmed four minutes later. Richard Walker looks set to celebrate his first senior Villa appearance in 26 months in style, when he climbs at the far post to head a Merson free kick back across the face of goal. It is met by an authoritative volley from Gareth Southgate, only for Flowers to hurl himself low to his right to tip the ball to safety.

It is the last major thrust from a Villa offensive that had increased in ferocity after the interval, only to be denied by City's massed ranks in their own half. The visitors do their job effectively enough for John Gregory to stoke up the fires for the second leg after the final whistle, when he sardonically expresses the hope that Leicester might be so good as to venture across the half-way line occasionally when battle is rejoined in a week's time.

Not that they are without their chances this evening. A long-range lob from 30 yards out by Theo Zagorakis in the final minute of the game looks capable of just sneaking beneath the bar, but David James is alert to the threat.

In contrast to the last 30 minutes, the game's opening phase was a timid affair, with 17 minutes ticking by before either side could manage a shot.

Julian Joachim is chivvied off the ball by a posse of defenders, after Ian Taylor has put him through, and the striker later opts for a conservative shot when a further advance into the area might have produced greater dividends, when he runs onto a misplaced header from Andy Impey.

Steve Stone almost benefits from another Foxes error when he seizes on a wayward pass from City's Gerry Taggart, only to watch his shot being deflected to safety.

David James is limited to keeping out a curling free kick from Stefan Oakes, meanwhile, and then throwing himself on the ball at Emile Heskey's feet when the big forward is put through by Muzzy Izzet.

Heskey is a constant threat in Leicester's rare attacks, although he is arguably fortunate to remain on the pitch when his leading arm crashes into Gareth Barry's head as the two contest a header.

Physical and uncompromising, Leicester's gameplan earns them little in the way of rave reviews from home fans, but it does its job in an unspectacular contest.

Villa's sole consolation as they look to Filbert Street is that their rivals at least have no away goals to sharpen their edge; just an ongoing ability to drive Villa to distraction.

Matt Elliott gives Gareth the cold shoulder

Sunday 30th January 2000 • Villa Park • 2.00pm

ASTON VILLA 3 LEEDS UNITED 2

Half-time 1-2 • Attendance 30,026

Referee Graham BARBER (Tring)

Referee's Assistants R.R. SHARP and M.A. WILLIAMS

Claret and Blue Striped Shirts, Claret Shorts		Goals	White Shirts, White Shorts		Goals
1	David JAMES		1	Nigel MARTYN	
2	Steve WATSON ❏ †		2	Gary KELLY (c)	
3	Alan WRIGHT		3	Ian HARTE	13
4	Gareth SOUTHGATE (c)		6	Jonathan WOODGATE	
5	Ugo EHIOGU		8	Michael BRIDGES †	
6	George BOATENG		10	Harry KEWELL	
10	Paul MERSON ‡		11	Lee BOWYER ❏	
12	Julian JOACHIM		14	Stephen McPHAIL	
15	Gareth BARRY		16	Jason WILCOX ❏	
18	Benito CARBONE ❏	32,58,69	19	Eirik BAKKE #	38
26	Steve STONE		22	Michael DUBERRY ‡	
	Substitutes			*Substitutes*	
11	Alan THOMPSON		12	Darren HUCKERBY #84	
13	Neil CUTLER (Gk)		13	Paul ROBINSON (Gk)	
17	Lee HENDRIE ‡73		17	Alan SMITH †70	
19	Richard WALKER		18	Danny MILLS ‡70	
24	Mark DELANEY †45		20	Matthew JONES	

Villa reach the FA Cup quarter-final for the first time in four years and will meet Everton at Goodison Park on 20th February... Carbone scores Villa's first hat-trick since Dion Dublin netted three times against Southampton on 14th November 1998... Villa announce a three-year kit deal with Diadora worth over £6m, to come into effect at the start of next season.

FACTFILE

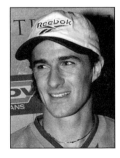

Hat-trick hero Benito Carbone

New footwear – change of fortune

Twelve hours before he is due to line up against Leeds United with his manager's call for more goals ringing in his ears, Benito Carbone is rummaging through a cupboard in the middle of the night, unable to sleep and smitten by the feeling that a change of footwear could be due.

Eventually he finds the boots he is looking for, painted in ostentatious blue. A happier man, he returns to his slumbers and if Leeds United had an inkling of what is about to hit them, they would stay in their own beds 'til tea-time.

As if he had been teasing his manager all along, Carbone unleashes his first hat-trick in Villa colours later this day, confounding a United side whose bid for a quarter-final slot starts so assuredly yet ends in disarray.

Villa are struggling for fluency and trailing to a 13th minute goal out of nothing by Ian Harte, when Carbone hits a firm drive into the corner of Nigel Martyn's goal, after Steve Watson heads a free-kick down to the little Italian, loitering on the edge of the penalty area.

The game is 32 minutes old and the hosts spurn the chance to take the lead just four minutes later, when George Boateng and Julian Joachim decide to go for the same cross to the far post, when either man might well have scored on his own.

Punishment follows, seven minutes from half-time, when Eirik Bakke heads home the crowning touch to a delightfully constructed move down the visitors' left flank.

Thirteen minutes into the second half, however, Carbone stuns Leeds and a 30,000 crowd with a goal of such breathtaking audacity that it irrevocably turns the tie's momentum.

From a distance where the Leeds goal is barely visible to the naked eye, Carbone spots a gap at Nigel Martyn's near post and finds it perfectly with a vast, curling shot that leaves the pundits' favourite for the England shirt looking decidedly embarrassed as he scrambles back helplessly.

If the Carbone show is now in full swing, there is an equally impressive support act being performed by Paul Merson.

Not quite managing to find his men as his passes probe the Leeds defences early on, the midfielder is getting into his stride as a plethora of crosses rain in on the United box in the first half's dying moments.

He saves his finest moment for the 69th minute and the game's *denouement*. Merson has a simple deal with his manager this season; all the freedom he wants on the field, as long as he gets his hands dirty when the occasion demands, by tracking back and getting stuck in.

As United finally succumb to incessant Villa onslaughts, Merson proves he'll even sweat blood for his team, as a couple of delicate flicks which transport the ball behind the Leeds defence bring him onto a collision course with Michael Duberry.

The last thing the Villa man remembers is heading the ball square to Carbone and then accidentally heading Duberry's skull in the follow-through. Only when the dazed twosome are having stitches inserted in the treatment room do they discover that Carbone had gleefully converted for his hat-trick.

Steve Stone has the beating of Jon Woodgate

Wednesday 2nd February 2000 • Filbert Street • 7.45pm

LEICESTER CITY 1 ASTON VILLA 0

Aggregate score 0-1

Half-time 1-0 • *Attendance* 21,843

Referee Paul DURKIN (Portland)

Referee's Assistants R. BURTON and D.S. BRYAN

Blue Shirts, White Shorts		Goals	Claret and Blue Striped Shirts, Claret Shorts		Goals
1	Tim FLOWERS		1	David JAMES	
3	Frank SINCLAIR		2	Steve WATSON †	
4	Gerry TAGGART ❑		3	Alan WRIGHT	
6	Muzzy IZZET #		4	Gareth SOUTHGATE (c)	
7	Neil LENNON ‡		5	Ugo EHIOGU	
9	Emile HESKEY		6	George BOATENG	
11	Steve GUPPY †		10	Paul MERSON	
14	Robbie SAVAGE		12	Julian JOACHIM	
15	Phil GILCHRIST		15	Gareth BARRY	
18	Matt ELLIOTT (c)	45	19	Richard WALKER ‡	
29	Stefan OAKES		26	Steve STONE	
Substitutes			*Substitutes*		
5	Steve WALSH		7	Ian TAYLOR ‡60	
16	Stuart CAMPBELL ‡84		13	Neil CUTLER (Gk)	
22	Pegguy ARPHEXAD (Gk)		17	Lee HENDRIE #82	
24	Andy IMPEY †73		24	Mark DELANEY †37 #	
37	Theo ZAGORAKIS #84		34	Colin CALDERWOOD	

Villa lose their first League Cup semi-final since their defeat over two legs by Oxford United in 1985-86... They have now failed to score in three of their last four games... Their winless run against Leicester City now stands at ten games.

FACTFILE

Ugo Ehiogu had his chances to keep Villa's cup dream alive

Cup run ends in anti-climax

Of all the times for the new-look Aston Villa to take a night off, they choose their most important game in four years. Whatever it is that has transformed John Gregory's side since mid-December, it is seriously lacking in a listless performance that meets its fate when City defender Matt Elliot heads home the tie's solitary goal on the stroke of half-time.

The spell which Leicester seem to hold over Villa can only thrive in games such as this. The Foxes' tactic of repeatedly running the ball into the corners in the final 10 minutes, hints at their own limitations, yet they have enough about them to mesmerise their opponents.

In the case for the defence, Paul Merson still seems to be suffering the effects of his collision with Michael Duberry three days earlier and is a shadow of the playmaker who helped destroy Leeds, while Villa's lack of height up front, where Richard Walker starts his first game for the first team, alongside Julian Joachim, makes for an easy night's work for Elliott and Gerry Taggart at the heart of the hosts' defence, thanks to their opponents' insistence on air-mail delivery to its forward line.

Leicester book their third Wembley visit in four years just as the interval beckons. A looping cross from Robbie Savage on the right seems to disorientate Ugo Ehiogu, thus giving Elliott time enough to head the ball into the top right hand corner.

It is the culmination of a half in which the chances had belonged almost entirely

to the Foxes. With their attack revolving around Emile Heskey, whose speed on the turn regularly takes several defenders out of the game, the hosts see Stefan Oakes hit the upright with a 20-yard drive after 33 minutes.

Earlier, James had to be smartly off his line to deny Heskey, following a mistake by Gareth Barry, and Ehiogu is the next to save his side, with a timely sliding tackle after James' attempted clearance of an under-hit back-pass is blocked to Elliott on the edge of Villa's area.

Ugo will rue two misses at the other end of the field after the break, as Villa substitute an ineffective Walker and press Merson into attack. Ehiogu heads wide under pressure when Tim Flowers commits in vain to a diagonal ball into the box from Gareth Barry, leaving his goal gaping open after 64 minutes. Three minutes before the end, Elliott misjudges the bounce to allow Ehiogu in behind him, but the Villa defender completely misses his kick as the travelling fans hold their breath.

While Villa are at least showing signs of getting back on terms, Steve Stone's shot from the edge of the box forcing a fingertip save from Flowers in the 76th minute, some players will later admit that their game-plan had been too passive; patiently waiting for the break to come instead of aggressively sniffing it out. A solemn John Gregory has no complaints in the post-game press conference.

"We didn't do enough in their half," he admits, "even though we were camped there after half-time."

This is a criticism that had dogged his team during the lean times of the autumn. Tonight it has come back – and it is haunting them with a vengeance.

Me and my shadow: Gerry Taggart guards Julian Joachim

Saturday 5th February 2000 • Villa Park • 3.00pm

ASTON VILLA 4 WATFORD 0

Half-time 0-0 • Attendance 27,647

Referee Paul JONES (Loughborough)

Referee's Assistants P. BARNES and R. GOULD

Claret and Blue Striped Shirts, Claret Shorts	Goals	Yellow Shirts, Red Shorts	Goals
1 David JAMES		13 Chris DAY	
3 Alan WRIGHT		4 Robert PAGE (c) ❑	
5 Ugo EHIOGU		5 Steve PALMER	
6 George BOATENG ‡		6 Paul ROBINSON ❑	
10 Paul MERSON (c) #	57,59	8 Micah HYDE	
12 Julian JOACHIM †		16 Nigel GIBBS	
15 Gareth BARRY		17 Tommy SMITH ‡	
18 Benito CARBONE		19 Clint EASTON †	
24 Mark DELANEY		24 Alex BONNOT	
26 Steve STONE	47	36 Neil COX #	
34 Colin CALDERWOOD		37 Heidar HELGUSON	
Substitutes		*Substitutes*	
2 Steve WATSON		1 Alec CHAMBERLAIN (Gk)	
13 Neil CUTLER (Gk)		2 Des LYTTLE	
17 Lee HENDRIE #84		3 Peter KENNEDY †45	
19 Richard WALKER †64	81	12 Allan SMART ‡45	
31 Jlloyd SAMUEL ‡71		14 Nordin WOOTER #64	

BEFORE	P	W	D	L	F	A	pts	AFTER	P	W	D	L	F	A	pts
9 Villa	23	8	7	8	22	23	31	8 Villa	24	9	7	8	26	23	34
20 Watford	23	4	2	17	21	50	14	20 Watford	24	4	2	18	21	54	14

FACTFILE

Steve Stone's second goal of the season and his first in the Premiership this term... Dion Dublin returns to training this week after making a rapid recovery from his neck injury... Roma striker Gustavo Bartelt signs on loan until the end of the season... Gareth Southgate is named Carling Player of the Month for January.

Merson magic exposes Hornets

He arrives in the visitors' dugout with a standing ovation ringing in his ears. He leaves it with damning proof that his team will need a miracle to avoid relegation. A bitter-sweet afternoon indeed, for Watford and ex-Villa manager Graham Taylor.

Two minutes of sublime skill from Paul Merson peel away what thin layer of credibility had accrued to the visitors by virtue of a 0-0 half-time scoreline and remind mundane Watford that spirit alone gets you only so far in the Premiership.

The message is first rammed home just two minutes into the second half, Steve Stone sliding in to volley Benito Carbone's cross into the bottom corner.

Watford later claim that their defence had stopped, under the impression that the throw-in which sent Carbone on his way, had been awarded to them, but they can offer no excuses for the two goals which condemn them to another barren Saturday afternoon. They are undone by brilliance, pure and simple.

Much better teams would have been similarly stretched when Merson takes the ball diagonally into Watford territory, before stabbing an inch-perfect chip over Watford keeper Chris Day and into the far corner.

The game is 57 minutes old and the encore is swift. Just two minutes later, Alan Wright is at Watford's back post to head Carbone's cross down to the waiting Merson, who turns on the spot to hook a shot home from just inside the penalty area.

Richard Walker and Robert Page in vertical take-off

It is hard to believe that such sparkling moments belong to the same game that had bored the crowd rigid for much of the first half, when 45 minutes of one-way traffic saw a succession of Villa chances fail to reach fruition.

Mark Delaney has a shot blocked by Paul Robinson, Ugo Ehiogu then heads wide from a Merson corner and Carbone scuffs his shot when connecting first time with a Stone cross.

Watford's sole contribution, meanwhile, is a shot from Micah Hyde, turning away from Stone, which proves fairly comfortable for David James in Villa's goal.

By the time they trouble Villa's defence again to any significant degree - Nigel Gibbs' fierce cross being just out of his team-mates' reach in the 73rd minute, the game is similarly beyond their grasp, Merson's goals and deft touches having lightened up the afternoon.

The game ends, as it began, with a heart-warming moment. Richard Walker has spent six years on Villa's books, patiently coming up through the ranks and biding his time for his big chance in the first team.

Barged out of contention by Leicester City's robust defence three days earlier, he may have wondered if that chance had come and gone, but after replacing Julian Joachim here, he rises to head home his first senior goal after an 81st minute cross from Alan Wright.

The talk afterwards is all of Merson, however. Wearing the captain's armband in Gareth Southgate's absence, Paul has responded in superb fashion, his only regret being that he had to turn on the style in front of the man who gave him his first England cap.

"It was a shame that Graham Taylor was on the receiving end," he says. A view no doubt shared by many Villa fans.

Monday 14th February 2000 • Riverside Stadium • 8.00pm

MIDDLESBROUGH 0 ASTON VILLA 4

Half-time 0-1 • *Attendance* 31,571

Referee Alan WILKIE (Chester-le-Street)
Referee's Assistants G. ATKINS and H. WEBB

Red Shirts, White Shorts		Goals	Turquoise Shirts with Black Trim, Black Shorts		Goals
13	Marlon BERESFORD		1	David JAMES #	
2	Curtis FLEMING #		3	Alan WRIGHT	
5	Gianluca FESTA ❏		4	Gareth SOUTHGATE (c)	
6	Gary PALLISTER		5	Ugo EHIOGU	
8	Paul GASCOIGNE †		6	George BOATENG ‡	
9	Paul INCE (c)		10	Paul MERSON †	
11	Keith O'NEILL ‡		12	Julian JOACHIM	70,76
18	Andy CAMPBELL		15	Gareth BARRY	
22	Mark SUMMERBELL		18	Benito CARBONE	11,66
23	JUNINHO		24	Mark DELANEY	
28	Colin COOPER ❏		26	Steve STONE	
Substitutes			*Substitutes*		
14	Philip STAMP †44		7	Ian TAYLOR ‡73	
15	Neil MADDISON #77		13	Neil CUTLER (Gk) #84	
20	Alun ARMSTRONG ‡73		17	Lee HENDRIE †63	
25	Ben ROBERTS (Gk)		19	Richard WALKER	
29	Jason GAVIN		31	Jlloyd SAMUEL	

BEFORE	P	W	D	L	F	A	pts	AFTER	P	W	D	L	F	A	pts
11 Villa	24	9	7	8	26	23	34	7 Villa	25	10	7	8	30	23	37
16 Boro	23	8	4	11	25	33	28	16 Boro	24	8	4	12	25	37	28

FACTFILE

Villa win by four clear goals away from home for the first time since their 4-0 defeat of Sunderland on 4th May 1985... Benito Carbone's first league goals for his new team... David James is substituted after a thigh injury... Stan Collymore signs for Leicester City on 10th February for a reported £500,000.

Double Strikes sink sad Boro

For those of us who have spent a decade giving Paul Gascoigne the benefit of the doubt, the well of tolerance finally runs dry.

Nine years ago, you could, at a pinch, put his two reckless fouls in the Cup Final down to a youthful red mist, but there are no get-outs for the forearm smash which the 32-year-old midfielder plants on the head of George Boateng this evening, as the two challenge for the ball just before half-time.

The potential consequences for Boateng hardly bear thinking about, but this is one of those occasions where life is fair. No harm is done to the Villa player, while Gazza, as at Wembley all those years ago, pays the price of his own madness when he is stretchered off with a broken arm.

By the time Villa have finished with his team, Boro too are in need of treatment. A shattered season, a nasty fall down the table and strained relations between manager Bryan Robson and the home fans: these are all the legacy of a trouncing by a Villa side with the Worthington Cup now well and truly out of its system.

Benito Carbone finally shows he can score in league games too, with two goals that break Middlesbrough's fragile spirit, leaving Julian Joachim to move in for the kill, with a brace of his own within a six minute spell during the second half.

It results in a happy ending to a night otherwise drenched in venom for Paul Merson, whose comments upon leaving Middlesbrough for Villa last season overshadowed anything he might have done for the club on the field, in the eyes of Boro supporters. With their man having missed this fixture last term, most of them have had almost 18 months to pool their bile, and it is to Merson's credit that he faces the music with aplomb before making way for Lee Hendrie.

He will take heart from his role in reducing his old club's starting midfield of Gascoigne, Juninho and Paul Ince to an irrelevance by the game's end, for Villa generally cope easily with their opponents, while Carbone puts them ahead in the 11th minute, driving a shot past goalkeeper Marlon Beresford from the edge of the area.

Not all Villa's attacks thereafter boast such clinical execution, but there is at least nothing wrong with their manager's strategy as regards substitution. Lee Hendrie finds Carbone with a cross-field pass in the 66th minute and the Italian encores his 18 yard shot from the first half, this time finding the net with a little help from a deflection.

This turns it into a practice game for the midlanders. Joachim scores from the rebound when Beresford saves a shot from Steve Stone after 70 minutes and he bags his second six minutes later, heading home an Alan Wright cross.

As for Middlesbrough, they need one of their exasperated fans to put the ball in the net, while David James is waiting to take a goal-kick deep into injury-time in the first half. Stupid behaviour, but when it's Paul Gascoigne who sets the tone around here, hardly surprising.

A triumphant return for Paul Merson

Sunday 20th February 2000 • Goodison Park • 4.00pm

EVERTON 1 ASTON VILLA 2

Half-time 1-2 • *Attendance* 35,331

Referee Dermot GALLAGHER (Banbury)
Referee's Assistants G. ATKINS and J. DEVINE

Blue Shirts, White Shorts		Goals	Claret and Blue Striped Shirts, Claret Shorts		Goals
1	Thomas MYHRE		39	Peter ENCKELMAN	
4	Richard GOUGH		3	Alan WRIGHT	
6	David UNSWORTH ❏		4	Gareth SOUTHGATE (c)	
7	John COLLINS		5	Ugo EHIOGU	
8	Nick BARMBY		6	George BOATENG ❏	
9	Kevin CAMPBELL		10	Paul MERSON †	
10	Don HUTCHISON (c)		12	Julian JOACHIM	
12	Mark PEMBRIDGE ‡		15	Gareth BARRY	
14	David WEIR		18	Benito CARBONE ❏ ■89	45
19	Abel XAVIER ❏ †		24	Mark DELANEY	
23	Joe-Max MOORE	20	26	Steve STONE	16
Substitutes			*Substitutes*		
3	Michael BALL		2	Steve WATSON	
15	Richard DUNNE		7	Ian TAYLOR †45	
16	Danny CADAMARTERI ‡76		13	Neil CUTLER (Gk)	
17	Francis JEFFERS †66		17	Lee HENDRIE	
35	Steve SIMONSEN (Gk)		19	Richard WALKER	

F A C T F I L E

Villa will face Bolton Wanderers at Wembley, in their first FA Cup semi-final in four years... Newcastle United play Chelsea, also at Wembley, in the other semi-final... Carbone scores in consecutive games for the first time since joining Villa... He and Stone have five goals between them in Villa's last three games... Villa's first away win in the FA Cup since 13th March 1996.

George Boateng

Goodison again the springboard

While Sheffield Wednesday will always appear the starting point of Villa's revival this season, it is arguable that a goalless draw at Goodison Park three weeks earlier was where the team rediscovered its resolve.

In a backs-to-the-wall, Rourke's Drift kind of a football game, Villa looked like they had decided enough was enough that day and not even a 1-0 defeat at home by Newcastle seven days later could dispel the notion that their act was coming together once more.

So there is a sense of the wheel turning full circle as John Gregory's men return to the blue quarter of Merseyside for their first FA Cup tie away from home this season, and go one better than when last here.

That they do so is down to an early lead taken through Steve Stone, regained by Benito Carbone on the stroke of half-time and then defended doggedly throughout a second half where Everton proffer everything but the kitchen sink, only to have to make do with a smack of the woodwork for their efforts.

They had hoped for better things when American Joe-Max Moore cancelled out Stone's goal after 20 minutes. Stone had been the recipient of Ugo Ehiogu's knockdown from a Paul Merson cross four minutes earlier, dipping his head to push the ball home via goalkeeper Thomas Myhre's shoulder.

Gareth Barry's failure to clear a header from Kevin Campbell lets in Moore to notch the equaliser, but Merson, despite generally making less of an impression than in recent games, helps restore the visitor's lead at the end of the half, when Myhre can only swat away his shot, leaving Carbone with a tap-in that is a piece of cake for the man who bombarded Leeds from all ranges in the previous round.

Everton are indignation personified as they fling themselves on the offensive after the break, only to find a Villa defence even more impenetrable than that which kept a clean sheet three months earlier.

Ehiogu and Gareth Southgate in particular are a bridge too far for the Toffees' strikers, and while the visitors' midfield had seemed in danger of being swamped in the game's early stages, Steve Stone and George Boateng are soon giving as good as they get, and using the ball constructively.

It allows Carbone to keep the hosts' defence honest, with three chances to increase his team's lead, but the day will end with an early bath for the man bidding to add a fresh chapter to the pantheon of Villa Cup heroes, when he hampers David Unsworth while the latter is trying to take a free-kick.

Having already been booked for kicking the ball away, it is not the most unavoidable red card in the world, and Villa will hope it doesn't come back to haunt them when Benito is forced to sit out the Arsenal game as a result of his actions.

Everton's problems are much more pressing, however. A second half of repeatedly blunted ambition reaches its nadir when Richard Gough, in his team's only gilt-edged chance in 45 minutes, volleys a Danny Cadamarteri cross against the face of the post, only for the ball to come back into play.

Steve Stone's header gives Villa the lead

Saturday 26th February 2000 • Valley Parade • 3.00pm

BRADFORD CITY 1 ASTON VILLA 1

Half-time 0-1 • *Attendance* 18,276

Referee Mark HALSEY (Welwyn Garden City)
Referee's Assistants C. WEBSTER and R. BOOTH

Claret and Amber Striped Shirts, Claret Shorts		Goals	Turquoise Shirts with Black Trim, Black Shorts		Goals
31	Aidan DAVISON		39	Peter ENCKELMAN	
4	Stuart McCALL (c)		3	Alan WRIGHT	
5	David WETHERALL		4	Gareth SOUTHGATE (c)	
7	Jamie LAWRENCE †		5	Ugo EHIOGU	
10	Gareth WHALLEY ‡		6	George BOATENG ❏	
11	Peter BEAGRIE		10	Paul MERSON ‡	39
14	Andrew O'BRIEN		12	Julian JOACHIM	
15	Dean WINDASS	76	15	Gareth BARRY	
18	Gunnar HALLE		18	Benito CARBONE	
22	Wayne JACOBS		24	Mark DELANEY	
28	Dean SAUNDERS		26	Steve STONE †	
Substitutes			*Substitutes*		
8	Robbie BLAKE †68		2	Steve WATSON	
16	Lee SHARPE		7	Ian TAYLOR †66	
20	John DREYER		13	Neil CUTLER (Gk)	
32	Neville SOUTHALL (Gk)		17	Lee HENDRIE ‡77	
33	Jorge CADETE ‡75		19	Richard WALKER	

BEFORE		P	W	D	L	F	A	pts	AFTER		P	W	D	L	F	A	pts
7	Villa	25	10	7	8	30	23	37	8	Villa	26	10	8	8	31	24	38
18	Bradford	25	6	6	13	25	41	24	18	Bradford	26	6	7	13	26	42	25

FACTFILE

Villa play a league game at Bradford for the first time in 13 years... A good week for Villa on the international front: Gareth Southgate plays in England's goalless draw with Argentina, Gareth Barry is in the squad, but misses out. Lee Hendrie score the game's only goal as England's U21s beat their Argentine counterparts.

Points dropped against strugglers

If you ever wanted to know just how small the football world has become, look no further than Jorge Cadete.

The last time Villa found his name on the opposing squad-list, they were facing an ultimately fruitless UEFA Cup tie against Spanish side Celta Vigo. Now he pops up again in the slightly less exotic climes of Bradford.

The Portuguese striker almost makes an immediate mark with his new club, when only a fingertip save onto the woodwork by Villa keeper Peter Enckelman prevents Cadete's 83rd minute header from turning a disappointing afternoon into a calamity.

There had been a time in this game when Villa looked as if they might breeze to three points, on the back of beautifully taken goal by Paul Merson. As the match wears on, however, Bradford's determination to continue the eight game unbeaten home run that is underpinning their tenuous prospects of Premiership football next term, forces the visitors back on their heels, and Villa end the game mightily glad of a solitary point, after Dean Windass' 76th minute equaliser.

The Yorkshiremen too will not be entirely dissatisfied with the draw, having originally looked like putty in Villa's hands.

Paul Merson might have seen some football in his career, but it is doubtful he has ever worked harder on a football field than he is at present. If he is not tormenting his hosts with the ball at his feet this afternoon, he is hounding them relentlessly whenever it is at theirs.

The man who was a peripheral figure in the 'wilderness months' that followed his arrival from Middlesbrough, is now involved in everything, to the point where Bradford full-back Gunnar Halle even requires treatment after one uncompromising Merson challenge.

The only disappointment was his goal after 39 minutes. When you've chipped the keeper at full tilt and fired in a shot on the turn only two games ago, merely curling an effort into the top corner of Bradford's goal from the front corner of the penalty box is fairly mundane stuff.

As is customary these days, a concession to his 31 years, Merson is substituted with 12 minutes of the game remaining, and he leaves a contest whose character has changed quite considerably.

For so long tormented by Benito Carbone and hustled by George Boateng, the home team come out clearly resolved to recover their dignity after the interval, and for the first time in the game, Villa's defence looks uncomfortable.

While Everton knocked at the door without getting their foot in it six days earlier, City ensure that Enckelman has more than just a watching brief this afternoon, and the Finn is forced to make good saves from Windass and Gareth Whalley before his team finally buckles.

Enckelman does really well to push David

Wetherall's far post header out, but is powerless to do anything about Windass' header from the corner. The Bradford striker finds himself wide open and suddenly, amazingly, so is the game.

Villa hold out in the last quarter of an hour, however; a point being the very least of their requirements as they must now face the visit of Arsenal without suspended Boateng and Carbone.

Peter Enckelman – crucial saves

Sunday 5th March 2000 • Villa Park • 3.00pm

ASTON VILLA 1 ARSENAL 1

Half-time 0-0 • Attendance 36,930

Referee Graham POLL (Tring)

Referee's Assistants K. HAWKES and S. BRAND

Claret and Blue Striped Shirts, Claret Shorts	Goals	Yellow Shirts with Navy Blue Trim, Navy Blue Shorts	Goals
39 Peter ENCKELMAN		1 David SEAMAN	
3 Alan WRIGHT		2 Lee DIXON (c)	83
4 Gareth SOUTHGATE (c)		4 Patrick VIEIRA	
5 Ugo EHIOGU		5 Martin KEOWN	
7 Ian TAYLOR		10 Dennis BERGKAMP †	
10 Paul MERSON		14 Thierry HENRY	
12 Julian JOACHIM		15 Ray PARLOUR	
15 Gareth BARRY		16 SILVINHO	
19 Richard WALKER †	62	17 Emmanuel PETIT ❑ #	
24 Mark DELANEY		18 Gilles GRIMANDI ‡	
26 Steve STONE		25 Nwankwo KANU	
Substitutes		*Substitutes*	
2 Steve WATSON		3 Nigel WINTERBURN #74	
13 Neil CUTLER (Gk)		8 Fredrik LJUNGBERG	
17 Lee HENDRIE †81		11 Marc OVERMARS †45	
25 Gustavo BARTELT		13 Alex MANNINGER (Gk)	
31 Jlloyd SAMUEL		22 Oleg LUZHNY ‡45	

BEFORE	P	W	D	L	F	A	pts	AFTER	P	W	D	L	F	A	pts
3 Arsenal	26	14	5	7	46	27	47	4 Arsenal	27	14	6	7	47	28	48
8 Villa	26	10	8	8	31	24	38	8 Villa	27	10	9	8	32	25	39

FACTFILE

Richard Walker scores on his full league debut... The crowd of 36,930 is Villa Park's best attendance since the Spurs game on 29th December... The end of a good week for Lee Dixon, who also scored in the midweek UEFA Cup game against Deportivo la Caruña.

Dixon rifles point for the Gunners

Not quite as dramatic as Villa's revival in this game last year, perhaps, but delight for Arsenal nevertheless, as full-back Lee Dixon's 83rd minute equaliser salvages a point from a game that might easily have been lost.

For much of the afternoon, the Gunners look to be there for the taking, their out-of-sorts demeanour typified by Frenchman Emannuel Petit, who will cause a storm in the press for the next few days after gesturing to the crowd when substituted: a response, he maintains, to racist abuse suffered while on the pitch. Villa strongly deny his claims.

Hesitant and ineffectual for much of the game, it is hard to believe this is the same Arsenal side which dismantled Spanish league leaders Deportivo la Coruña 5-1 only three days earlier, although Villa will rightly claim that this is down to their attentions rather than the Londoners' fatigue.

On another day, this might have proved fatal for the away side, as Julian Joachim has two one-on-one opportunities, but cannot convert either one of them. Instead, it needs Richard Walker's best moment for his club to date to open the scoring, as he beats Martin Keown and Petit to a Paul Merson free kick from the right before administering a glancing header that reaches home via the far post.

It lifts a game that had been threatening to become ragged, but not for the first time this season, Villa cannot find the killer touch, in spite of Paul Merson becoming more involved against his old club.

With Nwankwo Kanu coming increasingly to the fore, Arsenal finally claw back a point with seven minutes remaining, when Dixon picks up a pass from the Nigerian and charges into the Villa box. A slip by Gareth Barry doesn't help

his side any, and with no-one else close enough to launch a tackle, Dixon jubilantly slides the ball past the advancing Peter Enckelman.

Ironically, it is one of Arsenal's rare peeks at goal. Enckelman had to dive at Kanu's feet to cut out a Dennis Bergkamp cross in the 5th minute, but otherwise it is all Villa in the first half, with the visitors' midfield only starting to assert itself in the 10 minute before half-time.

After Walker and Ugo Ehiogu have both placed headers on the wrong side of David Seaman's crossbar, Joachim has the first of his gilt-edged chances when Steve Stone's through ball finds him unattended after 16 minutes. The striker bears down on Arsenal's goal but appears to run out of ideas as Seaman approaches and the keeper throws himself at Joachim's feet to knock the ball away.

23 minutes later, Julian goes for plan B when Walker's header from a goal-kick again springs his striking partner behind the Arsenal defence. This time, Joachim elects to shoot early, before Seaman can get to him, but the big goalkeeper parries the shot to his right. Just wide with a near-post shot five minutes before the interval, Joachim knows it's not his day.

Nor, mercifully, is it Marc Overmars'. The Dutchman replaces Dennis Bergkamp at half-time and is onto a Ray Parlour cross in injury time, only to see his volley go above the bar. Comebacks *that* dramatic really do only happen once in a blue moon.

Stone and Southgate pursue Thierry Henry

Saturday 11th March 2000 • Villa Park • 3.00pm

ASTON VILLA 1 COVENTRY CITY 0

Half-time 1-0 • *Attendance* 33,177

Referee Uriah RENNIE (Sheffield)

Referee's Assistants C. WEBSTER and J. PETTITT

Claret and Blue Striped Shirts, Claret Shorts	Goals	White Shirts with Black Trim, Black Shorts	Goals
39 Peter ENCKELMAN		1 Magnus HEDMAN	
3 Alan WRIGHT ❏		5 Richard SHAW	
4 Gareth SOUTHGATE (c)		7 Robbie KEANE †	
5 Ugo EHIOGU ❏	45	10 Gary McALLISTER (c)	
6 George BOATENG		11 Moustapha HADJI ❏	
7 Ian TAYLOR		16 Stephen FROGGATT	
10 Paul MERSON †		18 Youssef CHIPPO	
12 Julian JOACHIM ‡		24 John EUSTACE ‡	
15 Gareth BARRY		31 Cedric ROUSSEL ❏	
18 Benito CARBONE		32 Tomas GUSTAFSSON	
24 Mark DELANEY		35 Colin HENDRY	
Substitutes		*Substitutes*	
2 Steve WATSON		3 David BURROWS ‡74	
13 Neil CUTLER (Gk)		8 Noel WHELAN †45	
17 Lee HENDRIE		13 Morten HYLDGAARD (Gk)	
19 Richard WALKER ‡86		22 Barry QUINN	
26 Steve STONE †79		36 Craig PEAD	

AFTER	P	W	D	L	F	A	pts	AFTER	P	W	D	L	F	A	pts
8 Villa	27	10	9	8	32	25	39	7 Villa	28	11	9	8	33	25	42
14 Coventry	27	8	8	11	35	35	32	14 Coventry	28	8	8	12	35	36	32

FACTFILE

Villa end a two-game losing run against City... Steve Stone back on the bench after eight straight starts... Paul Merson is named Carling Player of the Month for February, keeping the award at the same club two months running for the first time since Manninger and Petit did it for Arsenal in March and April 1998.

Ugo gives City away-day blues

After their first ever league win at Villa Park last season, followed by an emphatic win at Highfield Road four months ago, Coventry City once again find themselves in the role of poor relations, as a header from Ugo Ehiogu resolves the latest instalment of the West Mids derby.

It continues a sequence of important, if rare goals from the central defender, who salvaged a point against Derby and also hit the winner versus Blackburn with his two strikes of last term.

More importantly for his team, it continues their opponents' dismal lack of success whenever they venture beyond Coventry's city limits. The Sky Blues remain the only team in the Premiership without an away win to their name this season and as manager Gordon Strachan played for the last top-flight side to 'achieve' such a feat, Leeds United in 1992-93, this latest loss rankles deeply.

He and his men can have little complaint, however, for they have looked like runners-up in waiting where this game is concerned, even before Ehiogu heads home Paul Merson's free-kick at the far post, deep into first-half injury time.

Not helped by their hosts' tigerish attendance when chasing possession, Coventry bear scant resemblance to the side which tormented Villa's defence when they last met, and Robbie Keane's suspect fitness sees him substituted at half-time.

In defence, meanwhile, despite the efforts of recent signing Colin Hendry to be in two places at once, City spend a half trying to plug a hole in their left-back position which Merson and Mark Delaney exploit to ensure a stream of crosses from both flanks.

Julian Joachim gets a touch to one of them, almost flicking the ball over Magnus Hedman in the Coventry goal, and George Boateng

senses glory against his former club when a clearance falls to him on the edge of the area, only for his shot to be deflected over the bar.

Finding some width of their own, the visitors begin to make their own mark on the game as the first half enters its latter stages and both Keane and Cedric Roussel go close as John Eustace sends a couple of crosses into the Villa area.

The initiative is handed back to their opponents after Ehiogu's goal, however. Hedman needs assistance from Richard Shaw to keep out a Joachim effort and later gets just enough of a touch to deny the striker once more after 'JJ' has jumped onto a weak back pass by Eustace.

Apart from a wayward shot by Noel Whelan late on, Coventry are muzzled for virtually the entire second half, and Villa might well have put more distance between them and their neighbours if only their ability to win the ball was matched by their use of it.

The game becomes ragged in its latter stages, which is more to City's advantage than Villa's, as John Gregory later acknowledges.

"We made heavy weather of the second half," says the Villa manager. "We limited the opposition to not a lot, which has been one of the hallmarks of our recent run, but ended up hanging on at the death."

Youssef Chippo tustles with Paul Merson

Wednesday 15th March 2000 • Anfield • 7.45pm

LIVERPOOL 0 ASTON VILLA 0

Half-time 0-0 • *Attendance* 43,615

Referee Steve BENNETT (Orpington)

Referee's Assistants M. SHORT and D. BABSKI

Red Shirts, Red Shorts	Goals	Turquoise Shirts with Black Trim, Black Shorts	Goals
1 Sander WESTERVELD		39 Peter ENCKELMAN	
2 Stephane HENCHOZ		3 Alan WRIGHT	
8 Emile HESKEY		4 Gareth SOUTHGATE (c) †	
10 Michael OWEN †		5 Ugo EHIOGU	
12 Sami HYYPIA (c)		6 George BOATENG	
15 Patrik BERGER		10 Paul MERSON ‡	
16 Dietmar HAMANN		12 Julian JOACHIM #	
21 Dominic MATTEO		15 Gareth BARRY ❑	
23 Jamie CARRAGHER		18 Benito CARBONE	
25 David THOMPSON #		24 Mark DELANEY	
28 Steven GERRARD ‡		26 Steve STONE	
Substitutes		*Substitutes*	
5 Steve STAUNTON		2 Steve WATSON	
11 Jamie REDKNAPP ‡78		7 Ian TAYLOR †52	
18 Erik MEIJER #83		13 Neil CUTLER (Gk)	
19 Brad FRIEDEL (Gk)		17 Lee HENDRIE ‡59	
22 Titi CAMARA †66		19 Richard WALKER #88	

BEFORE	P	W	D	L	F	A	pts	AFTER	P	W	D	L	F	A	pts
4 Liverpool	27	14	7	6	40	23	49	3 Liverpool	28	14	8	6	40	23	50
7 Villa	28	11	9	8	33	25	42	6 Villa	29	11	10	8	33	25	43

FACTFILE

Villa now unbeaten in all but one of their last 19 games... The first time these two clubs have shared two goalless draws in the league in the same season... The second-largest gate at a Villa away game this term, after Old Trafford.

Cautious Villa settle for point

Maybe it's that 'Welcome to Anfield' sign above the tunnel. Maybe it's the thought of facing a Liverpool side that is once again causing the stirring of vaulting ambition in the red half of Merseyside. Or maybe it's just the sight of Emile Heskey on the opponents' team sheet.

Something, definitely, has removed the trace of swagger that has marked Villa's resurgence of recent months and as Anfield empties this evening, there is a feeling that with a little more endeavour, Villa might have taken all three points with them down the M6, just as they did last season.

True, there is much of which to be wary. Stung by their defeat against Sunderland, Liverpool tear into Villa for much of the game, as if determined to prove that this is not yet another false dawn.

Michael Owen's joy at making his first start for two months due to his worrying hamstring injury, is short-lived after missing a 31st minute penalty, and Peter Enckelman has to make key saves from Owen, when the latter is put through in the 14th minute despite looking to be offside, and also from David Thompson's ferociously struck angled shot in the second half.

And then there is pesky Heskey. Relations between John Gregory and the burly striker, recently signed from Leicester City for £11m, remain chilly after Gareth Barry is left briefly teetering on the brink as Heskey tumbles under his challenge when the teenager is already on a booking.

"Heskey falls over an awful lot," seethes Gregory afterwards.

"He has so much ability that he doesn't need to resort to those kind of tactics."

While Heskey torments Villa by less questionable means in the first half, he has to join his strike partner Owen in eventually admitting defeat to a Villa defence that barely skips a beat, even after Gareth Southgate leaves the game with an ankle injury in the 52nd minute.

As the Reds' neighbours on t'other side of Stanley Park discovered in the FA Cup quarterfinal, it is one thing to have possession in your opponents' half, but it can be something else altogether to get within shooting range. With Ian Taylor deputising for his captain, Villa's back-line continues to keep their hosts at bay and as the second half develops, the visitors finally start to believe that this game could be their for the taking.

A Julian Joachim effort, cleared off the line, was their best, if not their only opportunity of the first half, but as they finally began to call a few shots of their own, Ian Taylor and Carbone both have chances to open the scoring.

The thought occurs that with a little more adventure in the first half, Villa might never have given Liverpool the chance to seize the initiative as forcibly as they did. Not for the first time, the aerial prowess of Dion Dublin is sorely missed. Joachim and Carbone are forced to work around the edges of the Liverpool defence, when Dublin would have been able to go head to head with Sami Hyypia and Stephane Henchoz in the air.

A point at Anfield should never be sneered at, but for the first time this season, the Villa supporters come away from Merseyside feeling just a little short-changed.

Skipper Gareth Southgate, forced out of the game with an ankle injury

Saturday 18th March 2000 • The Dell • 3.00pm

SOUTHAMPTON 2 ASTON VILLA 0

Half-time 1-0 • *Attendance* 15,218

Referee Mike RILEY (Leeds)

Referee's Assistants J.J. ROSS and P.V. NORMAN

Red and White Striped Shirts, Black Shorts		Goals	Claret and Blue Striped Shirts, Claret Shorts		Goals
1	Paul JONES		39	Peter ENCKELMAN	
2	Jason DODD (c)		2	Steve WATSON	
4	Chris MARSDEN ❏		3	Alan WRIGHT #	
6	Dean RICHARDS		5	Ugo EHIOGU ❏	
8	Matthew OAKLEY		6	George BOATENG	
10	Kevin DAVIES ❏	39,63	7	Ian TAYLOR	
17	Marian PAHARS †		10	Paul MERSON (c)	
18	Wayne BRIDGE		15	Gareth BARRY	
21	Jo TESSEM		17	Lee HENDRIE ‡	
27	Tahar EL KHALEJ ❏		18	Benito CARBONE	
30	Hassan KACHLOUL ❏		26	Steve STONE †	
Substitutes			*Substitutes*		
7	Matthew LE TISSIER		11	Alan THOMPSON #82	
13	Neil MOSS (Gk)		12	Julian JOACHIM †63	
15	Francis BENALI		13	Neil CUTLER (Gk)	
32	Trond SOLTVEDT †90		19	Richard WALKER	
35	Luis BOA MORTE		31	Jlloyd SAMUEL ‡71	

BEFORE	P	W	D	L	F	A	pts	AFTER	P	W	D	L	F	A	pts
6 Villa	29	11	10	8	33	25	43	6 Villa	30	11	10	9	33	27	43
16 Saints	28	8	6	14	33	51	30	15 Saints	29	9	6	14	35	51	33

FACTFILE

Southampton do the 'double' over Villa in the league for the first time since 1993-94... Villa fail to score in back-to-back Premiership matches for just the second time this season... Defender Colin Calderwood signs for Nottingham Forest for a reported £70,000.

Villa express grinds to a halt

Into every life a little rain must fall, but Villa have a habit of being caught when they least expect to require an umbrella.

Bolton and Barnsley two years ago, Charlton last season, relegation fodder all, managed to stop a Villa side on a roll. Now it's Southampton, fresh from a 7-2 drubbing at Spurs just a week earlier, who make a mockery of recent form, finally ending an unbeaten Villa league run that stretches back to mid-December.

"You can't castigate people for a poor performance, because that was the first bad one in 19 games," says John Gregory afterwards. "I'm not one for jumping up and down when we win and it's the same now."

A modest crowd that is similarly disinclined towards histrionics, and an unseasonably balmy afternoon by the Solent, appear to conspire to appease the hunger that has driven Villa on in recent weeks, although an enforced reshuffle does not help.

Like his team, Southampton's Kevin Davies seizes the moment for a spot of rehabilitation. While still feeling his way back to form after his Blackburn nightmare, the fact that manager Glenn Hoddle was prepared to let Mark Hughes go to Everton, will have given Davies fresh heart, and it shows this afternoon.

The barrel-chested striker had got stuck in with some bracing challenges when Villa put Saints out of the FA Cup two months earlier, but today his contribution, while equally uncompromising, is more in keeping with his position.

As Southampton build up momentum towards the interval, Villa's re-jigged defence, where Steve Watson replaces the rested Mark Delaney, allows a throw-in to bounce through their own area, past a forest of swinging feet. Dodd eventually sends it into the path of Davies on the left, who hits an angled shot from 20 yards past Peter Enckelman.

He adds a second in the 64th minute, when Matthew Oakley's pass catches the defence square and leaves Davies with time and space to pick his spot.

These are the peaks in a performance by the hosts which shows that opportunities for sheer willpower to outdo talent are not yet extinct within the Premiership. Southampton, their 90 minutes of shame in north London spurring them on, are seriously up for this. Villa, on the other hand, can't quite make up their minds.

Allied to this diffidence are the dilemmas of Ian Taylor, who has the thankless task of trying to replace the injured Gareth Southgate, while a beleaguered midfield is crying out for his presence, and Paul Merson, playing in the conventional forward's role which is yet to bring the best out of him.

The sum of these parts is a side lacking in drive and ideas, which has now squandered six points in the league this season, against opponents who have shipped more goals than all but three of their Premiership rivals and are now embroiled in their traditional fight against relegation.

Whether that is a fair trade for Saints' going belly-up against Villa in both Cups this term, remains to be seen.

"It never did me any good as a player when managers were shouting at me," comments a restrained Gregory.

"There are times to sit back and take stock and this is one of them."

Ian Taylor – replaced the injured Gareth Southgate

Saturday 25th March 2000 • Villa Park • 3.00pm

ASTON VILLA 2 DERBY COUNTY 0

Half-time 1-0 • *Attendance* 28,613

Referee Paul ALCOCK (Halstead, Kent)

Referee's Assistants C. BASSINDALE and J. DEVINE

Claret and Blue Striped Shirts, Claret Shorts		Goals	White Shirts, Black Shorts		Goals
1	David JAMES		21	Mart POOM	
3	Alan WRIGHT		2	Horacio CARBONARI	
5	Ugo EHIOGU		3	Stefan SCHNOOR ❑	
6	George BOATENG	57	4	Darryl POWELL (c)	
7	Ian TAYLOR ‡		7	Seth JOHNSON	
10	Paul MERSON (c)		10	Rory DELAP	
12	Julian JOACHIM †		16	Jacob LAURSEN	
15	Gareth BARRY		19	Steve ELLIOTT †	
18	Benito CARBONE #	41	27	Giorgi KINKLADZE	
24	Mark DELANEY		29	Stefano ERANIO ‡	
31	Jlloyd SAMUEL		35	Branko STRUPAR	

Substitutes			*Substitutes*		
2	Steve WATSON		5	Tony DORIGO	
9	Dion DUBLIN #80		8	Dean STURRIDGE ‡88	
17	Lee HENDRIE ‡75		12	Malcolm CHRISTIE †61	
26	Steve STONE †62		24	Andy OAKES (Gk)	
39	Peter ENCKELMAN (Gk)		31	Chris RIGGOTT	

BEFORE		P	W	D	L	F	A	pts	AFTER		P	W	D	L	F	A	pts
6	Villa	30	11	10	9	33	27	43	6	Villa	31	12	10	9	35	27	46
17	Derby	29	7	7	15	33	44	28	17	Derby	30	7	7	16	33	46	28

FACTFILE

Villa repeat the scoreline from their win at Derby shortly after Christmas... Boateng's first goal since scoring in that same game... Gareth Barry and Lee Hendrie are in the England U21 squad for next week's European Championship play-off with Yugoslavia.

Goals and Dion lift the gloom

A Villa side looking to put its upset at Southampton behind it, against a Derby County team with relegation on its mind, does not have the makings of a free-flowing contest on paper, and that is how it turns out, with a ragged 90 minutes made memorable only by the two goals which punctuate it. Plus one of the substitutions.

The return of Dion Dublin would have lifted the mood at a wake. Here is a man whom the experts would have us believe was just milli-metres away from life in a wheelchair only three months ago, returning to action well ahead of schedule, his broken neck now fixed and supported by a titanium brace, which makes it, if anything, even stronger than before. No wonder Benito Carbone greets his 80th minute replacement with a 'we are not worthy' bow.

Dublin's first touch, wouldn't you just know it, is a header, executed with unruffled aplomb and before long it's like he's never been away.

Villa Park needs the lift his arrival provides. In between two delightful goals either side of half-time, by Carbone and George Boateng, there has been little to write home about.

For all their problems, Derby still look a cut above fellow relegation-battlers Bradford and Watford, and could have emerged from this game with a point, had Villa been dependent on determined teamwork for their goals rather than the game-breaking flair of Carbone and Paul Merson.

Villa might get a fortuitous nod on several marginal offside calls early on, but County's defence are no mugs and Villa's attacks are soon harried into disjointed affairs, with Carbone having to track back inside his own half to see much of the ball.

Ironically, he is exactly where he should be

after 41 minutes, when Merson, who has picked incessantly at County, like a seamstress altering a hemline, lays the ball square to the Italian on the edge of the box. If Carbone's backlift is almost languid, his downswing is like a gun-hammer, and deposits the ball in the far corner, beyond Mart Poom's grasp.

It's perfect timing for Benito and his team. Embroiled in contract talks which are now becoming a tad tense, Carbone milks the moment with a flamboyance that clearly illus-trates why Italy is the spiritual home of grand opera, running the length of the pitch with his shirt off to salute an adoring Holte End.

The goal brings more cutting edge to Villa's attacks. Shortly after, Merson's curling shot strikes the woodwork and Ugo Ehiogu forces a low save from Poom when he meets a free-kick at the far post five minutes into the second half.

Game set and match arrives after 57 minutes, when Merson rips a stretched County defence asunder with a cross from the outside of his right boot that is met by the head of Boateng, hanging in the air like a kestrel, to give Poom no chance with a downward header at close range.

Three points and the return of Dublin send the fans home happy, at the end of a forget-table game which has been saved by its details.

George Boateng is a picture of concentration as Stefan Schnoor closes in

Sunday 2nd April 2000 • Wembley Stadium • 3.00pm

BOLTON WANDERERS 0   ASTON VILLA 0

after extra time (Villa win 4-1 on penalties)
Half-time 0-0 • *Attendance 62,828*
Referee David ELLERAY (Harrow-on-the-Hill)
Referee's Assistants P.R. SHARP and B. WADE

White Shirts with Navy Trim, Navy Blue Shorts	Goals	Claret and Blue Striped Shirts, Claret Shorts	Goals
22 Jussi JAASKELAINEN		1 David JAMES	
3 Mike WHITLOW (c) ❑		3 Alan WRIGHT	
4 Gudni BERGSSON ‡		4 Gareth SOUTHGATE (c)	
7 Michael JOHANSEN		5 Ugo EHIOGU ❑	
8 Claus JENSEN †		6 George BOATENG #	
10 Dean HOLDSWORTH ❑		7 Ian TAYLOR †	
12 Eidur GUDJOHNSEN		10 Paul MERSON	
15 Robbie ELLIOTT ❑		12 Julian JOACHIM	
17 Mark FISH		15 Gareth BARRY	
31 Paul RITCHIE		18 Benito CARBONE ‡	
32 Allan JOHNSTON		24 Mark DELANEY ❑ ■110	
Substitutes		*Substitutes*	
5 Paul WARHURST †61 ❑		9 Dion DUBLIN ‡69	
14 Bo HANSEN		17 Lee HENDRIE #118	
20 Steve BANKS (Gk)		26 Steve STONE †15	
24 John O'KANE ‡91		31 Jlloyd SAMUEL	
25 Franck PASSI		39 Peter ENCKELMAN (Gk)	

FACTFILE

PENALTY SHOOT-OUT – BOLTON				PENALTY SHOOT-OUT – VILLA			
1	Dean HOLDSWORTH	scored	1-1	1	Steve STONE	scored	1-0
2	Allan JOHNSTON	saved	1-2	2	Lee HENDRIE	scored	2-1
3	Michael JOHANSEN	saved	1-3	3	Gareth BARRY	scored	3-1
Villa took the first penalty.				4	Dion DUBLIN	scored	4-1

Villa reach their first FA Cup Final since beating West Brom 1-0 in a semi-final replay on 28th March 1957... They will be the first team to contest an FA Cup Final in three different centuries... Mark Delaney is the first man to be sent off at Wembley while playing for Villa.

Comeback kids end 43 year wait

Much-maligned as a means of settling a football match, you won't find anyone carping over penalties down Aston Villa way.

Six years after they opened the door for a famous League Cup Final win, the supposedly dreaded spot-kicks book Villa's place in the FA Cup Final after a 43 year absence and provide redemption for two of the club's most favoured sons.

Back from the injury that might have confined him to a wheelchair, comes Dion Dublin, stroking home the winning penalty that sets one half of Wembley alight.

Back from no-man's land after his Liverpool career fizzled out, comes David James, his status as one of the steals of the season confirmed as he denies two Bolton penalties to set up Dublin's moment of glory.

And back come Villa, who had looked a healthy prospect for semi-final woe for the second time this season, as 90 disappointing minutes erupt into extra-time drama.

Already forced to adapt to the loss of Ian Taylor with a bad hamstring injury, after 14 minutes, the favourites must again re-jig after two fouls in the opening four minutes of the extra half-hour earn Mark Delaney a red card.

For a Bolton side that has grown in confidence as the game progresses, it must seem like a pivotal moment in their bid for an upset, yet their own share of the heartbreak is just beginning.

Dean Holdsworth's free-kick following Delaney's infringement curls against James' far post, but far worse is to come for the ex-Wimbledon man, 12

Carbone and Bergsson seek inspiration from above

minutes into extra-time. As he has done several times in the game, Icelander Eidur Gudjohnsen loses his marker Ugo Ehiogu and evades the advancing James before pulling the ball back from the by-line.

Holdsworth is 12 yards out and despite the presence on the line of the two Gareths, has the chance of a lifetime yawning open in front of him, only for him to send the ball over the bar. The line about one's name being on the Cup springs to mind.

In truth, Villa would be glad of any supernatural assistance. They have the moves but not the finish this afternoon, while Bolton have enterprise and bravery in abundance but are without the wit to break down their opponents' doughty defence.

The result is a stodgy 90 minutes salvaged only by the absorbing tension of the moment, a mood heightened by Benito Carbone's annoyance at being substituted after 70 minutes.

In fairness, he had not found the kind of openings which had fallen to his strike partner Julian Joachim up to that point, although the latter's lack of success in front of goal continues. JJ is put clear by a one-two with the Italian on the half-hour but his shot is wastefully high.

Twice more in the first half will he find only Wanderers keeper Jussi Jaaskelainen between himself and the goal, but the keeper blocks his shot on both occasions.

So often Villa's saviour before his broken neck, it is Dublin who works the trick again. Sparking his team with a header against the post late in extra time, his is the name on the list with Bolton just a penalty kick from surrender.

"The script's been written, boys," Gareth Southgate tells his team, as Dion approaches the box. And so it had.

Wednesday 5th April 2000 • Hillsborough • 7.45pm

SHEFFIELD WEDNESDAY 0 ASTON VILLA 1

Half-time 0-0 • *Attendance* 18,136

Referee Graham POLL (Tring)

Referee's Assistants S.L. GAGEN and I. BLANCHARD

Blue and White Striped Shirts, Black Shorts		Goals	Claret and Blue Striped Shirts, Claret Shorts		Goals
1	Kevin PRESSMAN		1	David JAMES	
2	Peter ATHERTON (c)		2	Steve WATSON	
3	Andy HINCHCLIFFE		3	Alan WRIGHT #	
4	Wim JONK		5	Ugo EHIOGU (c)	
6	Des WALKER		9	Dion DUBLIN	
10	Andy BOOTH ‡		11	Alan THOMPSON	90
16	Niclas ALEXANDERSSON		15	Gareth BARRY	
17	Ian NOLAN		17	Lee HENDRIE ❑	
21	Lee BRISCOE †		19	Richard WALKER ‡	
23	Gilles DE BILDE		24	Mark DELANEY †	
33	Alan QUINN ❑		31	Jlloyd SAMUEL	
	Substitutes			*Substitutes*	
7	Danny SONNER †62		12	Julian JOACHIM ‡56	
12	Richard CRESSWELL ‡81		20	Najwan GHRAYIB #64	
13	Barry RICHARDSON (Gk)		26	Steve STONE †45	
22	Steven HASLAM		30	Jonathan BEWERS	
26	Barry HORNE		39	Peter ENCKELMAN (Gk)	

BEFORE		P	W	D	L	F	A	pts	AFTER		P	W	D	L	F	A	pts
7	Villa	31	12	10	9	35	27	46	6	Villa	32	13	10	9	36	27	49
19	Sheff Wed	30	5	6	19	27	57	21	19	Sheff Wed	31	5	6	20	27	58	21

FACTFILE

Villa have won five of their last six meetings with the Owls... Alan Thompson's first goal since scoring in the home leg of the Worthington Cup tie with Chester City on 21st September... There is tragedy in Turkey this night, when two Leeds fans are stabbed to death ahead of their team's UEFA Cup tie with Galatasaray.

'B Team' keeps up momentum

With the acclaim of Wembley's west end still ringing in their ears, Villa reconvene on a bleak night at Hillsborough, where the spectre of relegation casts a subdued pall around the stadium.

It should be an ideal setting for the Cup Finalists to be caught with their heads still in the clouds, yet Villa are commendably refocused, even if they need a goal from Alan Thompson deep into injury time to break what was looking increasingly like an intractable deadlock.

That they apply themselves so readily to the season's bread-and-butter is down partly to an enforced reshuffle that sees five changes from the team that beat Bolton; Benito Carbone, Ian Taylor, George Boateng, Paul Merson and Gareth Southgate, all being rested, either through injury or exhaustion after the rigours of 120 minutes at Wembley.

It opens the door for five replacements and with John Gregory already hinting that his Cup Final team will not be set in stone until the big day itself, every game between now and mid-May becomes an audition.

No one will relish the opportunity much more than Alan Thompson, making his first start since the Darlington game, although he is not the first to learn how finely-drawn is the line between success and failure in sport.

Gregory admits afterwards that several errors prior to his goal would have seen the Geordie hauled off but for the lack of a suitable replacement on the bench.

Thompson redeems himself

in the 92nd minute, sparing his side a frustrated journey home after a game they had controlled for long periods.

He is on the end of a Steve Stone cross from the right and heads the ball downwards to beat Wednesday goalkeeper Kevin Pressman. It rips another piece of hope away from the Owls, who may have thought that Lady Luck was making one of her rare appearances in blue and white stripes this season.

Dion Dublin, starting a game for the first time since his fateful injury in the corresponding fixture at Villa Park, is thwarted by the woodwork for the third time in three days when he hits the outside of the post from 12 yards after a Gareth Barry cross in the 29th minute and heads Lee Hendrie's cross against the upright once more, 12 minutes later.

One blank page remains in the Dublin horror story against Wednesday this season, which has seen him hit the timbers three times, miss a penalty and suffer a serious injury. Only a disallowed goal remains and that irritation duly arrives in the 62nd minute, when Julian Joachim's effort is wiped out after Dublin is adjudged to have fouled the goalkeeper.

It sparks Sheffield as much as it dismays Dion. The time for making do with draws has long passed for the Tykes and while they lack the imagination to make more of a plethora of crosses, they do manage threatening shots from Alan Quinn and Gilles de Bilde, while David James has to throw himself at the feet of Danny Sonner, seven minutes from time, to preserve the clean sheet.

It sets the stage for Thompson to clinch the game at the death and reassure anyone who might have feared seven weeks of anti-climax between Villa's two Wembley visits.

Goalscorer – Alan Thompson

Sunday 9th April 2000 • Villa Park • 3.00pm

ASTON VILLA 1 LEEDS UNITED 0

Half-time 1-0 • *Attendance* 33,889

Referee Barry KNIGHT (Orpington)

Referee's Assistants A.J. MARTIN and P. PROSSER

Claret and Blue Striped Shirts, Claret Shorts		Goals	White Shirts, White Shorts		Goals
1	David JAMES		1	Nigel MARTYN	
2	Steve WATSON		2	Gary KELLY ❑	
3	Alan WRIGHT †		3	Ian HARTE	
5	Ugo EHIOGU		5	Lucas RADEBE (c)	
6	George BOATENG		6	Jonathan WOODGATE	
10	Paul MERSON (c)		8	Michael BRIDGES †	
12	Julian JOACHIM	39	10	Harry KEWELL	
15	Gareth BARRY		11	Lee BOWYER	
17	Lee HENDRIE #		14	Stephen McPHAIL	
18	Benito CARBONE ‡		16	Jason WILCOX	
31	Jlloyd SAMUEL ❑		19	Eirik BAKKE	
Substitutes			*Substitutes*		
9	Dion DUBLIN ‡59		4	Alf Inge HAALAND	
11	Alan THOMPSON #67		12	Darren HUCKERBY †59	
20	Najwan GHRAYIB †51		13	Paul ROBINSON (Gk)	
24	Mark DELANEY		18	Danny MILLS	
39	Peter ENCKELMAN (Gk)		20	Matthew JONES	

BEFORE	P	W	D	L	F	A	pts	AFTER	P	W	D	L	F	A	pts
2 Leeds	31	19	3	9	49	34	60	3 Leeds	32	19	3	10	49	35	60
6 Villa	32	13	10	9	36	27	49	6 Villa	33	14	10	9	37	27	52

FACTFILE

A fourth consecutive Villa clean sheet (all competitions), the first time they have achieved this since 22nd December 1996... Joachim's first goal since his brace at Middlesbrough... Villa will face Chelsea in the Cup Final on 20th May, after the Londoners beat Newcastle United 2-1 at Wembley.

Joachim joy as United slump

If Leeds United thought a slump in form would be their abiding memory of a season turning sour, they have had a rude awakening in the days leading up to this game.

The death of two United supporters in a few hours of mayhem on the streets of Turkey in midweek has all but drawn a line under the Yorkshiremen's campaign, how ironic that a team so young should have its season sullied by problems more befitting to football's dark age of 20 years ago, and it is a sombre group of men who report to the visitors' dressing room.

All minute's silences should be as this one was. It is a truly poignant moment just before kick-off, when all that can be heard from a stadium filled with some 34,000 people is the occasional chirp of a bird and the light rattle of debris on the stand roofs.

While the Villa players form an arc around the centre circle, their opponents prefer to huddle rugby-style, as if trying to hang on to the last semblance of normality in a season which has crumbled into chaos.

It is a credit to their professionalism that they proceed to do just that in a busy first 45 minutes, before the game runs out of gas.

While the Holte Enders and the visiting supporters' section strike up a touching vocal rapport, as the home fans try to lift the spirits of their Leeds counterparts, the two teams fight out an engrossing nip-and-tuck first half, with Benito Carbone cannoning a shot off goal-keeper Nigel Martyn's chest and Gareth Barry having a long-range effort deflected against the post, before Julian Joachim settles the game and ends a 10-game goalless streak, in the 39th minute.

A through-ball from Gareth Barry sets up Joachim and Leeds defender Gary Kelly on a collision course that sees the latter fall to the floor, while Julian advances to fire the ball past Martyn. The visitors are adamant that Kelly was barged off the ball, but replays suggest that the Republic of Ireland international merely tripped over his own feet, and after a consultation with his linesman, the referee allows the goal to stand.

Leeds are not short of chances to get back on terms prior to the half-time whistle. David James is kept busy as he twice has to save an initial shot and then courageously gather the rebound as United players come steaming in.

His best stop comes when Lee Bowyer lunges at a low cross from the left just before half-time, forcing the Villa keeper to make a fine save low down to his left.

Not helped by a stiff breeze, the game tails off forlornly after the interval and tempers begin to flare, although no one has greater cause to rant and rave than Michael Bridges, who contrives to put a 58th minute cross from Harry Kewell over the bar when a goal appears to be nothing more than a formality.

Leeds may see more of the ball in general, but it is heartening to watch Villa threaten more with the fewer chances which come their way. In the end, though, a match to be got through rather than savoured, particularly for those players and patrons in white shirts.

Leeds' Michael Bridges – coming off second best to Ugo Ehiogu

Saturday 15th April 2000 • White Hart Lane • 3.06pm

TOTTENHAM HOTSPUR 2 ASTON VILLA 4

Half-time 1-0 • *Attendance* 35,304

Referee Rob HARRIS (Oxford)

Referee's Assistants G. BEALE and R. GOULD

White Shirts, Navy Blue Shorts		Goals
1	Ian WALKER	
2	Stephen CARR	
3	Mauricio TARICCO ❑	
4	Steffen FREUND	
5	Sol CAMPBELL (c) ❑	
6	Chris PERRY ❑	
7	Darren ANDERTON ❑	
10	Steffen IVERSEN	16
14	David GINOLA	
16	Chris ARMSTRONG	47
25	Stephen CLEMENCE	
	Substitutes	
11	Willem KORSTEN	
13	Espen BAARDSEN (Gk)	
19	John SCALES	
21	Luke YOUNG	
28	Matthew ETHERINGTON	

Claret and Blue Striped Shirts, Claret Shorts		Goals
1	David JAMES	
2	Steve WATSON †	
3	Alan WRIGHT	74
5	Ugo EHIOGU	
6	George BOATENG ❑	
9	Dion DUBLIN	62pen,69
10	Paul MERSON (c)	
11	Alan THOMPSON ❑	
15	Gareth BARRY	
18	Benito CARBONE	70
31	Jlloyd SAMUEL ❑	
	Substitutes	
19	Richard WALKER	
20	Najwan GHRAYIB	
24	Mark DELANEY †45 ‡	
30	Jonathan BEWERS ‡90	
39	Peter ENCKELMAN (Gk)	

BEFORE		P	W	D	L	F	A	pts
6	Villa	33	14	10	9	37	27	52
11	Spurs	32	12	7	13	47	40	43

AFTER		P	W	D	L	F	A	pts
6	Villa	34	15	10	9	41	29	55
12	Spurs	33	12	7	14	49	44	43

FACTFILE

The game kicked off at 3.06pm to commemorate the 11th anniversary of the Hillsborough disaster... Alan Wright's first goal since scoring at Wimbledon on 9th April 1997... Joachim misses game after flying out to represent St Vincent, only to learn that his England U21 and U18 appearances make him ineligible.

Villa toast absent friends

Whatever you think of George Graham, you can't fault his timing. Just a few days before Villa were in town, the Spurs manager was admitted to hospital with an arthritic condition and it soon became apparent that his touchline duties for this afternoon would have to be delegated to his coaching staff.

Wrench though it must have been for the dedicated Scot, if you have to while away one Saturday afternoon drinking Lucozade and listening to hospital radio, it might as well be one like this.

Because the simmering discontent that has bubbled among White Hart Lane devotees for some time now is brought to the boil as Spurs surrender a 2-0 lead in the face of a second-half onslaught that sees Aston Villa submit their 'Goal of the Season' entries *en masse* in the space of 12 minutes.

If it is devastating for the hosts, it is uplifting for their jubilant opponents, and with Chelsea losing 1-0 at Sheffield Wednesday on the same afternoon, some of that smart Cup Final money steaming in on the Londoners suddenly doesn't look quite so clever.

And yet the sensation has such humble beginnings. Even as Dion Dublin steps up to stroke home a penalty past Ian Walker shortly before the hour, attention is more focused on the handball which preceded it, Steffen Iversen being fortunate still to be on the pitch in the opinion of the Villa camp, who believed the contact was more deliberate than reflex.

With referee and linesman unable to identify the culprit, to the rueful amusement of the visitors, the Norwegian stays, but his presence swiftly becomes an irrelevance as Villa find three goals from the top drawer to leave Spurs gasping.

Dublin displays a rather touching faith in the quality of British spinal surgery, when he launches himself into an overhead kick with all the trimmings to divert Benito Carbone's 69th minute cross for the equaliser and then he returns the favour to equally telling effect a minute later.

David James' booming kick is headed by Dublin into Carbone's path, and the Italian kills the ball on his chest before thumping a dipping 25-yard volley over Walker.

The hosts get just four minutes' respite this time, before Alan Wright hits his first goal in three years, returning Sol Campbell's headed clearance with interest, as he strikes a sweet half-volley home from roughly the same range as Carbone.

While it is not an extensive trend, Villa have never lost a game when the wing-back scores, but even if they aren't aware of that statistic, Spurs probably don't need persuading that their goose is cooked.

They had ironically subdued a lively start by their opponents in the first half, to take the lead when Iversen converted a precise cross from David Ginola, and when Chris Armstrong redeemed himself for an awful miss by beating the offside trap with the second half a mere two minutes old, to make it 2-0, Villa appear doomed.

That they recover in such dramatic fashion hints at a confident side that is hopefully poised to peak just as the season reaches its climax.

Goalscorer extraordinaire – Alan Wright

Saturday 22nd April 2000 • Villa Park • 3.00pm

ASTON VILLA 2 LEICESTER CITY 2

Half-time 1-1 • Attendance 31,229

Referee Graham BARBER (Tring)

Referee's Assistants D. DRYSDALE and J. HOLBROOK

Claret and Blue Striped Shirts, Claret Shorts		Goals	Yellow Shirts with Blue Trim, Blue Shorts		Goals
1	David JAMES		1	Tim FLOWERS	
2	Steve WATSON ❑		3	Frank SINCLAIR	
3	Alan WRIGHT		4	Gerry TAGGART ❑	
5	Ugo EHIOGU		6	Muzzy IZZET ‡	
6	George BOATENG ❑		7	Neil LENNON ❑	64
9	Dion DUBLIN ‡		14	Robbie SAVAGE	
10	Paul MERSON (c)	47	15	Phil GILCHRIST	
11	Alan THOMPSON †	31	18	Matt ELLIOTT (c)	36
15	Gareth BARRY		24	Andy IMPEY	
18	Benito CARBONE		27	Tony COTTEE	
31	Jlloyd SAMUEL		29	Stefan OAKES †	
Substitutes			*Substitutes*		
12	Julian JOACHIM ‡80		5	Steve WALSH	
17	Lee HENDRIE †71		20	Ian MARSHALL	
20	Najwan GHRAYIB		22	Pegguy ARPHEXAD (Gk)	
30	Jonathan BEWERS		28	Lawrie DUDFIELD †59	
39	Peter ENCKELMAN (Gk)		37	Theo ZAGORAKIS ‡72	

BEFORE	P	W	D	L	F	A	pts	AFTER	P	W	D	L	F	A	pts
6 Villa	34	15	10	9	41	29	55	6 Villa	35	15	11	9	43	31	56
11 Leicester	33	13	6	14	46	48	45	11 Leicester	34	13	7	14	48	50	46

FACTFILE

Villa concede four goals over two consecutive games for the first time since 6th November... Villa fans will be situated at the tunnel end of Wembley Stadium on Cup Final day, the opposite end from that where they sat for their semi-final with Bolton and both their successful League Cup Finals in the '90s.

Neighbours from hell

If Fox-hunting was as futile generally as it is where Aston Villa are concerned, the League Against Cruel Sports would have decamped to the bull-rings of Spain some years ago.

John Gregory won't have any talk of Leicester City and 'hoodoos', yet it becomes harder and harder to find an alternative pigeon-hole in which to place a fixture that has now not yielded a Villa win on the last 12 occasions.

With a third defeat of Leeds this season under their belts and last weekend's sensational victory at Spurs, Villa hit the ground running against their Midlands rivals, and taking the lead twice would be enough, you might think, to erase the memory of two grim trips to Filbert Street this term.

Not a bit of it. No sooner does neat work by Geordie duo Alan Thompson and Steve Watson unlock City's defences to push Villa in front, than Matt Elliott and Neil Lennon negate the advantage each time, like card-sharks slipping a trump card down their sleeve.

Elliott being asked to exchange the destructive role of centre-half for the creative intricacies of centre-forward always carries vague echoes of Fred Flintstone being asked to advise on fabric combinations for Royal Ascot, yet full credit to him; he gets the job done.

Scorer of the goal that removed Villa from the Worthington Cup, today he shows an aplomb of which Gary Lineker would have been proud, to tie the game up at 1-1 after 36 minutes, when he calmly thumps the ball past David James, after Gareth Barry's wild swipe at Stefan Oakes' cross meets only air.

Then there's Lennon, who makes the contention that Leicester City are nothing but graft look ridiculous, when Elliott nods a cross down to him in Villa's penalty area in the 64th minute. With Alan Wright hurtling towards him at a tangent, the Ulsterman executes a delightful sleight-of-foot to take the defender out of the game, before side-footing the ball into the right-hand corner of James' goal.

It wipes out some creditable work by their hosts, who have the better of a scrappy opening. Thompson draws first blood, emerging on the blind side of City's defence to thump a Dion Dublin back-heel past Tim Flowers after 31 minutes.

City respond by sending Elliott to join Tony Cottee and it almost proves a master-stroke, as the converted striker nods an Oakes centre across the face of goal, 11 minutes after he has levelled the scores, only for Cottee to be inches away from giving Leicester the lead.

A fine run and cross from the right by Steve Watson allows Paul Merson to restore Villa's edge with the easiest of headers two minutes after the interval, but Villa cannot derive the inspiration from the goal that City did.

Missing Ian Taylor's trademark cavalry charges from midfield and bereft of telling passes, they remain vulnerable, and it would be wrong to suggest that Lennon's equaliser comes as a bolt from the blue.

Ending 43 years of FA Cup misery is one thing. Giving your regional rivals their comeuppance, it would seem, is very much another.

No way through for Paul Merson

Saturday 29th April 2000 • Villa Park • 3.00pm

ASTON VILLA 1 SUNDERLAND 1

Half-time 0-0 • Attendance 33,949

Referee Andy D'URSO (Billericay)
Referee's Assistants R. BURTON and M. TINGEY

Claret and Blue Striped Shirts, Claret Shorts	Goals	Red and White Striped Shirts, White Shorts	Goals
1 David JAMES		1 Thomas SORENSEN	
4 Gareth SOUTHGATE (c)		2 Chris MAKIN (c)	
5 Ugo EHIOGU		3 Michael GRAY	
6 George BOATENG		4 Kevin KILBANE †	
10 Paul MERSON		6 Paul BUTLER	
11 Alan THOMPSON ‡		7 Nicky SUMMERBEE	
12 Julian JOACHIM †		9 Niall QUINN	85
15 Gareth BARRY ❏	59	10 Kevin PHILLIPS ❏	
18 Benito CARBONE		17 Jody CRADDOCK ❏	
20 Najwan GHRAYIB #		19 Paul THIRLWELL	
24 Mark DELANEY		29 Eric ROY	
Substitutes		*Substitutes*	
2 Steve WATSON		12 Danny DICHIO	
9 Dion DUBLIN †60		13 Andy MARRIOTT (Gk)	
17 Lee HENDRIE ‡77		18 Darren WILLIAMS	
31 Jlloyd SAMUEL #87		27 Thomas BUTLER	
39 Peter ENCKELMAN (Gk)		28 John OSTER †45	

BEFORE	P	W	D	L	F	A	pts	AFTER	P	W	D	L	F	A	pts
6 Villa	35	15	11	9	43	31	56	6 Villa	36	15	12	9	44	32	57
7 Sunderland	35	15	9	11	54	52	54	7 Sunderland	36	15	10	11	55	53	55

FACTFILE

Sunderland's first visit to Villa Park since 1st February 1997... Gareth Barry's first goal since scoring in the final home game of last season, against Charlton... Najwan Ghrayib makes his first Premiership start... Gareth Southgate returns to the side after recovering from his ankle injury.

Quinn's late goal dents Euro hopes

The old superstition about a black cat crossing your path being lucky has had its day in north-east Birmingham, after Sunderland snatch a late equaliser from nowhere to leave Villa's hopes of European qualification via the league in tatters.

As wasted chances go, not even the previous Saturday's fare comes close. Even when trailing, Leicester always induced the suspicion that they might have something in reserve, but Sunderland look a spent force the moment they go behind to a Gareth Barry goal on the hour.

As their manager Peter Reid has admitted, behind the indefatigable goalscoring exploits of Kevin Phillips, ably supported by Niall Quinn, is an unspectacular team that will most certainly need bolstering before 2000-01.

Its shallow reserves are exposed when Barry gets his head to an Alan Thompson corner and the ball squeezes between a defender and the post. Disappointment at going behind, coupled with a sense of injustice that the goal should stand, despite goalkeeper Thomas Sorensen claiming he was unfairly impeded, reduces the visitors to headless chickens in the absence of injured old stager Steve Bould.

The boot is suddenly on the other foot for a Villa team that was similarly shaken by a controversial goal at The Stadium of Light six months earlier. Unlike Sunderland on that autumn evening, however, Villa cannot find the killer touch.

His confidence even higher than normal, Barry sees Sorensen tip his 18-yard effort over the bar four minutes after his goal, and Benito Carbone shoots narrowly wide of the far post when Dion Dublin's back-header to David James' huge goal kick sets Carbone clear of the defence.

George Boateng is then released by Carbone into a similarly generous space, with Sunder-land's now-hapless defence scattered across several counties, but the Dutchman scuffs an easy shot to the goalkeeper.

Despite Paul Merson having similarly mis-cued his shot after a burst into the area early in the half, the newly-christened 'Black Cats' ('Rokermen' having become somewhat obso-lete) show so little sign of being able to run to two lives, let alone nine, that three points for a generally desultory performance seems to be Villa's destiny long before the final whistle.

Sunderland's best moments are confined to the first half-hour, when David James has to be alert to deny Phillips and keep out a shot from Paul Thirlwell, but even then, so effective is the containment of Phillips that Sunderland offer little hint of the team which stormed up the table in the first five months of the campaign.

Sadly for Villa, they learn with five minutes to go that having kept Eric Morecambe gagged throughout, it was Ernie Wise who had the punch-line all along. Ugo Ehiogu commits to a low corner but fails to intercept it and with two deft touches, Niall Quinn steadies the ball and pokes it past James.

Four points gone begging in the space of seven days. If there is any consolation, it is the hope that Villa are getting the mistakes out of their system now, rather than being confronted by them on 20th May, in a Cup Final which is now as crucial to their European plans as it is to their trophy cabinet.

Beni Carbone plays footsie with Paul Thirlwell

Saturday 6th May 2000 • Selhurst Park • 3.00pm

WIMBLEDON 2 ASTON VILLA 2

Half-time 1-0 • *Attendance* 19,188

Referee Mark HALSEY (Welwyn Garden City)

Referee's Assistants D. BABSKI and C. WEBSTER

Dark Blue Shirts, Dark Blue Shorts		Goals	Claret and Blue Striped Shirts, Claret Shorts		Goals
1	Neil SULLIVAN		1	David JAMES	
2	Kenny CUNNINGHAM (c) †		3	Alan WRIGHT †	
5	Dean BLACKWELL		4	Gareth SOUTHGATE (c)	
6	Ben THATCHER		5	Ugo EHIOGU	15og
7	Carl CORT #		9	Dion DUBLIN ❑ ‡	74
10	Jason EUELL		10	Paul MERSON	
11	Marcus GAYLE		11	Alan THOMPSON	
12	Neal ARDLEY		15	Gareth BARRY	
16	Michael HUGHES ‡		17	Lee HENDRIE	56
29	Trond ANDERSEN		18	Benito CARBONE	
30	Hermann HREIDARSSON		24	Mark DELANEY ❑	
	Substitutes			*Substitutes*	
3	Alan KIMBLE		12	Julian JOACHIM ‡81	
9	John HARTSON #76	90	27	Michael STANDING	
13	Paul HEALD (Gk)		31	Jlloyd SAMUEL †65	
21	Duncan JUPP †28		38	John McGRATH	
24	Damien FRANCIS ‡45		39	Peter ENCKELMAN (Gk)	

BEFORE		P	W	D	L	F	A	pts	AFTER		P	W	D	L	F	A	pts
6	Villa	36	15	12	9	44	32	57	6	Villa	37	15	13	9	46	34	58
18	Wimbledon	36	7	11	18	44	70	32	17	Wimbledon	37	7	12	18	46	72	33

FACTFILE

A third straight draw with the Dons... Villa can now no longer qualify for Europe via the Premiership... Lee Hendrie's first goal since scoring twice at home to Chester City in September... John Gregory signs a new three-year contract to remain Villa manager, two days before the game.

Late equaliser gives Dons hope

They are a lot better placed in the Premiership but Villa cannot match Wimbledon when it comes to party-pooping.

The only blots on Benito Carbone's glittering debut back in October were that he failed to score and his new club failed to win, as Wimbledon kept their heads at a buzzing Villa Park, the vast majority of whose occupants were willing the new signing to clinch three points with a goal.

Locked in battle with Bradford to avoid the final relegation spot, the stakes are infinitely higher for the hosts in the return fixture, yet Villa fail to return the compliment by just 45 seconds.

That's how close they are to a come-from-behind 2-1 victory, when substitute John Hartson, villain of the piece a week earlier when his red card at Bradford ruled him out of the Dons' crucial last game of the season, turns hero by nodding in a Neal Ardley corner in the 92nd minute, after David James has found his path to the ball blocked.

Hartson's outrageous timing, his transformation from pariah to prince; both suggest that Wimbledon's mercurial spirit is returning, following the replacement in midweek of manager Egil Olsen with Terry Burton, who immediately did his own bit for the 'Crazy Gang' mentality, by threatening to throw any journalist who questioned the commitment of Dons players, into the Thames.

Certainly, the manner in which his side gives itself hope for next week's game at Southampton would warm the heart of any Wimbledon traditionalist. You let the opposing team score your first goal, shrug off the little matter of losing your captain to a groin injury and your best player to a broken leg, and somehow still manage to send your fans home in raptures.

This loopiness ultimately reduces Villa to bystanders at someone else's party, yet for long enough they had looked emphatic gatecrashers, even if poor Ugo Ehiogu has one of those days where nothing goes right.

As if fate hadn't done enough by turning his attempted back-pass following a cross into an own goal after 15 minutes, it then decrees that he shall be the recipient of a superb chipped pass by Paul Merson after the interval, which leaves the big defender one-on-one with goalkeeper Neil Sullivan, only for Ehiogu to send his shot over the bar.

The miss is forgotten when Lee Hendrie heads the equaliser following an Alan Wright cross in the 56th minute and the unravelling of Wimbledon looks complete 18 minutes later, when Gareth Southgate's clearance bypasses the Dons' back line, leaving Dion Dublin in the clear to atone for an earlier miss by slamming the ball past Sullivan.

It cannot quite unclog the pipes, however, as Jlloyd Samuel is the next man to spurn a goalscoring chance, when the young defender is unable to control the ball at his feet in the Wimbledon penalty area, when a shot is his for the asking.

Missing skipper Kenny Cunningham and Michael Hughes, whose leg is broken following an accidental collision with Mark Delaney, the Londoners take their last throw of the dice shortly after going behind, with the arrival of substitute Hartson. For the third week in a row, Villa are about to suffer for missed opportunities.

Lee Hendrie – headed Villa back into the game

Saturday 15th April 2000 • Villa Park • 3.00pm

ASTON VILLA 0 MANCHESTER UNITED 1

Half-time 0-0 • Attendance 39,217

Referee Paul DURKIN (Portland)
Referee's Assistants M.A. WILLIAMS and P. CANADINE

Claret and Blue Striped Shirts, Claret Shorts	Goals	Navy Blue Shirts, White Shorts	Goals
39 Peter ENCKELMAN		17 Raimond VAN DER GOUW	
3 Alan WRIGHT		3 Denis IRWIN	
4 Gareth SOUTHGATE (c)		10 Teddy SHERINGHAM	64
5 Ugo EHIOGU		11 Ryan GIGGS	
6 George BOATENG #		12 Phil NEVILLE	
9 Dion DUBLIN		18 Paul SCHOLES ❑	
10 Paul MERSON		19 Dwight YORKE	
15 Gareth BARRY		20 Ole Gunnar SOLSKJAER †	
17 Lee HENDRIE ‡		21 Henning BERG	
18 Benito CARBONE †		27 Mickael SILVESTRE	
24 Mark DELANEY ❑		28 Danny HIGGINBOTHAM ‡	
Substitutes		*Substitutes*	
7 Ian TAYLOR ‡64		14 Jordi CRUYFF †33 ❑	
11 Alan THOMPSON #80		25 Quinton FORTUNE	
12 Julian JOACHIM †58		30 Ronnie WALLWORK ‡45	
13 Neil CUTLER (Gk)		34 Jonathan GREENING	
31 Jlloyd SAMUEL		43 Michael STEWART	

BEFORE	P	W	D	L	F	A	pts	AFTER	P	W	D	L	F	A	pts
1 United	37	27	7	3	96	45	88	1 United	38	28	7	3	97	45	91
6 Villa	37	15	13	9	46	34	58	6 Villa	38	15	13	10	46	35	58

FACTFILE

*Villa's first home defeat since losing to Newcastle United on 4th December...
They are goalless in their final league game of the season for the first time since
1996... They fail to score for the first time in open play since the semi-final with
Bolton Wanderers.*

Going through the motions

Two teams with their minds elsewhere end another season at Villa Park, and if John Gregory is critical of the 'testimonial' pace of a listless encounter, the analogy is fitting, given that the club is saying farewell to its most famous stretch of bricks and mortar.

One only wishes that the Trinity Road stand could have had a more stirring send-off. The first game it witnessed was the 2-0 defeat of Blackburn Rovers in August 1922. The last is a distinctly second-gear affair, with Villa's players anxious not to be crocked six days ahead of the Cup Final and United's players, their sixth Premiership crown secured some three weeks ago, probably already imagining the sand between their toes.

If pre-game rumours of United fielding their *creche* at Villa Park for the second time this season prove to be unfounded, so does any talk that Sir Alex Ferguson's men are committed to being the first team to break the 100 goal barrier in the Premiership.

That requires four goals to be conceded by Villa at home for the first time since they lost 4-3 to Charlton in their final home game of last season, but the point is academic as the visitors make do with just one, Teddy Sheringham being the happy recipient of an inadequate clearance from a Jordi Cruyff cross, as he sidefoots the ball past Peter Enckelman with the clock showing 64 minutes.

The young Finn is deputising for David James, who is under orders not to aggravate a groin injury. He isn't missing much, in a game where the sight of Dwight Yorke playing in midfield sums up the general absence of cutting edge.

When United score Villa are stung into action and after a generally quiet afternoon, Dion Dublin is denied twice in the last few minutes, his volley from an Ian Taylor header being deflected for a corner, which leads to an Alan Wright cross that the big striker heads onto the crossbar. Earlier, his downward header had deceived Raimond Van Der Gouw, the United keeper being saved by a goalline clearance from Phil Neville.

Paul Merson, toiling as ever to give the home fans something to cheer, also has his chances to open the hosts' account. His chipped shot from a Lee Hendrie back-heel after 20 minutes had to be clawed away by Raimond Van Der Gouw, but Merson cannot find anything like the same touch when a Julian Joachim cross falls to his feet seven minutes from full-time.

Pressing to level the scores, Villa are vulnerable to United's counter-attack and Gareth Barry and Gareth Southgate both make timely tackles to deny Sheringham and Paul Scholes, the latter's assured performance throughout the game marred only by a caution for a silly foul on Hendrie.

The final whistle is met with the general relief once reserved for the bell at the end of double maths on a hot Friday afternoon. Only the thought of quitting the Trinity for the final time gives pause to the exodus.

Villa deserve credit for not succumbing to anti-climax over these last seven weeks, but it is nevertheless a relief that the phony wars are now over. Bring on Chelsea.

Dion Dublin – foiled by the crossbar

Saturday 20th May 2000 • Wembley • 3.00pm

ASTON VILLA 0 CHELSEA 1

Half-time 0-0 • *Attendance* 78,217

Referee Graham POLL (Tring)

Referee's Assistants G. ATKINS and D. DRYSDALE

Claret and Blue Striped Shirts, Claret Shorts	Goals	Blue Shirts, Blue Shorts	Goals
1 David JAMES		1 Ed DE GOEY	
3 Alan WRIGHT #		3 Celestine BABAYARO	
4 Gareth SOUTHGATE (c)		5 Frank LEBOEUF	
5 Ugo EHIOGU		6 Marcel DESAILLY	
6 George BOATENG ❑		7 Didier DESCHAMPS	
7 Ian TAYLOR ‡		8 Gustavo POYET ❑	
9 Dion DUBLIN		11 Dennis WISE (c) ❑	
10 Paul MERSON		15 Mario MELCHIOT ❑	
15 Gareth BARRY ❑		16 Roberto DI MATTEO	72
18 Benito CARBONE †		25 Gianfranco ZOLA ‡	
24 Mark DELANEY		31 George WEAH †	
Substitutes		*Substitutes*	
12 Julian JOACHIM †79		19 Tore Andre FLO †87	
17 Lee HENDRIE #88		20 Jody MORRIS ‡90	
26 Steve STONE ‡79		23 Carlo CUDICINI (Gk)	
31 Jlloyd SAMUEL		26 John TERRY	
39 Peter ENCKELMAN (Gk)		34 Jon HARLEY	

Villa lose their third FA Cup Final... They are yet to score when losing in an FA Cup Final... The defeat condemns them to InterToto Cup football beginning in mid-July... Ian Taylor wins his battle against the hamstring injury sustained against Bolton Wanderers in the semi-final... Carbone and Boateng are first players from outside British Isles to play for Villa in an FA Cup Final... Johnny Dixon and Peter McParland, central figures from the 1957 Final, are the club's guests at Wembley... Di Matteo's goal the only goal scored by a Chelsea player against Villa in 4-and-a-half hours of football this season.

Forty-three years and counting

At first sight, this sad end to Aston Villa's season comes down to an error by David James. Yet the roots go far deeper, for as the man from *The Times* points out afterwards, how unbearable must the pressure be on a goalkeeper when his team looks so incapable of scoring at the other end?

As Villa's league schedule has falteringly wound down during these last three weeks, the consolatory hope has been that some players were preserving themselves for their date with destiny in north London.

What this has gained in healthy bodies, it has lost in terms of fading momentum, and as the last Final in the shadow of the twin towers unfolds, it becomes apparent that Villa cannot instantly revert to the crushing form that confounded Spurs, back on the same April day when Chelsea were losing 1-0 at Sheffield Wednesday and prospects looked bright for the famous trophy finding its way back to Villa Park.

Time and again, Villa find themselves with the ball at their feet and room to manoeuvre, midway into Chelsea's half, only for a lack of support and ideas to reduce their attacking gameplan to a dispirited fudge.

Chelsea, in contrast, look like a team that knows precisely what it is about, even when thwarted, and when the trio of Deschamps, Poyet and Wise, finally gets the measure of its opponents in a midfield battle that is as blood-curdling as it is crucial, the Londoners slip into an ominous gear that hits maximum revs with 18 minutes left.

Ian Taylor's tussle with Mario Melchiot yields a free-kick just to the left of Villa's area, and Gianfranco Zola fires a cross like a tracer bullet to the near post.

Momentarily distracted by the throng, James

can only slap the ball downwards, where it rebounds off Gareth Southgate and is poked home from close range by Roberto Di Matteo. The disconsolate keeper had surrendered his 'get out of jail' card 18 minutes earlier, when he could not hold a shot that rebounded to Dennis Wise, only for the Chelsea captain's goal to be ruled out through George Weah being offside. It is one of the few things the Liberian does wrong this afternoon, in a performance full of deft flicks and imaginative runs that sadly find no echo amongst his opponents.

With Desailly making it a very different Wembley occasion for Dion Dublin this time around, and the supposedly suspect Frank Leboeuf not missing a step, it is not one of Ed de Goey's more hectic afternoons.

On the one occasion Villa manage a shot on goal Chelsea's Dutch keeper even has the luxury of delegating his duties, Leboeuf blocking with ease a scuffed shot by a wide-open Benito Carbone from 12 yards, in the 75th minute.

This, and Ugo Ehiogu's wayward header when unmarked at the back post in injury-time, sum up the afternoon. All that fervour against Leeds in Round Five; all that irresistible sparkle at White Hart Lane: whither now?

If there is a lesson to be learned from Villa's conquerors this afternoon, it is the art of timing. When you can pull the fat from the fire in games which matter, it is remarkable how quickly those embarrassing little hiccups at Hillsborough are forgotten.

Gustavo Poyet goes over the top to deny Ugo

Friday 16th July 1999 • Stevenage Stadium • 7.45pm

STEVENAGE BOROUGH 0 ASTON VILLA 3

Half-time 0-0 • Attendance 3,886

Referee W. JORDAN

Referee's Assistants S. TINCKNELL and R. SIDLIN

Sky Blue Shirts, Sky Blue Shorts		Goals	White Shirts, White Shorts		Goals
1	Chris TAYLOR		1	David JAMES §	
2	Lee HARVEY		2	Steve WATSON †	
3	Ross HARRISON §		3	Alan WRIGHT (c)	
4	Mark SMITH		4	Colin CALDERWOOD	
5	Robin TROTT #		5	Gareth BARRY	
6	Ryan KIRBY ‡ ‡‡61		6	Lee HENDRIE	74
7	Michael LOVE		7	Steve STONE #	
8	Sam McMAHON		8	Mark DRAPER ‡	
9	Carl ALFORD ‡‡		9	Julian JOACHIM	61,78
10	Richard LEADBEATER ‡ ††61		10	Paul MERSON ††	
11	Jimmy STROUTS ††		11	Darius VASSELL ‡‡	
	Substitutes			*Substitutes*	
12	Lee HOWARTH ‡45		12	Mark DELANEY †45	
14	Chris PEARSON †30		13	Michael OAKES (Gk) §74	
15	Michael McLARNON #61		14	Ian TAYLOR ‡45	
16	Dwaynne PLUMMER §61		15	Simon GRAYSON ††74	
			16	Neil TARRANT ‡‡74	
			17	Jlloyd SAMUEL #45	

FACTFILE

Villa started off this game playing in a 4-4-2 formation, but didn't really come to life until the second half when they changed to their more familiar 3-5-2 pattern. When Jlloyd Samuel came on to create the third central defender and Ian Taylor moved into mid-field, it allowed Paul Merson to get in behind the two strikers and the goals soon began to flow. A neat chip from Merson gave Julian Joachim the chance to give Villa the lead; the second came 13 minutes later, when Hendrie side-footed home after combining well with Darius Vassell and Joachim rounded off the scoring when put through by Hendrie and Mark Delaney.

Tuesday 20th July 1999 • Middlefield Lane • 7.30pm

HINCKLEY UNITED 1 ASTON VILLA 6

H.U.F.C

Half-time 0-3 • *Attendance* 330

Referee Paul DANSON (Leicester)

Referee's Assistants A. PARSONS and M. DINGLEY

Yellow and Black Striped Shirts, Black Shorts	Goals	Claret and Blue Shirts, White Shorts	Goals
1 Wayne STARKEY		1 Peter ENCKELMAN ‡‡	
2 David SADLER †		2 Simon GRAYSON (c)	
3 John HASSALL ‡		3 David CURTOLO #	
4 Mark HARBOTTLE		4 Aaron LESCOTT	
5 Charlie PALMER		5 Jlloyd SAMUEL ‡	
6 Marvin MARSTON		6 Tommy JASZCZUN	
7 Adi DOUGHTY		7 Gavin MELAUGH §	33
8 Morton TITTERTON (c)		8 Michael STANDING †	
9 Paul HUNTER		9 Richard WALKER	35,52,65
10 Lee McGLINCHEY		10 Darren BYFIELD ††	20
11 Jason KNIGHT #		11 Neil TARRANT	
Substitutes		*Substitutes*	
12 Ian DREWITT †45		12 Stephen EVANS ‡52	
14 Richard SELBY ‡45		13 Matthew GHENT (Gk) ‡‡80	
15 Steve ADAMS #45		14 Graham EVANS #52	
16 Gary RICKETTS §45	69	15 Danny HAYNES ††65	
17 Jamie LENTON		16 Fraser MURRAY †23	90
		17 John McGRATH §52	

A Villa team, comprising a mixture of reserve team players and youths, proved to be too strong for a Hinckley team which was never really in the running. A hat-trick from striker Richard Walker was the highlight of the evening, strike partner Darren Byfield weighed in with one and the second was tucked away nicely by midfielder Gavin Melaugh, who should be a regular in the reserve side this season. Although substitute Gary Ricketts scored a well-deserved consolation to pull the score back to 5-1, triallist, Fraser Murray closed the scoring at the death.

FACTFILE

Friday 23rd July 1999 • Giants Stadium, New Jersey • 7.00pm

AJAX 2 ASTON VILLA 2

(No extra time – Villa won penalty shoot-out 3-2)

Half-time 1-2 • Attendance 23,500

Referee Kevin TERRY

Referee's Assistants G. BARKEY and C. LOWRY

Red and White Shirts, White Shorts		Goals	Turquoise Shirts with Black Trim, Black Shorts		Goals
1	Fred GRIM		1	David JAMES	
4	Jan VAN HALST		2	Mark DELANEY	
5	Frank VERLATT (c) §		3	Alan WRIGHT ❏	
8	Richard WITSCHGE		4	Gareth SOUTHGATE (c)	
9	Nikos MACHLAS ‡	39	5	Ugo EHIOGU #	
10	Brian LAUDRUP ††		6	Gareth BARRY	
13	Richard KNOPPER †		7	Ian TAYLOR	
14	DANI #		8	George BOATENG ‡	
24	Shora ARVELADZE		9	Dion DUBLIN †	29
30	Mitchell PIQUE		10	Julian JOACHIM ††	13
37	Aaron MOKOENA		11	Alan THOMPSON §	
	Substitutes			*Substitutes*	
7	WAMBERTO ††84	84	12	Paul MERSON §66	
12	Stanley MENZO (Gk)		13	Michael OAKES (Gk)	
15	Tim DE CLER #64		14	Mark DRAPER ‡56	
23	Martijn REUSER †45		15	Steve STONE ††80	
29	Kevin BOBSON ‡45		16	Colin CALDERWOOD #62	
36	Quido LANZAAT §80		17	Steve WATSON	
			18	Darius VASSELL †53	

PENALTY SHOOT-OUT – AJAX				PENALTY SHOOT-OUT – VILLA			
1	Jan VAN HALST	missed	0-0	1	Gareth SOUTHGATE	missed	0-0
2	Martijn REUSER	missed	0-0	2	Steve STONE	scored	1-0
3	Shora ARVELADZE	scored	1-1	3	Gareth BARRY	missed	1-1
4	Tim DE CLER	scored	2-1	4	Mark DRAPER	scored	2-2
5	Richard WITSCHGE	missed	2-2	5	Alan WRIGHT	scored	3-2

Saturday 24th July 1999 • Sixfields Stadium • 3.00pm

NORTHAMPTON TOWN 1 ASTON VILLA 1

Half-time 1-0 • *Attendance* 1,340

Referee P. REJER (West Midlands)

Referee's Assistants K. TOWNSEND and S. BRATT

Claret and White Striped Shirts, White Shorts		Goals	Turquoise Shirts with Black Trim, Turquiose Shorts		Goals
1	Keith WELCH ‡‡		1	Peter ENCKELMAN	
2	Ian CLARKSON		2	Simon GRAYSON (c)	
3	John FRAIN (c)		3	David CURTOLO #	
4	Garry HUGHES #		4	Aaron LESCOTT	
5	Lee HOWEY		5	Jlloyd SAMUEL §	
6	Richard HOPE ‡		6	Tommy JASZCZUN	
7	Dave SAVAGE		7	Jay SMITH	
8	Steve McGAVIN ††		8	Gavin MELAUGH	
9	Steven HOWARD §		9	Richard WALKER †	
10	Simon STURRIDGE	1	10	Darren BYFIELD ‡	
11	Roy HUNTER †		11	Neil TARRANT ††	

	Substitutes			*Substitutes*	
12	Duncan SPEDDING †51		12	Stephen EVANS †55	83
13	Tony DOBSON (Gk) ‡‡81		13	Michael PRICE	
13	Ryan THOMPSON ‡51		14	Graham EVANS ††83	
14	Sean PARRISH §79		15	Gary McSEVENEY	
15	Amadu DONGAR		16	Danny HAYNES	
16	Christian LEE ††79		17	Stephen COOKE §75	
17	Andrew MORROW #51		18	Jonathan BEWERS ‡63	
			19	John McGRATH #68	

FACTFILE

Once again, Villa fielded a team which was a mixture of reserves and youths and they put in a highly creditable performance against an experienced Northampton side. They got off to the worst possible start when Simon Sturridge beat Enckelman from close range, but they stuck to their task well and were rewarded when striker Stephen Evans scored with seven minutes left.

DLJ DIRECT GOTHAM CUP – FINAL

Sunday 25th July 1999 • Giants Stadium, New Jersey • 4.00pm

FIORENTINA 4 ASTON VILLA 0

Half-time 2-0 • *Attendance* 25,500

Referee Tim WEYLAND

Referee's Assistants G. VERGARA and N. CLEMENT

Purple Shirts, Purple Shorts		Goals	White Shirts with Claret and Blue Sash, White Shorts		Goals
1	Francesco TOLDO		1	David JAMES	
2	Thomas REPKA		2	Steve WATSON #	
3	Stefano BETTARINI		3	Alan WRIGHT	
4	Fabio ROSSITO ††		4	Gareth SOUTHGATE (c)	
5	Pasquale PADALINO		5	Ugo EHIOGU	
6	Alessandro PIERINI		6	Gareth BARRY	
7	Angelo DI LIVIO #		7	Ian TAYLOR §	
8	Predrag MIJATOVIC §	19	8	George BOATENG †	
9	Gabriel BATISTUTA ‡	35pen,48	9	Dion DUBLIN	
10	Manuel RUI COSTA	87	10	Julian JOACHIM	
11	Enrico CHIESA †		11	Alan THOMPSON ‡	

	Substitutes			*Substitutes*	
13	Aldo FIRICANO		12	Paul MERSON	
14	Daniele ADANI		13	Michael OAKES (Gk)	
15	Paul OKON †20		14	Mark DRAPER †45	
16	Mauro BRESSAN #72		15	Steve STONE §68	
17	Andrea TAROZZI		16	Colin CALDERWOOD	
18	Abel BALBO ‡68		17	Lee HENDRIE ‡45	
19	Guillermo AMOR §78		18	Mark DELANEY #45	
20	Christian AMOROSO				
22	Giuseppe TAGLIALARELA (Gk)				
25	Luis OLIVEIRA ††78				

Despite the competition's name, Fiorentina's prize is not a cup but a crystal block with an image of the the Gotham Cup logo created inside it by firing direct computer laser beams into the crystal.

FACTFILE

Tuesday 27th July 1999 • Croft Park • 7.30pm

BLYTH SPARTANS 0 ASTON VILLA 5

Half-time 0-1

Referee Keith MILLER

Referee's Assistants C. SEACH and B. DAVISON

Green and White Striped Shirts, Green Shorts		Goals	Claret and Blue Shirts, White Shorts		Goals
1	Sean MUSGRAVE		1	Michael PRICE ‡‡	
2	Michael FARREY (c)		2	Gary McSEVENEY #	
3	David BURT		3	David CURTOLO	
4	Andy BLOWER		4	Aaron LESCOTT	
5	Craig MELROSE		5	Jlloyd SAMUEL (c)	
6	Matty HYSEN †		6	Tommy JASZCZUN	65
7	Ross LUMSDEN §		7	Graham EVANS §	
8	Richie PITT		8	Gavin MELAUGH	66,80
9	Wayne EDGCUMBE		9	Neil TARRANT ‡	43
10	Steven HUTCHINSON ‡ §62		10	Darren BYFIELD †	
11	Derek ATWELL #		11	John McGRATH ††	
	Substitutes			*Substitutes*	
12	Jon ATKINSON †45		12	David HARDING #56	
14	Michael IRVING		13	Boaz MYHILL (Gk) ‡‡70	
15	Ian IRVING ‡45		14	Danny HAYNES ††62	
16	Lawrie PEARSON #45		15	Richard WALKER §59	
17	Paul JOISCE		16	Jay SMITH †45	67
			17	Stephen EVANS ‡45	

FACTFILE

A young Villa side made the long trip to Blyth Spartans, where an even first-half was followed by a second-half in which the visitors' superior fitness saw them comfortably home with a four goal burst. The first 45 minutes were closely fought and some entertaining, end-to-end play entertained the small crowd. The deadlock was broken two minutes from the break when Scottish striker Neil Tarrant forced the ball home. The second-half was slightly more one-sided and four goals, all coming from midfield, made it look easier than it really was.

Friday 30th July 1999 • The Lamb • 7.30pm

TAMWORTH 3 ASTON VILLA 4

Half-time 3-2 • Attendance 1,254

Referee B. MILLERSHIP (Atherstone)

Referee's Assistants R. JONES and J. VALLANCE

Red Shirts, Red Shorts	Goals	Turquoise Shirts with Black Trim, Turquiose Shorts	Goals
1 Harvey WILLETTS ††		1 Michael PRICE	
2 Rob WARNER		2 Jonathan BEWERS	
3 Rob MURCHELL		3 John McGRATH ††	
4 Darren GROCUTT §		4 Aaron LESCOTT	4og
5 Jon HOWARD (c) #		5 Danny HAYNES	
6 Michael GRAY ‡‡		6 Tommy JASZCZUN (c) #	
7 David FOY		7 Steve STONE	66
8 Gary SMITH † ##71	41	8 Gavin MELAUGH	42
9 Mark HALLAM		9 Richard WALKER †	
10 Warren HAUGHTON ‡		10 Paul MERSON	44
11 Mark WOLSEY ##	24	11 Neil TARRANT ‡	55
Substitutes		*Substitutes*	
12 Mickey COTTER †45		12 Graham EVANS ‡68	
14 Paul HATTON ‡45		13 Boaz MYHILL (Gk)	
15 Richard CLARKE #45		14 David HUGHES †53	
16 Nick COLLEY §45		15 Michael STANDING ††76	
17 Wayne DYER ‡‡60		16 Jay SMITH #70	
18 Darren ACTON (Gk) ††45			

FACTFILE

A fine first-half performance from Tamworth saw them go into a three goal lead by the 41st minute, thanks to an Aaron Lescott own goal followed by strikes from Mark Wolsey and Gary Smith. But Paul Merson and Steve Stone then inspired a fight-back and by half-time goals from the impressive Gavin Melaugh and Paul Merson had brought Villa back into the game. It was a goal from Neil Tarrant ten minutes into the second-half that gave Villa parity. And it was only fitting that Steve Stone should score the winner to round off a thrilling encounter.

PRE-SEASON FRIENDLY

Sunday 1st August 1999 • Feyenoord Stadium • 2.30pm

FEYENOORD 0 ASTON VILLA 0

Half-time 0-0 • *Attendance* 26,500

Referee J.H. UILENBERG
Referee's Assistants J.C. RIJSER and A. INIA

Red and White Halved Shirts, Black Shorts	Goals	Claret and Blue Striped Shirts, White Shorts	Goals
1 Jurek DUDEK		1 David JAMES	
3 Thomasz RZASA		2 Mark DELANEY ‡	
6 Paul BOSVELT #		3 Alan WRIGHT †	
7 Bonaventure KALOU		4 Gareth SOUTHGATE (c)	
10 Jon Dahl TOMASSON †		5 Colin CALDERWOOD §	
14 Peter VAN VOSSEN ‡		6 Gareth BARRY	
16 Bert KONTERMAN		7 Ian TAYLOR ‡‡	
17 Patrick PAAUWE		8 George BOATENG ††	
18 Igor KORNEEV §		9 Dion DUBLIN #	
19 Jan DE VISSER		10 Julian JOACHIM	
22 Ulrich VAN GOBBEL		11 Alan THOMPSON	
Substitutes		*Substitutes*	
2 Christian GYAN		12 Steve STONE ††62	
11 Henk VOS		13 Michael PRICE (Gk)	
13 TININHO †62		14 Mark DRAPER ‡‡72	
20 Ferry DE HAAN		15 Steve WATSON ‡49	
21 Edwin ZOETEBIER (Gk)		16 Neil TARRANT	
23 Mohammed ALLACH #76		17 Najwan GHRAYIB †45	
24 SOMALIA		18 Darius VASSELL #51	
28 Thomas BUFFEL §83		19 Ugo EHIOGU §51	
30 Ellery CAIRO ‡62			

FACTFILE

*Villa return to Rotterdam for first time since their European Cup win in 1982...
Villa's first goalless draw in a pre-season game since their local derby with
Birmingham City on 30th July 1997... Najwan Ghrayib makes his Villa debut.*

Monday 2nd August 1999 • Aggborough • 7.30pm

KIDDERMINSTER HARRIERS 1 ASTON VILLA 0

Half-time 1-0 • *Attendance* 4,003

Referee Mick FLETCHER (Oldbury)

Referee's Assistants G. CHAPMAN and G. PEARSON

Red Shirts, Red Shorts	Goals	White Shirts with Claret and Blue Sash, White Shorts	Goals
1 Stuart BROCK		1 David JAMES #	
2 Craig HINTON		2 Steve WATSON	
3 Leslie HINES		3 Najwan GHRAYIB	
4 Paul WEBB		4 Colin CALDERWOOD ‡‡	
5 Martin WEIR (c) †		5 Ugo EHIOGU	
6 Adie SMITH		6 David HUGHES	
7 James COLLINS #		7 George BOATENG §	
8 Rene PETERSON ††		8 Mark DRAPER	
9 Dean BENNETT ‡		9 Dion DUBLIN (c) ‡	
10 Stewart HADLEY ‡‡	31	10 Paul MERSON ††	
11 Thomas SKOVBJERG §		11 Alan THOMPSON †	

Substitutes		*Substitutes*	
12 Steve TAYLOR ‡64		12 Lee HENDRIE †25	
13 Shaun CUNNINGTON ††80		13 Michael PRICE (Gk) #45	
14 Gary BARNETT #72		14 Darius VASSELL ‡30	
15 Andrew BROWNRIGG †60		15 Neil TARRANT ††72	
16 Stuart PAYNE ‡‡80		17 Michael STANDING §45	
17 Vadim MIKOUTSKI §72		18 Tommy JASZCZUN ‡‡72	

FACTFILE

This testimonial for stalwart defender, Martin Weir, saw Harriers pull off a deserved win in a thoroughly entertaining encounter. Villa should have taken the lead in the 20th minute when Paul Merson, running on to a through ball from Steve Watson, thundered in a fierce shot which cannoned back off the post with Brock well beaten. Shortly afterwards, however, it was Kiddy who took the lead when a long-range cross into the box by Dean Bennett found the head of Stewart Hadley and he finished with aplomb. Merson again went close just before half-time, Brock tipping a delightful chip shot over the bar.

Tuesday 3rd August 1999 • The Lawn • 7.45pm

FOREST GREEN ROVERS 2 ASTON VILLA 5

Half-time 1-2 • *Attendance* 810

Referee D. CURTIS (Wotton-under-Edge)

Referee's Assistants R. DYER and A. BOULTON

Black and White Striped Shirts, Black Shorts	Goals	Turquoise Shirts with Black Trim, Turquiose Shorts	Goals
1 Justin SHUTTLEWOOD ‡		1 Wayne HENDERSON †	
2 Chris HONOUR (c)		2 Jonathan BEWERS #	
3 Wayne HATWELL	5	3 Danny JACKMAN §	
4 Chris BURNS		4 Aaron LESCOTT	
5 Mike KILGOUR		5 Danny HAYNES	70
6 Adie RANDLE		6 Tommy JASZCZUN (c)	
7 Rob COOK §		7 Jay SMITH ‡‡	7
8 Andrew CARLEY #		8 Gavin MELAUGH ††	
9 Marc McGREGOR †		9 Richard WALKER ‡	53
10 David MEHEW		10 Stephen EVANS	
11 Jason DRYSDALE	63	11 John McGRATH	14
Substitutes		*Substitutes*	
12 Paul HUNT †51		12 Graham EVANS §67	88
13 Steve PERRIN (Gk) ‡71		13 Boaz MYHILL (Gk) †48	
14 Steve WINTER #71		14 Jamie KEARNS #66	
15 Shaun CHAPPLE §71		15 Michael STANDING ††78	
16 Bill CLARKE		16 Andy MORROW ‡60	
		17 Gordon COWANS ‡‡78	

This turned out to be a good work-out for a Villa team of reserves and youths, with a late appearance for coach Gordon Cowans thrown in to delight the crowd. After giving away an early lead, Villa came back strongly and won comfortably with a couple of goals late on underlining their superiority.

Jay Smith – scored Villa's equaliser.

FRIENDLY MATCH

Thursday 2nd September 1999 • Valley Stadium • 7.45pm

REDDITCH UNITED 2 ASTON VILLA 2

Half-time 1-1 • Attendance 812

 Redditch United

Referee Brian ELLICOTT

Referee's Assistants A. MARRINER and A. HEADLEY

Red Shirts, Red Shorts		Goals	Turquoise Shirts with Black Trim, Black Shorts		Goals
1	Dave ADEY		1	Adam RACHEL	
2	Stuart RANDALL † ††69		2	Jlloyd SAMUEL	
3	Paul MOLLOY ††		3	Gareth BARRY	
4	James COPE ‡		4	Liam FOLDS	
5	Craig GILLETT	85	5	Karl JOHNSON †	
6	Jan MULDERS		6	David HUGHES	35
7	Dean TILLEY ‡‡		7	Greg WALTERS ‡	
8	Paul BURTON #		8	Marco RUSSO	65pen
9	Nicky CROSS §		9	Graham EVANS	
10	Peter SUTTON	11	10	Aaron LESCOTT #	
11	Mark SMITH		11	John McGRATH	

	Substitutes			Substitutes	
12	Jamie HART †45		12	Tommy JASZCZUN †57	
14	Rob SMITH ‡45		13	Matthew GHENT (Gk)	
15	Adam NICHOLLS #45		14	Richard WALKER ‡60	
16	James BURKE §45		15	Gordon COWANS #63	
17	Andy YAPP ‡‡75				

FACTFILE

A game which was organised to celebrate the switching on of Redditch's new floodlighting system turned out to be closely fought encounter and the final stalemate was a fair enough result. Going behind to an early goal from Peter Sutton, Villa upped the tempo and were rewarded in the 35th minute when central defender David Hughes joined the attack to notch the equaliser. It was not until 20 minutes into the second-half that Villa went in front, Italian triallist Marco Russo converting a spot-kick. Just when it looked as if Villa would hold out for a win, defender Craig Gillett came upfield to score a deserved equaliser.

120

Aston Villa Review 2000

Monday 13th September 1999 • Avenue Stadium • 7.30pm

DORCHESTER TOWN 1 ASTON VILLA 5

Half-time 1-1 • *Attendance 658*

Referee Roystan MITCHELL

Referee's Assistants G. MASTERS and N. DALKINS

Black and White Striped Shirts, Black Shorts	Goals	Turquoise Shirts with Black Trim, Turquoise Shorts	Goals
1 James DUNGEY †		1 Wayne HENDERSON	
2 Jeff MacLEAN		2 Jamie KEARNS §	
3 Martyn SULLIVAN ‡		3 David CURTOLO	
4 Neil COATES (c) ††		4 Aaron LESCOTT	
5 Andy HARRIS		5 David HUGHES (c)	22
6 Ryan CROSS		6 Tommy JASZCZUN	
7 Roy O'BRIEN		7 Darren BYFIELD †	54
8 Rob TAYLOR		8 Graham EVANS	
9 Danny O'HAGAN		9 Neil TARRANT #	
10 Owen PICKARD #	40	10 Gavin MELAUGH	50,80
11 Dave LOVELL §		11 John McGRATH ‡	
Substitutes		*Substitutes*	
Gk Chris HIGGS †45		12 Michael STANDING #76	
14 Scott COMIE ‡45		13 Matthew GHENT (Gk)	
15 Sufyan GHAZGHAZI #45		14 Stephen EVANS †57	76
16 David WRIGHT §45		15 Luke PRINCE ‡63	
17 Chris FERRETT ††45		16 David HARDING §79	

A young Villa side went to Dorchester and returned with a comfortable win under their belts. After an evenly contested first-half in which central defender David Hughes was again on target, Villa dominated the second period and two goals from Gavin Melaugh were the highlights of the half.

Two-goal Gavin Melaugh put the game beyond Dorchester's reach.

Tuesday 8th February 2000 • Victoria Ground • 7.30pm

BROMSGROVE ROVERS 0 ASTON VILLA 5

Half-time 0-1 • *Attendance* 1,504

Referee Gavin BARROW

Referee's Assistants C. FOX and D. SATTERTHWAITE

White Shirts with Green Trim, White Shorts	Goals	Claret and Blue Striped Shirts, Claret Shorts	Goals
1 Nore GABBIDON		1 Neil CUTLER †	
2 Quentin TOWNSEND		2 Lee HENDRIE	
3 Steve ULFIG §		3 John McGRATH ‡‡	45
4 Tom DAVIES ††		4 Steve WATSON	
5 Mark BOWATER		5 Jlloyd SAMUEL	
6 Kevin JINKES †		6 Leon HYLTON §	
7 Mark BENBOW ‡		7 Aaron LESCOTT ††	
8 Patrick BANNISTER (c)		8 Jay SMITH #	
9 Peter SUTTON		9 Gustavo BARTELT	65
10 Ryan DALEY #		10 Stephen EVANS ‡	
11 Andy BIDDLE		11 Alan THOMPSON (c)	

Substitutes		*Substitutes*	
12 Robbie COLEWALL †70		12 Michael STANDING ‡‡83	
14 Tim LANGFORD #80		13 Peter ENCKELMAN (Gk) †45	
15 Robert HUNTER §80		14 Gavin MELAUGH ††72	
16 Richard BALL ††80		15 Mark DEBOLLA #50	
17 James COOPER ‡70		16 Jamie KEARNS §62	
18 Russell PHILPOT		17 Graham EVANS ‡45 82,83,87	
19 Alex McROBERTS			

FACTFILE

This match was arranged to help out Bromsgrove, who are struggling financially. It marked the debut in claret and blue of Gustavo Bartelt, signed on loan to the end of the season from Roma. Bartelt opened his account for Villa, scoring with a sweetly struck shot from 20 yards. The hero of the night, however, was substitute Graham Evans who scored a hat-trick in five minutes to round off the night's scoring. The first goal of the night was scored by John McGrath, who swept the ball home on the stroke of half-time, after good work from Stephen Evans.

Tuesday 25th April 2000 • Whaddon Road • 7.30pm

CHELTENHAM TOWN 1 ASTON VILLA 6

Half-time 0-3 • Attendance 3,009

Referee Dermot GALLAGHER (Banbury)

Referee's Assistants R.P. DESMOND and G. CHAPMAN

Red and White Striped Shirts, Black Shorts	Goals	Claret and Blue Striped Shirts, Blue Shorts	Goals
13 Shane HIGGS §§		1 David JAMES †	
3 Jamie VICTORY ## ≠80		2 Steve WATSON ##	
4 Chris BANKS (c) ‡		3 Alan WRIGHT ≠	
7 Lee HOWELLS †		4 Gareth SOUTHGATE (c) ‡‡	
8 Bob BLOOMER		5 Ugo EHIOGU §	
10 Jason EATON ‡‡		9 Dion DUBLIN §§	66
11 Antony GRIFFIN		11 Alan THOMPSON ‡	
17 Neil HOWARTH ††		15 Gareth BARRY ††	
19 Michael JACKSON		16 Mark DELANEY	
20 Gareth HOPKINS §		17 Lee HENDRIE	19,20,68,83
29 Steve COTTERILL #		18 Benito CARBONE #	10
Substitutes		*Substitutes*	
5 Mark FREEMAN ‡45		6 George BOATENG ‡45	
6 John BROUGH		7 Jim WALKER ≠≠84	
9 Neil GRAYSON ##60 ≠		8 Jlloyd SAMUEL ‡‡60	
14 Hugh McAULEY #45		10 Ross MacLAREN §45	
15 Richard WALKER §45	61	12 Julian JOACHIM #45	
16 Mark YATES †25		13 Peter ENCKELMAN †31	
18 Russell MILTON ††45		14 Kevin MacDONALD ##66	
22 Steve BENBOW (Gk) §§78		18 Chris BANKS ††45 ≠≠	
23 Martin DELANEY ‡‡45		19 Richard WALKER §§75	
		20 Steve HARRISON ≠75	

FACTFILE

A full-strength Villa squad turned out in support of long-serving Robins' centre-half, Chris Banks, who swapped sides to captain Villa in the second half. After Benito Carbone opened the scoring with a chip shot, Lee Hendrie, still recovering from injury, went on the rampage, Dion Dublin also getting on the scoresheet.

KEITH WALKER TESTIMONIAL

Tuesday 9th May 2000 • Vetch Field • 7.30pm

SWANSEA CITY 0 ASTON VILLA 3

Half-time 0-2 • Attendance 5,726

Referee Ceri RICHARDS (Llanelli)
Referee's Assistants S. HAMES and R. THOMAS

White Shirts, White Shorts	Goals	Turquoise Shirts with Black Trim, Turquoise Shorts	Goals
1 Roger FREESTONE † ≠≠85		1 David JAMES §	
2 Steve JONES ##		3 Alan WRIGHT ‡‡	19
3 Michael HOWARDS		4 Gareth SOUTHGATE (c) ††	
4 Nick CUSACK ‡‡		5 Ugo EHIOGU #	
8 Martin THOMAS §§		6 George BOATENG	
11 Jonathan COATES		9 Dion DUBLIN ‡	
14 Kristian O'LEARY ≠		11 Alan THOMPSON †	
16 Keith WALKER ††		15 Gareth BARRY §§	
17 Stuart ROBERTS		17 Lee HENDRIE ≠	
18 Jason PRICE ≠≠		18 Benito CARBONE ##	31
20 Lee JENKINS		24 Mark DELANEY	
Substitutes		*Substitutes*	
13 Jason JONES †45		7 Ian TAYLOR †36	
19 Ryan CASEY ‡45		10 Neil TARRANT §§74	
21 Gareth PHILIPS ‖47		12 Julian JOACHIM ‡45	90
23 Bari MORGAN ‡‡67		14 Jlloyd SAMUEL #45	
25 Michael KEEGAN #45		16 Jonathan BEWERS ††55	
26 Leigh DE-VULGT ##70		19 Richard WALKER ##60	
28 Tommy MURTON §45		20 John McGRATH ‡‡60	
32 Alan CURTIS §§77		21 Michael STANDING ≠74	
34 Colin PASCOE ≠77		39 Peter ENCKELMAN §45	
John HOLLINS 87 *(extra player)*			

FACTFILE

This testimonial game to honour former Swansea defender, Keith Walker, was tinged with sadness as a minute silence was observed before the kick-off in memory of Swans fan, Terry Coles, who was killed at the previous weekend's game at Rotherham. Ian Taylor made his comeback in an attempt to be fit for the cup final.

Aston Villa's final first team squad photograph of the 20th century. Back row, left to right: Aaron Lescott, Jlloyd Samuel, Colin Calderwood (now Nottingham Forest), Peter Enckelman, David James, Neil Cutler, Mark Delaney, Mark Draper, Najwan Ghrayib.

Middle row: Kevin MacDonald (Reserve Team Coach), Darren Byfield, Paul Merson, Steve Watson, Ugo Ehiogu, Ian Taylor, Gareth Barry, Alan Thompson, Darius Vassell, Tommy Jaszczun (now Blackpool), Jim Walker (Physiotherapist);

Front row: Steve Stone, Lee Hendrie, Benito Carbone, Gareth Southgate, Paul Barron (Goalkeeping Coach), John Gregory (Manager), Steve Harrison (First Tream Coach), Dion Dublin, Julian Joachim, Alan Wright, George Boateng.

THE MANAGEMENT TEAM

If John Gregory thought last season was one of contrasts, it was merely different shades of grey compared to the extremes he experienced in this, his second full season in charge of Aston Villa.

Wins over Newcastle United and Everton gave the 46-year-old a perfect start, but when West Ham United snatched a 2-2 draw in the 93rd minute at Villa Park, it triggered a discontent among fans and pundits that seemed to fester throughout the autumn.

Villa couldn't beat the Premiership's elite sides and when they dutifully picked off those lower down the table, they were accused of not being sufficiently entertaining.

Attendances were dipping, Leicester City still couldn't be beaten, and the penalty-call from hell ruined a potentially uplifting Monday night at Sunderland. By the time Robbie Keane, of all people, helped condemn Villa to defeat at Coventry, certain quarters of the Press were convinced that Gregory's days were numbered.

Several factors contributed to the U-turn in fortunes which ensued – Doug Ellis making a mockery of his 'Deadly' sobriquet by keeping faith with his manager; the relocation of George Boateng into central midfield, and Villa players in general waking up to the talent they had in their ranks. Oh yes, and there was the ban that became a boon.

What a poor show it was that in the players' voting for 'Clubman of the Year' at the season's end, there wasn't so much as a proposer for the FA official who decided to ban John Gregory from the touchline for 28 days in mid-season. If the intention was to open his eyes to the

JOHN GREGORY   STEVE HARRISON

error of his more contentious remarks concerning Premiership referees, the effect was to reveal the whole new perspective one gets of a game when one is sat in the directors' box instead of on the touchline.

By his own admission, Gregory actually benefited from the enforced move, which soon became permanent, saying that it enabled him to take a more detached view of the action.

By now, his team were on the roll that would turn around their season, although nowhere near as much as their manager would wish, Wembley notwithstanding. Behind Gregory's effervescent personality there remains a dour determination to bring his team up to the level of the five teams which headed it in the Premiership table.

Objective to the point of ruthlessness when deciding whose name goes on the team-sheet, he continues to preside over a strict meritocracy that spurs on his younger players, and prevents the veterans from ever resting on their laurels.

KEVIN MacDONALD   TONY McANDREW   GORDON COWANS   PAUL BARRON

THE MANAGEMENT TEAM

Gregory is the first to acknowledge the invaluable help he receives from his support staff, no more so than in the case of first team coach Steve Harrison, whose afternoon 'workshops' at Bodymoor Heath with the younger members of the first team, played a considerable part in the development of talents such as Mark Delaney and Gareth Barry. Harrison can take pride in the fact that no team was harder to score against at home in the Premiership last season, Villa's overall defensive record was bettered only by Chelsea and Liverpool.

As important as his technical contribution is his irrepressible personality. One of the best ways to stay cheerful is to surround yourself with cheerful people and anyone who has seen Harrison's sense of humour and his talent for mimicry will understand why glumness is only an occasional visitor to the Villa camp.

Goalkeeping coach Paul Barron didn't need to hire an advertising agency in 1999-00. His players did a good enough job themselves, with David James, Peter Enckelman and Neil Cutler all fulsome in their praise of the former Arsenal keeper. James in particular has been delighted to have had someone with whom he can discuss his game and maintains that Barron must take a large share of the credit for the former Liverpool keeper having returned to peak form during the season.

Several players also owe much to physio Jim Walker, whose dedication to duty earned him a simple tribute in John Gregory's list of 'thankyous' in the final home match programme of the season - "... good job we don't pay you by the hour, we'd never be able to afford you!"

With key players such as Ugo Ehiogu, Lee Hendrie, Ian Taylor, Gareth Southgate and Dion Dublin all requiring lengthy periods of treatment this season, Jim's services and those of assistant physio Terry Standring were much in demand. It was a mark of the esteem in which he is held throughout the game when Brian Clough turned up at the Midland Football Writers' dinner to present Walker with a special award for services to Midlands football.

The purchase of Belgian striker Luc Nilis showed that Villa continue to keep a watchful eye on the Continent as a source of playing talent, which should ensure plenty more mileage next season for chief scout Ross MacLaren, as the club looks to strengthen its squad.

Away from the first team, a reshuffle saw Kevin MacDonald take over as coach of the Reserves, a job he combined with his 'watching brief' with the first team on matchdays.

This created a vacancy in the running of the youth teams, which was ably filled by former Middlesbrough player Tony McAndrew, who became youth team manager alongside coach Gordon Cowans.

Ensuring that Villa's players of tomorrow are properly brought on is Villa's Football Academy run by director Bryan Jones, his assistant Steve Burns and Youth Development Officer Alan Miller.

The succession of young hopefuls introduced to the Villa Park crowd while signing Academy forms during the season is a reminder of the tireless job these men do in trying to ensure that football's next young phenomenon has a Villa badge on his shirt.

ROSS MacLAREN   JIM WALKER   TERRY STANDRING   BRYAN JONES

GARETH BARRY

Born Hastings,
23rd February 1981.
Joined Villa on YTS terms
in 1997, signed profes-
sional forms 23/2/98.
Villa debut as sub v
Sheffield Wednesday,
Lge (a) 2/5/98.

Onwards and upwards for Villa's hottest young property. Gareth Barry quickly showed that he was no one-season wonder with another progressive campaign in the defence.

Superbly poised and relaxed on the ball, he is learning to spot the situation which calls for the unsophisticated hoof upfield, but his first preference remains ball control and careful distribution, and Villa are a better team for it.

Off the field, the shy teenager is also growing more poised in handling the media and general hoopla which accompanies the successful footballer, and he was a popular winner of the Midland Football Writers' Young Player of the Year award for last season.

Called up twice to the full England squad during this season, it is a measure of Barry's progress that he was draughted into England's Euro 2000 squad as a late replacement for Jason Wilcox, he made his full England debut as a substitute v Ukraine at Wembley in a 2-0 win and was later named in Kevin Keegan's final 22-man squad for the Championships.

Career Record:

Season	Club	League		Cups	
		Apps	Gls	Apps	Gls
97-98	Aston Villa	1 (1)	-	-	-
98-99	Aston Villa	27 (5)	2	5	-
99-00	Aston Villa	30	1	13	-
TOTAL		58 (6)	3	18	-

★ *England Full (1 cap), Under-18 (4 caps, 4 goals) and Under-21 International (4 caps).*

JONATHAN BEWERS

Born Kettering,
10th September, 1982.
Joined Villa July 1997 as
an Academy player.
Villa debut as sub v
Tottenham Hotspur, Lge
(a) 15/4/00.

A brief first team debut at Tottenham in April, when he went on as a late substitute, heralded what could be an exciting career for versatile youngster Jonathan Bewers.

Attached to Villa since he was eight and one of the final graduates of Lilleshall's National School of Excellence, the Kettering born 17-year-old is happy at full back, in the centre of defence or in midfield.

He has occupied all three positions with distinction and certainly has the potential, having been called up to the England under-18 squad this season, to add further international honours to his caps at Under-15 and Under-16 levels.

Career Record:

Season	Club	League		Cups	
		Apps	Gls	Apps	Gls
99-00	Aston Villa	- (1)	-	-	-

VILLA PLAYERS ON LOAN

Stan Collymore to Fulham from *July 99* - Lge 3(3) apps; Cup 1(2) apps, 1 goal.
Darren Byfield went on three loan spells: from *Aug 99* - Northampton Town - Lge 6 apps, 1 goal; WC 1 app, 1 goal. *Sept 99* - Cambridge United - Lge 3(1) apps. *Mar 2000* - Blackpool - Lge 2 apps.
Michael Blackwood to Chester City for two months from *Sept 99* - 8 apps, 2 goals.
Neil Tarrant to Ayr United from *Dec 99* for season - Lge 15 apps 4 goals; Cup 5 apps, 3 goals.
Aaron Lescott to Lincoln City from *Mar 2000* - Lge 4(1) apps.

GEORGE BOATENG

Born Nkawkaw, Ghana, 5th September 1975. *Joined Villa* July 1999 from Coventry City, £4.5m. *Villa debut* v Newcastle United, Lge (a) 7/8/99.

The relocation of Villa's £4.5m signing to central midfield was one of the turning points of Villa's season.

Initially a peripheral figure on the wing, Boateng's tenacious tackling and eye for an opening were immediately apparent, but it was only when John Gregory re-jigged his side in a bid to arrest its autumnal slide, that Villa fans finally saw what their money had bought.

Moved to the engine room alongside Ian Taylor, the Dutchman was a revelation, stamping his authority on game after game and freeing Taylor to go on his mid-season scoring spree that powered the Villa revival.

Off the field, the ex-Feyenoord player is a complete contrast to his combative footballing persona. Happily married since arriving at Villa, the laid-back Boateng is a breath of fresh air in a game that is prone to taking itself far too seriously.

Career Record:

Season	Club	League Apps	League Gls	Cups Apps	Cups Gls
94-95	Excelsior (Hol)	9	-	-	-
95-96	Feyenoord	21 (3)	1	-	-
96-97	Feyenoord	25 (1)	-	-	-
97-98	Feyenoord	15 (3)	-	-	-
	Coventry C.	14	1	5	-
98-99	Coventry C.	29 (4)	4	6	2
99-00	Aston Villa	30 (3)	2	11	1
TOTAL		143 (14)	8	22	3

★ *Dutch Under-21 International.*

COLIN CALDERWOOD

Born Glasgow, 20th January 1965. *Joined Villa* March 1999 from Tottenham Hotspur, £225,000. *Villa debut* v West Ham United, Lge (h) 2/3/99.

Ugo Ehiogu's return to the starting line-up on a regular basis this season meant that opportunities were limited for Colin Calderwood, especially once Gareth Barry became a fixture in central defence. He was therefore allowed to go to Forest in mid-season, after a job well done.

Career Record:

Season	Club	League Apps	League Gls	Cups Apps	Cups Gls
81-82	Mansfield T.	1	-	-	-
82-83	Mansfield T.	28	-	3	-
83-84	Mansfield T.	27 (3)	1	4	1
84-85	Mansfield T.	41	-	10	-
85-86	Swindon T.	46	2	10	-
86-87	Swindon T.	46	1	13	-
87-88	Swindon T.	33 (1)	1	13	-
88-89	Swindon T.	43	4	7	-
89-90	Swindon T.	46	3	12	-
90-91	Swindon T.	22 (1)	2	-	-
91-92	Swindon T.	46	5	11	1
92-93	Swindon T.	46	2	6	-
93-94	Tottenham H.	26	-	8	-
94-95	Tottenham H.	35 (1)	2	7	-
95-96	Tottenham H.	26 (3)	1	7	-
96-97	Tottenham H.	33 (1)	-	5	-
97-98	Tottenham H.	21 (5)	4	2 (2)	1
98-99	Tottenham H.	11 (1)	-	5	-
	Aston Villa	8	-	-	-
99-00	Aston Villa	15 (3)	-	3 (1)	-
Villa record		*23 (3)*	*-*	*3 (1)*	*-*
TOTAL		600 (19)	28	126 (3)	3

● *At Swindon also appeared in four Play-Offs, making 13 appearances.*

★ *Full Scotland international (38 caps, 1 goal).*

BENITO CARBONE

Born Begnara, Italy,
14th August 1971.
Joined Villa October 1999
for a nominal fee from
Sheffield Wed.
Villa debut v Wimbledon,
Lge (h) 23/10/99.

In retrospect, Benito Carbone made a rod for his own back with the dazzling debut that followed his arrival from Sheffield Wednesday last October.

The diminutive Italian turned on the style against Wimbledon, and in doing so he sent expectations through the roof.

No-one could maintain such form over a whole season, yet Benito offered ample evidence of his worth to the team through the months which followed.

His hat-trick against Leeds in the FA Cup confirmed his status as one of the most exciting players in the Villa ranks and his willingness to chase back and harry opponents left no-one in doubt as to his commitment to the cause.

Career Record:

Season	Club	League Apps	Gls	Cups Apps	Gls
88-89	Torino	3	-	-	-
89-90	Torino	5	-	-	-
90-91	Reggina	31	5	-	-
91-92	Casertana	31	4	-	-
92-93	Ascoli	28	6	-	-
93-94	Torino	25 (3)	3	-	-
94-95	Napoli	27 (2)	4	-	-
95-96	Inter Milan	25 (6)	2	-	-
96-97	Inter Milan	- (1)	-	-	-
	Sheff. Wed.	24 (1)	6	2	-
97-98	Sheff. Wed.	28 (5)	9	3	-
98-99	Sheff. Wed.	31	8	5	1
99-00	Sheff. Wed.	3 (4)	2	- (1)	-
	Aston Villa	22 (2)	4	6	5
TOTAL		283 (24)	53	16 (1)	6

NEIL CUTLER

Born Birmingham,
3rd September 1976.
Joined Villa November
1999 from Chester City
on a free transfer.
Villa debut as sub v
Middlesbrough, Lge (a)
14/2/2000.

The 1999-00 season became a rags-to-riches story for goalkeeper Neil Cutler, when he left cash-strapped Chester City for Premiership football.

Hailing from the West Midlands, Cutler had worked with Villa's goalkeeping coach Paul Barron at both Lilleshall and West Brom, hence the interest which brought him to Villa Park, where he was offered a contract until the end of the season, with a view to staying on for another year. Neil is third choice keeper behind James and Enckelman.

Career Record:

Season	Club	League Apps	Gls	Cups Apps	Gls
93-94	W.B. Albion	-	-	-	-
94-95	W.B. Albion	-	-	-	-
95-96	W.B. Albion	-	-	-	-
(loan)	Coventry City	-	-	-	-
(loan)	Chester City	1	-	-	-
96-97	Crewe A.	-	-	-	-
(loan)	Chester City	5	-	-	-
97-98	Crewe A.	-	-	-	-
98-99	Chester City	23	-	3	-
99-00	Chester City	-	-	-	-
	Aston Villa	- (1)	-	-	-
TOTAL		29 (1)	-	3	-

★ *England Schoolboy and Youth international.*

● *NOTE: Career records of goalkeepers Neil Cutler (above) and Peter Enckelman (p133) and David James (p134) list number of goals conceded for Aston Villa in the goals columns.*

● *NOTE: All international records are up to the 31st May 2000.*

MARK DELANEY

Born Haverfordwest,
13th May 1976.
Joined Villa March 1999
from Cardiff C., £500,000.
Villa debut as sub v
Nottingham Forest, Lge
(h) 24/4/99.

Not even his red card at Wembley in the FA Cup semi-final could alter the fact that this has been an impressive first full season for Mark Delaney.

Handed his chance to make a name for himself at the outset, with Steve Watson suspended, the Welshman accepted with gusto, even responding to his manager's half-time observation that he was playing 'like a tart' at Watford, by going out and scoring the winning goal!

It would be his only one for the season, but no-one was complaining, as he effortlessly continued to bridge the gap between the Third Division with Cardiff City just over a year ago and Premiership football with Villa.

Ironically, he was one of Villa's best attacking options early in the season, his surging runs forward counter-balanced by a sliding tackle executed with the precision of a locksmith.

It was not long before he felt the dragon breathing down his neck, and he made his full international debut in Wales' game with Switzerland in September.

Career Record:

Season	Club	League Apps	Gls	Cups Apps	Gls
98-99	Cardiff City	28	-	10 (2)	1
98-99	Aston Villa	- (2)	-	-	-
99-00	Aston Villa	25 (3)	1	5 (3)	-
Villa record		*25 (5)*	*1*	*-*	*-*
TOTAL		53 (5)	1	15 (5)	1

★ *Welsh international at Full (2 caps) and Under-21 levels.*

MARK DRAPER

Born Derby, 11th
November 1970.
Joined Villa July 1995
from Leicester City,
£3.25m.
Villa debut v Manchester
Utd, Lge (h) 19/8/95.

Mark Draper's hopes that his career might be back on track after he recovered from surgery on a niggling ankle injury last term, were dashed when he was confined to a solitary substitute's appearance at Chelsea early in the season.

The outcome was a loan spell at Spanish side Rayo Vallecano, which began in mid-January until the end of the season, where he teamed up with another former Leicester player, goalkeeper Kasey Keller, with a view to a permanent move at the end of the season.

Career Record:

Season	Club	League Apps	Gls	Cups Apps	Gls
88-89	Notts County	16 (4)	3	3 (1)	-
89-90	Notts County	29 (5)	3	6	1
90-91	Notts County	41 (4)	9	12 (1)	1
91-92	Notts County	32 (3)	1	4 (1)	2
92-93	Notts County	44	11	5	1
93-94	Notts County	44	13	15	4
94-95	Leicester City	39	5	4	-
95-96	Aston Villa	36	2	13	3
96-97	Aston Villa	28 (1)	-	3 (1)	-
97-98	Aston Villa	31	3	12	-
98-99	Aston Villa	13 (10)	2	5 (1)	1
99-00	Aston Villa	- (1)	-	-	-
loan	Rayo Vallecano	1 (3)	-	-	-
Villa record		*108 (12)*	*7*	*33 (2)*	*4*
TOTAL		354 (31)	52	82 (5)	13

★ *England Under-21 international.*

DION DUBLIN

Born Leicester,
22nd April, 1969.
Joined Villa November
1998 from Coventry
City, £5.75m.
Villa debut v Tottenham,
Lge (h) 7/11/98.

Dion Dublin would head the queue if they were handing out medals for bravery. What at first seemed a minor knock against Sheffield Wednesday in December turned out to be a broken bone in his neck, after a collision with an opponent, and the striker was told he was lucky he could still walk.

Yet Dublin was back in the fray before March was over and went on to score the penalty that booked Villa's Cup Final place, as well as finishing the club's leading scorer for the season.

Career Record:

Season	Club	League Apps	Gls	Cups Apps	Gls
88-89	Cambridge U.	12 (9)	6	1 (1)	1
89-90	Cambridge U.	37 (9)	15	14 (2)	6
90-91	Cambridge U.	44 (2)	16	13	7
91-92	Cambridge U.	40 (3)	15	9	4
92-93	Manchester U.	3 (4)	1	-	-
93-94	Manchester U.	1 (4)	1	2 (3)	1
94-95	Manchester U.	-	-	-	-
94-95	Coventry City	31	13	7	3
95-96	Coventry City	34	14	4 (1)	2
96-97	Coventry City	33 (1)	13	4 (1)	-
97-98	Coventry City	36	18	7	5
98-99	Coventry City	10	3	2	-
	Aston Villa	24	11	-	-
99-00	Aston Villa	23 (3)	12	5 (1)	3
Villa record		*47 (3)*	*23*	*5 (1)*	*3*
TOTAL		328 (35)	138	68 (9)	32

● *At Cambridge also appeared in two Play-Offs, making 5 appearances, 2 goals.*

★ *England international (4 caps).*

UGO EHIOGU

Born Hackney, London,
3rd November 1972.
Joined Villa July 1991
from West Bromwich
Albion, £40,000.
Villa debut v Arsenal,
Lge (h) 24/8/91.

Many Villa fans will tell you there is no coincidence in the fact that their team won just one of the eight games in which it was without Ugo Ehiogu in the autumn.

While this frustrated goalscorer will not be happy with his solitary addition to the scoresheet this season, he carried out his primary job with aplomb and without fanfare, the latter characteristic perhaps a stumbling block to his ambition to add to his solitary England cap.

His value to his club was further illustrated when he became the central defence's 'senior partner' during Gareth Southgate's enforced absence late in the season, and responded by marshalling Jlloyd Samuel and Gareth Barry to help record three clean sheets in six games.

Career Record:

Season	Club	League Apps	Gls	Cups Apps	Gls
90-91	W.B.A.	- (2)	-	-	-
91-92	Aston Villa	4 (4)	-	1 (1)	-
92-93	Aston Villa	1 (3)	-	1	-
93-94	Aston Villa	14 (3)	-	- (2)	-
94-95	Aston Villa	38 (1)	3	9	1
95-96	Aston Villa	36	1	13	1
96-97	Aston Villa	38	3	7	1
97-98	Aston Villa	37	2	11	-
98-99	Aston Villa	23 (2)	2	6	-
99-00	Aston Villa	31	1	12	-
Villa record		*222 (13)*	*12*	*60 (3)*	*3*
TOTAL		222 (15)	12	60 (3)	3

★ *England international at Full (1 cap) and Under-21 levels.*

PETER ENCKELMAN

Born Turku, Finland,
10th March 1977.
Joined Villa February
1999 from Jalkapallo TPS
(Finland), for £200,000.
Villa debut as sub v
Arsenal, Lge (a) 11/9/99.

If Villa are inclined to think they got a
steal in David James, the purchase of his
understudy can hardly be described as an
extravagance, either.

Peter Enckelman has been something
of a revelation this season, proving a
highly competent replacement in the 12
games when James was forced to stand
down.

Cool and collected off the pitch, the
young Finn brought those same qualities
to bear when unexpectedly making his
Premiership debut in front of Highbury's
North Stand after James was injured
during the game.

That half of Peter's eight Premiership
starts produced clean sheets is testament
to an exciting prospect who has so far
made a nonsense of traditional English
reservations about foreign goalkeepers!

Career Record:

Season	Club	League Apps	Gls	Cups Apps	Gls
1995	TPS	5 (1)	-	-	-
1996	TPS	-	-	-	-
1997	TPS	24 (1)	-	-	-
1998	TPS	24	-	-	-
99-00	Aston Villa	9 (1)	9	4	1
Total		62 (3)	9	4	1

★ *Finland Full and Under-21 international.*

● Following the two-legged Worthington
Cup tie with Chester City in September Villa
took two Chester players, defender Martyn
Lancaster and Darren Moss, on a short loan
spell, but neither player was taken on.

NAJWAN GHRAYIB

Born Nazareth (Israel),
30th January 1974.
Joined Villa July 1999
from Hapoel Haifa (Israel)
for £1m.
Villa debut v Chester
City, League Cup (h)
10/9/99.

Having gained a wife and lost his
appendix since moving to England last
summer, Najwan Ghrayib will not forget
his first season in English football in a
hurry, but on the field, patience has had
to be the wing-back's watchword as he
waits for his chance to claim a regular
first team place.

Alan Wright's consistent performances
limited Ghrayib to just two starts this
term, and if initial impressions were
uncertain, his performance against
Sunderland late in the season suggested
that he is getting to grips with
Premiership football.

Blessed with a fine turn of pace and a
blistering shot, there is hopefully much
more to come from the Israeli
international.

Career Record:

Season	Club	League Apps	Gls	Cups Apps	Gls
94-95	Maccabi Haifa	13 (10)	4	-	-
95-96	M. Petach-Tikva	26 (1)	10	-	-
96-97	M. Petach-Tikva	17 (5)	4	-	-
97-98	Hapoel Haifa	26	2	-	-
98-99	Hapoel Haifa	29	7	-	-
99-00	Aston Villa	1 (4)	-	1	-
TOTAL		112 (20)	27	1	-

★ *Full Israeli International (15 caps, 4 goals).*

● Whilst playing for the England Under-18
side against San Marino on 9th September
1999, **Gareth Barry,** playing in his
accustomed centre-back position, scored a
hat-trick in a 9-0 win.

LEE HENDRIE

Born Birmingham, 18th May 1977. *Joined Villa* July 1993 as YTS trainee. July 1994 on professional forms. *Villa debut* As sub v Queens Park Rangers, Lge (a) 23/12/95.

Coming into the season as a new dad, Lee Hendrie was entitled to feel as optimistic as anyone about the months ahead, yet no-one will be happier to see the back of it.

At a time when he needed to be at his peak to stake a claim in Villa's midfield, Lee suffered a cruel double blow in mid-season. A crunching challenge by Newcastle United's Temuri Ketsbaia in December gashed skin and ligament and left Lee spending the festive season in the treatment room. He returned for a few moments as a substitute in the FA Cup game with Southampton, only to have the same injury aggravated by a foul committed by Hassan Kachloul.

That ruled him out for another four games and there followed a lengthy string of subs appearances upon his return. Ironically, his season at inter-national level was in stark contrast to his domestic woes. Hendrie scored key goals for England U21s in their trip to this summer's European Championships.

Career Record:

Season	Club	League Apps	Gls	Cups Apps	Gls
94-95	Aston Villa	-	-	-	-
95-96	Aston Villa	2 (1)	-	-	-
96-97	Aston Villa	- (4)	-	1 (2)	-
97-98	Aston Villa	13 (4)	3	4 (3)	-
98-99	Aston Villa	31 (1)	3	5	-
99-00	Aston Villa	18 (11)	1	4 (5)	3
TOTAL		64 (21)	7	14 (10)	3

★ *England Full international (1 cap); 'B' (1 cap) and Under-21 international (11 caps, 5 goals).*

DAVID JAMES

Born Welwyn, 1st August 1970. *Joined Villa* June 1999 from Liverpool, £1.8m. *Villa debut* v Newcastle United, Lge (a) 7.8.99.

The fumble which led to Chelsea's goal in the Cup Final should not overshadow David James' superb debut season.

David's insistence on being master of his own penalty area inevitably entailed going where angels fear to tread on occasion, yet that same trait proved inspirational to his defence throughout.

His shot-stopping abilities were amply illustrated when he saved two penalties to get his team to the Final, and his prodigious kicking and throwing were valuable qualities in turning defence into attack. The impact made by James was shown when Villa fans voted him runner-up to Paul Merson in the Player of the Year poll.

Career Record:

Season	Club	League Apps	Gls Ag	Cups Apps	Gls Ag
88-89	Watford	-	-	-	-
89-90	Watford	-	-	-	-
90-91	Watford	46	-	3	-
91-92	Watford	43	-	6	-
92-93	Liverpool	29	-	2	-
93-94	Liverpool	13 (1)	-	-	-
94-95	Liverpool	42	-	15	-
95-96	Liverpool	38	-	15	-
96-97	Liverpool	38	-	14	-
97-98	Liverpool	27	-	10	-
98-99	Liverpool	26	-	6	-
99-00	Aston Villa	29	26	9	6
TOTAL		302 (1)	-	80	6

★ *England Full international (1 cap); 'B'; Under-21 and Youth international.*

JULIAN JOACHIM

Born Peterborough, 12th September 1974. *Joined Villa* February 1996 from Leicester City, £1.5m. *Villa debut* as sub v Wimbledon, Lge (a) 24/2/96.

A frustrating season for last year's leading scorer, with Joachim unable to find a consistent goal output.

Goals in the first two games of the schedule boded well, but as Villa struggled to find form before Christmas, too much dependency was placed upon JJ's pace, and opposing defences grew wise to the ploy of setting up a sprint race between Julian and his marker.

His cause was not helped by the loss of injured Dion Dublin. Arguably at his best when feeding off a genuine target man, Joachim was forced to fill that role himself, and while he never shied away from some uneven contests, he inevitably struggled in the air.

Once Dublin returned, JJ had to adjust to alternating between a place in the starting line-up and a place on the bench.

Career Record:

Season	Club	League Apps	Gls	Cups Apps	Gls
92-93	Leicester City	25 (1)	10	5 (1)	4
93-94	Leicester City	27 (9)	11	5 (2)	1
94-95	Leicester City	11 (4)	3	2	-
95-96	Leicester City	12	2	2	-
	Aston Villa	4 (7)	1	-	-
96-97	Aston Villa	3 (12)	3	2	-
97-98	Aston Villa	16 (10)	8	2 (2)	-
98-99	Aston Villa	29 (7)	14	7	2
99-00	Aston Villa	27 (6)	6	10 (3)	3
Villa record		*79 (42)*	*32*	*21 (5)*	*5*
TOTAL		154 (56)	58	35 (8)	10

★ *England Youth and Under-21 International (8 caps).*

PAUL MERSON

Born Northolt, Middlesex, 20th March 1968. *Joined Villa* September 1998 from Middlesbrough, £6.75m. *Villa debut* v Wimbledon, Lge (h) 12/9/98.

After a season with no shortage of candidates, Paul Merson was the worthy winner of both the supporters' and players' Player of the Year titles.

In and out of the side and clearly ill at ease with life in general during the first half of the campaign, his season was turned around by the delightful goal with which he began Villa's comeback against Sheffield Wednesday in December.

Career Record:

Season	Club	League Apps	Gls	Cups Apps	Gls
86-87	Arsenal	5 (2)	3	-	-
(loan)	Brentford	6 (1)	-	1 (1)	-
87-88	Arsenal	7 (8)	5	1 (1)	-
88-89	Arsenal	29 (8)	10	7 (1)	4
89-90	Arsenal	21 (8)	7	4 (3)	-
90-91	Arsenal	36 (1)	13	12	3
91-92	Arsenal	41 (1)	12	9	1
92-93	Arsenal	32 (1)	6	17	2
93-94	Arsenal	24 (9)	7	15 (1)	5
94-95	Arsenal	24	4	11 (1)	3
95-96	Arsenal	38	5	9	-
96-97	Arsenal	32	6	8	3
97-98	Middlesbrough	45	12	10	4
98-99	Middlesbrough	3	-	-	-
98-99	Aston Villa	21 (5)	5	1	-
99-00	Aston Villa	24 (8)	5	10 (2)	-
Villa record		*45 (13)*	*10*	*11 (2)*	*-*
TOTAL		388 (52)	100	115 (10)	25

★ *England Youth International; Under-21 (4 caps); 'B' (4 caps); Full International (21 caps, 2 goals).*

JLLOYD SAMUEL

Born Trinidad & Tobago 29th March 1981. *Joined Villa* July 1997 as YTS trainee. January 1999 on professional forms. *Villa debut* As sub v Chester C., Worthington Cup (h) 21/9/99.

Years from now, Jlloyd Samuel will be able to say how pressmen everywhere were talking about him, the moment he made his first team debut in 2000. Admittedly, it was mainly to check with each other how you spell his Christian name, but the young Londoner is entitled to hope they will one day be talking about his defensive abilities, after a competent start to his first team career.

After three appearances as substitute, the 19-year-old's full debut came in the home game against Derby County and with Gareth Southgate taking an enforced breather following his ankle injury, Jlloyd was the beneficiary, with four consecutive starts in the centre of defence, late in the season.

Acquitting himself well in that time, Samuel showed that Villa have an able deputy at their disposal should their back line be in need of back-up.

Career Record:

Season	Club	League Apps	Gls	Cups Apps	Gls
99-00	Aston Villa	5 (4)	-	- (1)	-

★ *England Under-18 international (2 caps).*

● In November 1999 wing-back **Alan Wright** signed a new 3-and-a-half year contract which will keep him at the club until 2003.

● Midfield dynamo **Ian Taylor** has also signed a new contract with the club, this one being for three years and is effective from March 2000.

GARETH SOUTHGATE

Born Watford, 3rd September 1970. *Joined Villa* June 1995 from Crystal Palace, £2.5m. *Villa debut* v Manchester United, Lge (h) 19/8/95.

It was gratifying to see the skipper pick up one Player of the Year award this season, courtesy of the club's South African supporters, for he has spent the season making the art of defending look easier than it is.

He has not lacked for headlines, whether for managing an own goal and red card as he did at Leicester, or for missing from the penalty spot in the game-that-wasn't at Upton Park.

These were transitory downers in a polished season for Gareth, who picked up January's Carling Player of the Month award after scoring three goals in two games. Named in England's final 22-man squad for the Euro 2000 Championships.

Career Record:

Season	Club	League Apps	Gls	Cups Apps	Gls
88-89	Crystal Palace	-	-	-	-
89-90	Crystal Palace	-	-	-	-
90-91	Crystal Palace	1	-	1 (1)	-
91-92	Crystal Palace	26 (4)	-	9	-
92-93	Crystal Palace	33	3	6	2
93-94	Crystal Palace	46	9	7	3
94-95	Crystal Palace	42	3	15	2
95-96	Aston Villa	31	1	12	1
96-97	Aston Villa	28	1	6	-
97-98	Aston Villa	32	-	11	-
98-99	Aston Villa	38	1	6	-
99-00	Aston Villa	31	2	11	1
Villa record		160	5	46	2
TOTAL		308 (4)	20	84 (1)	9

★ *Full England international (35 caps, 1 goal).*

STEVE STONE

Born Gateshead, 20th August 1971. *Joined Villa* March 1999 from Nottingham Forest for £5.5m. *Villa debut* v Tottenham Hotspur, Lge (a) 13/3/99.

A casualty of Villa's preference for a 3-5-2 formation, winger Steve Stone nevertheless made the most of his regular late arrivals from the substitutes' bench, proving himself to be a tenacious tackler when required to defend as well as being an enterprising force in attack.

It will be scant consolation that his presence on the bench with the likes of Lee Hendrie, Steve Watson, Julian Joachim and, for a time, Dion Dublin, gave Villa far more strength in depth than they enjoyed in the previous season.

The midwinter months saw him force his way into the starting line-up 13 times in 16 games, in which time he chipped in with two timely goals, firstly against Watford and in the FA Cup quarter-final win at Everton.

Career Record:

Season	Club	League Apps	Gls	Cups Apps	Gls
91-92	Nottingham F.	- (1)	-	-	-
92-93	Nottingham F.	11 (1)	1	- (1)	-
93-94	Nottingham F.	45	5	9	-
94-95	Nottingham F.	41	5	6	-
95-96	Nottingham F.	34	7	16	2
96-97	Nottingham F.	5	-	-	-
97-98	Nottingham F.	27 (2)	2	-	-
98-99	Nottingham F.	26	3	4	2
	Aston Villa	9 (1)	-	-	-
99-00	Aston Villa	10 (14)	1	5 (6)	2
Villa record		*19 (15)*	*1*	*5 (6)*	*2*
TOTAL		208 (19)	24	40 (7)	6

★ *Full England international (9 caps, 2 goals).*

IAN TAYLOR

Born Birmingham, 4th June 1968. *Joined Villa* December 1994 in straight swop deal with Guy Whittingham from Sheffield Wed. *Villa debut* v Arsenal, Lge (a) 26/12/94.

His reaction to being nicknamed 'Mildred' once George Boateng joined him in central midfield is unrecorded, but Ian Taylor revelled in the freedom it afforded him to combine a taste for goals with his regular duties.

The 31-year-old's nine goals equalled his best ever haul in a Villa shirt and he would have beaten it with ease, had not injury marred the second half of his season just as he was getting into his stride.

An ankle injury restricted him to four substitute's appearances in five games and then a damaged hamstring sustained in the FA Cup semi-final with Bolton knocked him out of action until the Final itself.

A vintage season rewarded with a new contract will be consolations for the ever-popular midfielder.

Career Record:

Season	Club	League Apps	Gls	Cups Apps	Gls
92-93	Port Vale	41	15	15	4
93-94	Port Vale	42	13	8	3
94-95	Sheff. Wed.	9 (5)	1	2 (2)	1
	Aston Villa	21	1	2	-
95-96	Aston Villa	24 (1)	3	7 (2)	2
96-97	Aston Villa	29 (5)	2	3	1
97-98	Aston Villa	30 (2)	6	12	3
98-99	Aston Villa	31 (2)	4	4 (1)	-
99-00	Aston Villa	25 (4)	5	10 (2)	4
Villa record		*160 (14)*	*21*	*38 (5)*	*10*
TOTAL		252 (19)	50	63 (7)	18

ALAN THOMPSON

Born Newcastle,
22nd November 1973.
Joined Villa June 1998
from Bolton Wanderers,
£4.5m.
Villa debut v Everton,
Lge (a) 15/8/98.

This was a season of extremes for the likable Geordie, who started as a regular, disappeared off the team-sheet altogether and then took advantage of Villa's pre-Cup Final 'rotation scheme', to make his case for a place in the Final itself.

As Boateng, Merson and Taylor became entrenched as the midfield hub, Thompson found himself making just two appearances from the bench in four months.

Then a place became available in the side for the game at Sheffield Wednesday, when several of the FA Cup semi-final team were rested. The former Bolton player took his chance, hitting the winner late in injury time and then adding another goal in the game against Leicester.

Career Record:

Season	Club	League Apps	Gls	Cups Apps	Gls
91-92	Newcastle U.	12 (2)	-	1	-
92-93	Newcastle U.	1 (1)	-	3	-
93-94	Bolton W.	19 (8)	6	10 (2)	2
94-95	Bolton W.	34 (3)	7	11 (1)	2
95-96	Bolton W.	23 (3)	1	6	1
96-97	Bolton W.	34	11	5 (1)	2
97-98	Bolton W.	33	9	5	1
98-99	Aston Villa	20 (5)	2	3 (1)	-
99-00	Aston Villa	16 (5)	2	4 (2)	1
Villa record		36 (10)	4	7 (3)	1
TOTAL		192 (27)	38	48 (7)	9

★ *English Youth International; Under-21 (2 caps).*

DARIUS VASSELL

Born Birmingham,
30th June 1980.
Joined Villa July 1996 as
YTS trainee. March 1998
on professional forms.
Villa debut as sub v
Middlesbrough, Lge (h)
23/8/98.

Injuries spoiled a promising season for Darius Vassell. His first Premiership start at Sunderland led to a hamstring pull and he was not able to regain full fitness.

Career Record:

Season	Club	League Apps	Gls	Cups Apps	Gls
98-99	Aston Villa	- (6)	-	- (5)	2
99-00	Aston Villa	1 (10)	-	1 (4)	-
TOTAL		1 (16)	-	1 (9)	2

★ *England Under-18 International (5 caps, 5 goals), Under-21 international (2 caps).*

RICHARD WALKER

Born Birmingham,
8th November, 1977.
Joined Villa on YTS terms
in 1993 at the age of 16,
now full time professional.
Villa debut as sub v Leeds
Utd, Lge (a) 28/12/97.

Used his brief spell in the limelight to serve notice of his ability before the return from injury of Dion Dublin.

Career Record:

Season	Club	League Apps	Gls	Cups Apps	Gls
97-98	Aston Villa	- (1)	-	-	-
98-99	Aston Villa	-	-	-	-
loan	Cambridge U.	7 (13)	3	1 (2)	1
99-00	Aston Villa	2 (3)	2	1 (1)	-
Villa record		2 (4)	2	1 (1)	-
TOTAL		9 (17)	5	2 (3)	1

STEVE WATSON

Born North Shields,
1st April 1974
Joined Villa October 1998
from Newcastle United,
£3.5m.
Villa debut as sub v
Leicester C., Lge (h)
24/10/98

Locked in competition with Mark
Delaney for the most hotly-contested
shirt in the team, Steve Watson has had
to make do with a series of intermittent
runs in the first team this season, yet
hardly put a foot wrong whenever his
chance came.

Suspended for the first game of the
season at St James' Park, the Geordie
may have wondered if he had left the
door open for Delaney to claim the right
wing-back's spot on a permanent basis,
yet he managed to battle his way back
into the starting line-up.

John Gregory cited the versatile
Watson as one of the reasons he felt able
to let Colin Calderwood go.

Career Record:

Season	Club	League Apps	Gls	Cups Apps	Gls
90-91	Newcastle Utd	22 (2)	-	4	-
91-92	Newcastle Utd	23 (5)	1	2	-
92-93	Newcastle Utd	1 (1)	-	2 (1)	-
93-94	Newcastle Utd	29 (3)	2	5 (1)	-
94-95	Newcastle Utd	22 (5)	4	4 (4)	1
95-96	Newcastle Utd	15 (8)	3	3 (3)	1
96-97	Newcastle Utd	33 (3)	1	7 (3)	-
97-98	Newcastle Utd	27 (2)	1	13 (2)	-
98-99	Newcastle Utd	7	-	1	-
98-99	Aston Villa	26 (1)	-	3	-
99-00	Aston Villa	13 (1)	-	8 (1)	1
Villa record		*39 (2)*	*-*	*11 (1)*	*1*
TOTAL		218 (31)	12	52 (15)	3

★ *England Youth; England Under-21 (12 caps);*
England 'B' (1 cap).

ALAN WRIGHT

Born Ashton-under-Lyme,
28th September 1971.
Joined Villa March 1995
from Blackburn Rovers,
£900,000.
Villa debut v West Ham
Utd, Lge (h) 18/3/95.

If a stomach muscle injury early in the
season dented his hopes of another ever-
present campaign, Alan Wright at least
had the consolation of scoring his first
goal in three years, in the win at Spurs.

Wright acknowledged in mid-season
that the arrival of Najwan Ghrayib last
summer, provided a welcome incentive
for him to hang on to the place which
he has made his own since arriving from
Blackburn Rovers five years ago and he
has again turned in another dependable
season on the left side of defence.

Career Record:

Season	Club	League Apps	Gls	Cups Apps	Gls
87-88	Blackpool	- (1)	-	-	-
88-90	Blackpool	14 (2)	-	3 (1)	-
89-90	Blackpool	20 (4)	-	9 (3)	-
90-91	Blackpool	45	-	12	-
91-92	Blackpool	12	-	5	-
	Blackburn R.	32 (1)	1	5	-
92-93	Blackburn R.	24	-	9	-
93-94	Blackburn R.	7 (5)	-	2	-
94-95	Blackburn R.	4 (1)	-	- (1)	-
	Aston Villa	8	-	-	-
95-96	Aston Villa	38	2	13	-
96-97	Aston Villa	38	1	7	-
97-98	Aston Villa	35 (2)	-	13	-
98-99	Aston Villa	38	-	7	-
99-00	Aston Villa	31 (1)	1	10	-
Villa record		*188 (3)*	*4*	*50*	*-*
TOTAL		346 (17)	5	95 (5)	-

★ *England Under-21 International.*

FA CARLING PREMIERSHIP STATISTICS 1999-2000

FINAL TABLE

			Home				Away					Total					
	Pl	W	D	L	F	A	W	D	L	F	A	W	D	L	F	A	Pts
1 Manchester United	38	15	4	0	59	16	13	3	3	38	29	28	7	3	97	45	91
2 Arsenal	38	14	3	2	42	17	8	4	7	31	26	22	7	9	73	43	73
3 Leeds United	38	12	2	5	29	18	9	4	6	29	25	21	6	11	58	43	69
4 Liverpool	38	11	4	4	28	13	8	6	5	23	17	19	10	9	51	30	67
5 Chelsea	38	12	5	2	35	12	6	6	7	18	22	18	11	9	53	34	65
6 **Aston Villa**	38	8	8	3	23	12	7	5	7	23	23	15	13	10	46	35	58
7 Sunderland	38	10	6	3	28	17	6	4	9	29	39	16	10	12	57	56	58
8 Leicester City	38	10	3	6	31	24	6	4	9	24	31	16	7	15	55	55	55
9 West Ham United	38	11	5	3	32	23	4	5	10	20	30	15	10	13	52	53	55
10 Tottenham Hotspur	38	10	3	6	40	26	5	5	9	17	23	15	8	15	57	49	53
11 Newcastle United	38	10	5	4	42	20	4	5	10	21	34	14	10	14	63	54	52
12 Middlesbrough	38	8	5	6	23	26	6	5	8	23	26	14	10	14	46	52	52
13 Everton	38	7	9	3	36	21	5	5	9	23	28	12	14	12	59	49	50
14 Coventry City	38	12	1	6	38	22	0	7	12	9	32	12	8	18	47	54	44
15 Southampton	38	8	4	7	26	22	4	4	11	19	40	12	8	18	45	62	44
16 Derby County	38	6	3	10	22	25	3	8	8	22	32	9	11	18	44	57	38
17 Bradford City	38	6	8	5	26	29	3	1	15	12	39	9	9	20	38	68	36
18 Wimbledon	38	6	7	6	30	28	1	5	13	16	46	7	12	19	46	74	33
19 Sheffield Wednesday	38	6	3	10	21	23	2	4	13	17	47	8	7	23	38	70	31
20 Watford	38	5	4	10	24	31	1	2	16	11	46	6	6	26	35	47	24

ROLL OF HONOUR

Champions: Manchester United.
Runners-up: Arsenal.
Third place: Leeds United.
UEFA Cup Qualifiers: Liverpool, Chelsea, Leicester City.
Relegated: Wimbledon, Sheffield Wednesday, Watford.
FA Cup winners: Chelsea.
Worthington Cup winners: Leicester City.

FACTS & FIGURES

Of the 380 games played in the Premiership, 187 resulted in home wins, 101 in away wins and 92 draws. A total of 1060 goals were scored at an average of 2.79 per game, with 635 being scored by the home clubs and 425 by the visitors

Most goals scored: 97, Manchester United
Most home goals: 59, Manchester United
Most away goals: 38, Manchester United
Least goals scored: 35, Watford
Least home goals: 21, Sheffield Wednesday
Least away goals: 9, Coventry City

Least goals conceded: 30, Liverpool
Least home goals conceded: 12, Aston Villa and Chelsea
Least away goals conceded: 17, Liverpool
Most goals conceded: 77, Watford
Most home goals conceded: 31, Watford
Most away goals conceded: 47, Sheffield Wed.

Highest goals aggregate: 142, Manchester Utd
Lowest goals aggregate: 81, Liverpool

Best home record: 49 pts, Manchester United
Best away record: 42 pts, Manchester United
Worst home record: 19 pts, Watford
Worst away record: 5 pts, Watford

Highest home score:
Newcastle Utd 8 Sheffield Wed. 0, 19.9.99

Highest away score:
Derby County 0 Sunderland 5, 18.9.99

Penalties scored: 63
Hat-tricks: 13
Own goals: 30
Yellow cards: 1,245
Red Cards: 69
Bookings per game: 3.46

GOALSCORERS & ATTENDANCES

LEADING SCORERS
(Including Cup & European games)

30 Kevin Phillips (Sunderland)
30 Alan Shearer (Newcastle United)
26 Thierry Henry (Arsenal)
23 Dwight Yorke (Manchester United)
22 Andy Cole (Manchester United)
21 Michael Bridges (Leeds United)
19 Tore Andre Flo (Chelsea)
18 Gustavo Poyet (Chelsea)
17 Steffen Iversen (Tottenham Hotspur)
17 Harry Kewell (Leeds United)
17 Paulo di Canio (West Ham United)
17 Nwankwo Kanu (Arsenal)
15 Carl Cort (Wimbledon)
15 Dion Dublin (Aston Villa)
15 Ole Gunnar Solskjaer (Manchester United)
15 Paulo Wanchope (West Ham United)
14 Chris Armstrong (Tottenham Hotspur)
14 Niall Quinn (Sunderland)
14 Hamilton Ricard (Middlesbrough)
13 Tony Cottee (Leicester City)
13 Frank Lampard (West Ham United)
13 Gary McAllister (Coventry City)
13 Marc Overmars (Arsenal)
13 Marian Pahars (Southampton)
13 Gary Speed (Newcastle United)
12 Kevin Campbell (Everton)
12 Robbie Keane (Coventry City)
12 Roy Keane (Manchester United)
12 Michael Owen (Liverpool)
12 Paul Scholes (Manchester United)

GOLDEN BOOT WINNER
(Premiership games only)
30 Kevin Phillips.

QUICK OFF THE MARK
There is a tie for the fastest goal of this season, both goals were scored by Dion Dublin at Villa Park in the fifth minute of the game.
 The first was against West Ham United on 16th August 1999 and the second was against Middlesbrough on 28th August.

THE GATE LEAGUE

	Total	Best	Lowest	Average
Manchester Utd	1,102,269	61,629	54,941	58,014
Liverpool	837,402	44,929	40,483	44,074
Sunderland	776,131	42,192	30,105	40,849
Leeds United	743,932	40,192	34,112	39,154
Arsenal	722,576	38,147	37,271	38,030
Newcastle Utd	690,112	36,619	35,614	36,322
Tottenham	663,324	36,233	28,701	34,912
Everton	661,728	40,052	30,490	34,828
Chelsea	656,083	35,113	31,591	34,531
Middlesbrough	634,537	34,800	31,400	33,397
Aston Villa	602,237	39,217	23,885	31,697
Derby County	557,678	33,378	24,045	29,351
West Ham Utd	476,769	26,044	22,438	25,093
Sheffield Wed	472,253	39,640	18,077	24,855
Coventry City	395,369	23,098	17,685	20,809
Leicester City	376,718	22,170	17,550	19,827
Watford	352,338	21,590	15,511	18,544
Bradford City	342,563	18,286	16,864	18,030
Wimbledon	325,188	26,129	8,248	17,115
Southampton	287,516	15,257	14,208	15,132

Highest attendance:
61,629, Manchester Utd v Tottenham, 6.5.2000

Lowest attendance:
8,248, Wimbledon v Sheffield Wed, 12.4.2000

Five goals in a game:
Alan Shearer (Newcastle) v Sheff Wed 19.9.99

Four goals in a game:
Andy Cole (Man U.) v Newcastle 30.8.99
Ole Gunnar Solskjaer (Man U.) v Everton 4.12.99

Three goals in a game:
Michael Bridges (Leeds U.) v Southampton 11.8.99
Kevin Phillips (Sunderland) v Derby Co. 18.9.99
Nwankwo Kanu (Arsenal) v Chelsea 23.10.99
Marc Overmars (Arsenal) v Middlesbro' 20.11.99
Nick Barmby (Everton) v West Ham U. 26.2.00
Stan Collymore (Leicester C.) v Sunderland 5.3.00
Dwight Yorke (Man U.) v Derby Co. 11.3.00
Steffen Iversen (Spurs) v Southampton 11.3.00
Paul Scholes (Man U.) v West Ham U. 1.4.00
Dean Windass (Bradford) v Derby Co. 21.4.00

FIRST TEAM APPEARANCES & GOALSCORERS

	LEAGUE Apps	LEAGUE Gls	FA CUP Apps	FA CUP Gls	LGE CUP Apps	LGE CUP Gls	TOTAL Apps	TOTAL Gls
Gareth BARRY	30	1	6	-	7	-	43	1
Jonathan BEWERS	- (1)	-	-	-	-	-	-	-
George BOATENG	30 (3)	2	5	-	6	1	41 (3)	3
Colin CALDERWOOD	15 (3)	-	-	-	3 (1)	-	18 (4)	-
Benito CARBONE	22 (2)	4	6	5	-	-	28 (2)	9
Neil CUTLER	- (1)	-	-	-	-	-	-	-
Mark DELANEY	25 (3)	1	4 (1)	-	1 (2)	-	30 (6)	1
Mark DRAPER	- (1)	-	-	-	-	-	- (1)	-
Dion DUBLIN	23 (3)	12	2 (1)	1	3	2	28 (4)	15
Ugo EHIOGU	31	1	6	-	6	-	43	1
Peter ENCKELMAN	9 (1)	-	1	-	3	-	13 (1)	-
Najwan GHRAYIB	1 (4)	-	-	-	1	-	2 (4)	-
Lee HENDRIE	18 (11)	1	- (4)	-	4 (1)	3	22 (16)	4
David JAMES	29	-	5	-	4	-	38	-
Julian JOACHIM	27 (6)	6	4 (2)	-	6 (1)	3	37 (9)	9
Paul MERSON	24 (8)	5	6	-	4 (2)	-	34 (10)	5
Jlloyd SAMUEL	5 (4)	-	-	-	- (1)	-	5 (5)	-
Gareth SOUTHGATE	31	2	6	1	5	-	42	3
Steve STONE	10 (14)	1	2 (4)	1	3 (2)	1	15 (20)	3
Ian TAYLOR	25 (4)	5	4 (1)	-	6 (1)	4	35 (6)	9
Alan THOMPSON	16 (5)	2	1	-	3 (2)	1	20 (7)	3
Darius VASSELL	1 (10)	-	- (1)	-	1 (3)	-	2 (14)	-
Richard WALKER	2 (3)	2	-	-	1 (1)	-	3 (4)	2
Steve WATSON	13 (1)	-	2	-	6 (1)	1	21 (2)	1
Alan WRIGHT	31 (1)	1	6	-	4	-	41 (1)	1

Unused Substitutes: (figures in brackets refer to cup matches)
Neil Cutler 13(7), Peter Enckelman 14(3), Steve Watson 13(1), Najwan Ghrayib 10(2),
Michael Oakes 9(3), Colin Calderwood 5(3), Jlloyd Samuel 5(3), Paul Merson 5(1),
Richard Walker 4(2), Alan Thompson 3(2), Mark Draper 3(1), Steve Stone 3(1), Mark Delaney 2(1),
Darius Vassell 2(1), Jonathan Bewers 2, George Boateng 1(1), Lee Hendrie 1(1), Alan Wright 2,
Gareth Barry 1, Gustavo Bartelt 1, Benito Carbone 1, John McGrath 1, Michael Standing 1.

Goalscorers in friendly games:
Gavin Melaugh 6, Lee Hendrie 5, Graham Evans 4, Julian Joachim 4, Richard Walker 4,
Darren Byfield 2, Benito Carbone 2, Dion Dublin 2, Stephen Evans 2, David Hughes 2,
John McGrath 2, Jay Smith 2, Neil Tarrant 2, Gustavo Bartelt 1, Danny Haynes 1,
Tommy Jaszczun 1, Paul Merson 1, Fraser Murray 1, Marco Russo 1, Steve Stone 1, Alan Wright 1.

VILLA FACTS & FIGURES 1999-2000

HIGHEST AND LOWEST

Highest home attendance: 39,217 (3 times)
v Liverpool 2.10.99,
v Tottenham Hotspur 29.12.99,
v Manchester United 14.5.2000.

Lowest home attendance: 17,608
v Southampton (Worthington Cup, Fourth Round) 1.12.99

Highest away attendance: 55,211
v Manchester United 30.10.99
(not counting Wembley, a neutral venue)

Lowest away attendance: 4,364
v Chester City (Worthington Cup, 2/1) 14.9.99

Biggest victory:
5-0 v Chester City (Worthington Cup, 2/2) (h) 21.9.99;

Heaviest defeat:
0-3 v Manchester United (a) 30.10.99

Most goals in a match:
3 - Benito Carbone v Leeds United (h) (FA Cup Fifth Round) 30.1.00

Most goals against:
2 - Davor Suker (Arsenal) (a) 11.9.99,
Kevin Phillips (Sunderland) (a) 18.10.99,
Kevin Davies (Southampton) (a) 18.3.00

Clean Sheets: 23
Failed to score in: 14
Villa scored first: 28
Scored first and won: 20
Scored first and drew: 6
Scored first and lost: 2
Opponents scored first: 17
Lost after opponents scored first: 10
Drew after opponents scored first: 3
Won after opponents scored first: 4
Highest League position: 1st
Lowest League position: 15th

SEQUENCE RECORDS

Most matches undefeated:
11, Dec 11 - Jan 30
Most home matches undefeated:
14, Dec 11 - Apr 29
Most away matches undefeated:
5, Nov 27 - Jan 15
Most wins in succession:
3, Sep 14 - Sep 21; Dec 11 - Dec 26;
Jan 3 - Jan 11; Feb 5 - Feb 20 and
Apr 5 - Apr 15

Most home wins in succession:
3, Aug 28 - Sept 21 and Mar 11 - Apr 9
Most away wins in succession:
3, Dec 26 - Jan 11
Longest run without a win:
6, Oct 18 - Nov 27
Longest run without a home win:
3, Apr 22 - May 14
Longest run without an away win:
5, Sep 25 - Nov 27
Most defeats in succession:
3, Oct 30 - Nov 22
Goals for in successive matches:
8, Dec 11 - Jan 15
Goals against in successive matches:
6, Oct 18 - Nov 22 and Apr 15 - May 20
Longest run without scoring:
278 minutes, Jan 15 - Jan 30
Longest run without conceding a goal:
433 minutes, Mar 18 - Apr 15
Most consecutive appearances:
33 - Gareth Barry, Nov 27 - May 20.
Ever Presents: None, but Ugo Ehiogu and
Gareth Barry both played in 43 games
(League and Cup), more than any other
player.

DEBUTANTS
Eight players made their Villa debuts this
season:
David James v Newcastle United (a)
George Boateng v Newcastle United (a)
Peter Enckelman as sub v Arsenal (a)
Najwan Ghrayib v Chester City (WC) (a)
Jlloyd Samuel as sub v Chester City (WC) (h)
Benito Carbone v Wimbledon (h)
Neil Cutler v Middlesbrough (h)
Jonathan Bewers as sub v Tottenham H. (a)

PENALTIES
Villa were awarded five penalties during the
season, only one was converted and four were
missed.
Scored: Dion Dublin v Tottenham Hotspur
(a) (15.4.2000) beat Ian Walker.
Missed: Alan Thompson v Middlesbrough,
Schwarzer saved at Witton End (23.8.99). Lee
Hendrie v Chester City (WC2/1) (a) Brown
saved, Hendrie scored from rebound (14.9.99).
Dion Dublin v Sheffield Wednesday, Srnicek

saved at Witton End (18.12.99). Paul Merson v Sheffield Wednesday, Srnicek saved at Holte End (18.12.99).

Penalties conceded were: Luke Beckett for Chester City (WC2/2) Enckelman saved retaken penalty. Kevin Phillips at Sunderland (18.10.99), scored. Peter Duffield for Darlington, James saved, Heckingbottom scored from rebound at Holte End (11.12.99). Gilles de Bilde for Sheffield Wednesday (18.12.99), scored at Holte End. Paolo di Canio for West Ham (Restaged WC5) (a), James saved (11.1.00). Michael Owen for Liverpool (a), hit bar, Enckelman in goal (15.3.00). Also Paolo di Canio v West Ham (WC5) (a), scored, goal void, game restaged.

RED CARDS

Three Villa players were sent off during the course of this season:
Gareth Southgate in the League game at Leicester City (25.9.99) for two bookable offences.
Benito Carbone in the FA Cup Sixth Round at Everton (20.2.00) for two bookable offences.
Mark Delaney in the FA Cup Semi-Final at Wembley (2.4.00) for two bookable offences.

Three opposing players were sent off in games against Villa:
Alan Shearer (Newcastle United) 7.8.99 at St James' Park for two bookable offences.
John Collins (Everton) 11.8.99 at Villa Park for two bookable offences.
Steve Staunton (Liverpool) 2.10.99 at Villa Park for two bookable offences. (Sending-off was later rescinded as second booking was found to be incorrect.)

HOLTE END v WITTON END

Of the 56 goals scored at Villa Park in all competitions during the season, 35 were scored at the Holte End (29 for Villa and 6 against) and 21 at the Witton End (12 for Villa and 9 against).

ARRIVALS

David James 17.6.99 from Liverpool for £1.5m.
Najwan Ghrayib 20.7.99 from Hapoel Haifa (Israel) for £1m.
George Boateng from Coventry City 20.7.99 for £4.5m.

Benito Carbone from Sheffield Wednesday 20.10.99 for nominal fee until end of season.
Neil Cutler 27.7.99 from Chester City, free transfer.
Gustavo Bartelt 4.2.00 from Roma (Italy) on loan to end of season.
Luc Nilis 5.3.00 from PSV Eindhoven (Holland), Bosman signing, will join club in summer of 2000.

DEPARTURES

Reserve team players Reuben Hazell and Martin Ridley were released by the club in the summer of 1999.

Alan Lee went to Burnley 7.7.99 for £150,000. Riccardo Scimeca to Nottingham Forest 23.7.99 for £3m. Simon Grayson to Blackburn Rovers 29.7.99 for £750,000. David Hughes to Shrewsbury Town 21.9.99 on a Free transfer. Adam Rachel to Blackpool 28.9.99, Free. Michael Oakes to Wolves 29.10.99 for £400,000. Tommy Jaszczun to Blackpool 20.1.00 for £50,000. Stan Collymore to Leicester City 10.2.00 for fee based on appearances. 2.3.00 Colin Calderwood to Nottingham Forest 14.3.00 for £70,000.

At the end of the season Darren Byfield was released by the club. As were young professionals: Graham Evans, Michael Blackwood, David Harding, Jamie Kearns, Brian Mulholland, Michael Price and Luke Prince.

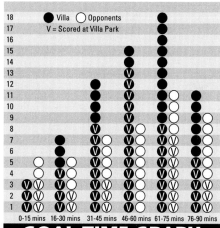

| | 0-15 mins | 16-30 mins | 31-45 mins | 46-60 mins | 61-75 mins | 76-90 mins |

● Villa   ○ Opponents
V = Scored at Villa Park

GOAL TIME GRAPH

FIFA CALLS FOR CHAIRMAN

Villa chairman Doug Ellis was appointed to FIFA's influential Marketing & Advisory Board towards the end of the season.

The game's governing body recognised the experience gained by Mr Ellis in his involvement with TV rights negotiations for both the FA and the Premiership, and for his part, the Chairman was delighted that English football again has a voice in the international corridors of power.

JOHN'S FAREWELL

Aston Villa said goodbye to its Safety/ Operations Manager, John Hood when the season ended, and the term 'end of an era' would not be out of place.

John's retirement concludes a decade in which he has had responsibility for implementing the quantum leap in ground safety and security which followed the Hillsborough disaster and the Taylor Report.

In his time at Villa Park, the former police officer established standards for stewarding and ground safety that have been used as a model by clubs both in Britain and on the Continent.

He will be succeeded in the post by another former policeman, Graham Hodgetts.

TRINITY END

The walls caved in on 77 years of history, shortly after the season finished, when the demolition crews set about felling the Trinity Road stand to make way for its modern replacement, part of the club's plans for an eventual 50,000-seater stadium.

Built in the early 1920s and officially opened by the future George VI, the stand's last stand, so to speak, was the 1-0 home defeat by Manchester United. The club planned to have between 8,000 and 10,000 seats available in the new stand by the time the Premiership resumed in August, with the new Trinity Stand, its capacity in the region of 13,500, being finished by the end of 2000.

EARLY VIEWING RECOMMENDED

Villa Park went 'on show' twice during the season, firstly when a FIFA party flew in to inspect the stadium in connection with England's 2006 World Cup bid and secondly

when the Mayor of Rotterdam and other city officials came to gain an insight into hosting a major international tournament. The Dutch party had an eye to its own responsibilities when Euro 2006 came around, and were drawing on Villa's experience from being one of the clubs whose stadium was used in Euro 96.

ANY OTHER BUSINESS?

On 2nd September 1999, Aston Villa held its last AGM of the century and informed shareholders that the company had made a profit after player trading of £20.2m, compared to £3.7m in the previous financial year. This was achieved on a turnover of £34.9m, up £3.1m on the previous year.

SOMETHING FOR A RAINY DAY

Villa clinched two lucrative commercial deals during the season, when cable company and new main sponsor, NTL, injected a £26m loan into the club, and Diadora became Villa's new official kit suppliers, in a deal worth more than £6m.

In return for its loan, NTL secures media rights and a 9.999% shareholding in the club after five years.

ABSENT FRIENDS

The club sadly lost two of its former servants during the season.

● **ERIC WOODWARD**, Villa's and football's first commercial manager when appointed by Doug Ellis in 1968, died after a long illness, at the age of 69.

Formerly chief sports writer with the *Evening Mail*, Eric was faced with the daunting task of helping stabilise the club following its change of ownership in the late 1960s. As well as his commercial work, the journalist in him also revamped the matchday programme, making it an informative and entertaining line of communication with the supporters, and he introduced organised press conferences for the benefit of the media.

● On the playing side, former Villa left-back **ALBERT VINALL** also died, having spent seven years at the club shortly after the Second World War.

Academy success is spreading

The growing success of Villa's Football Academy system was illustrated at reserve as well as youth level during the 1999-2000 campaign.

The club's FA Premier Reserve League team often boasted more teenagers than senior professionals, particularly in the closing stages of the season.

It was only a pity that Villa Park was so sparsely populated for games such as the 3-1 home win against Barnsley in mid-April, when a second team packed with youngsters produced some scintillating football and tremendous goals.

Results over the season were mixed, the side losing just one of its first seven games, but then collecting only two victories from the following 13.

Having to regularly make personnel changes was, as ever, a problem when it came to producing consistency of performance and thus results.

But the campaign ended on an optimistic note as youth came to the fore. As well as the impressive win against Barnsley, there was an excellent 4-1 victory at Middlesbrough to cheer.

The team was captained in several of those latter games by 17-year-old Jonathan Bewers, who also made his first team debut as a substitute at Tottenham during April. Hopefully Bewers, along with several of his Academy colleagues, will follow in the footsteps of former trainees such as Lee Hendrie and Gareth Barry into first team football.

The signs are certainly good if international recognition is anything to go by. No fewer than nine of this year's Under-17 Villa side are now international players, six having won England Under-16 caps, while three have represented the Republic of Ireland at Under-16 level.

The Villa Under-17s had a fine Academy League season, proving themselves one of the top teams at this level in the country. They won their regional League section comfortably then reached the semi-finals of the national play-offs.

The Under-19 side did not fare so well in terms of results, finishing fourth in their League section then going out in the last 16 of the play-offs.

While the season for the Under-19s might be seen as disappointing, there were some mitigating circumstances: ie – Gareth Barry and Jlloyd Samuel!

Both players were eligible for the Under-19s, but first team duties totally ruled Barry out, while Samuel played only a couple of Under-19 games.

So, if the object of Academy soccer is to prepare players for the Premier League, the Villa Under-19 section did not fare so badly after all.

PREMIER ACADEMY LEAGUE - UNDER-19

	P	W	D	L	F	A	Pts
Nottingham F.	22	15	2	5	63	29	47
Leicester City	22	11	5	6	32	29	38
Coventry City	22	11	4	7	38	33	37
Aston Villa	22	8	6	9	34	31	30
Derby County	22	6	5	11	26	33	23
Peterborough U.	22	5	6	11	29	41	21
Birmingham C.	22	6	3	13	23	36	21
Stoke City	22	3	5	14	17	47	14

PONTIN'S PREMIER LEAGUE TABLE

	P	W	D	L	F	A	Pts
Liverpool	24	16	7	1	55	18	55
Sunderland	24	12	5	7	35	27	41
Blackburn Rovers	24	11	6	7	37	26	39
Bradford City	24	12	3	9	44	45	39
Newcastle Utd	24	11	4	9	37	35	37
Manchester Utd	24	11	3	10	46	32	36
Leeds United	24	10	6	8	48	38	36
Middlesbrough	24	10	6	8	34	33	36
Everton	24	7	10	7	44	40	31
Aston Villa	24	8	5	11	37	42	29
Bolton Wanderers	24	6	4	14	22	59	22
Sheffield Wed.	24	5	4	15	35	52	19
Barnsley	24	3	5	16	22	49	14

PREMIER ACADEMY LEAGUE - UNDER-17

	P	W	D	L	F	A	Pts
Aston Villa	22	14	6	2	57	29	48
Leicester City	22	9	6	7	29	25	33
Coventry City	22	8	7	7	40	33	31
Nottingham F.	22	9	3	10	31	45	30
Birmingham C.	22	3	6	13	27	60	15

FA YOUTH CUP

Nov	16	A	Fulham (Rd 3)	4-1	Debolla (3), Smith J. (pen)
Jan	18	A	Derby County (Rd 4)	0-2	

RESERVE TEAM RESULTS & SCORERS 1999-2000

FA PREMIER RESERVE LEAGUE (NORTH)

Aug	31	A	Sheffield Wednesday	4-2	Walker 2, Draper, Boateng
Sept	7	**H**	**Liverpool**	1-1	Walker
Sept	23	A	Manchester United	3-2	McGrath, Lescott, Ghrayib
Sept	29	**H**	**Middlesbrough**	1-4	Lescott
Oct	5	A	Leeds United	1-0	Walker
Oct	14	**H**	**Bolton Wanderers**	2-0	Vassell, og
Oct	20	A	Barnsley	1-1	Melaugh
Oct	27	**H**	**Blackburn Rovers**	1-2	Stone
Nov	9	A	Bradford City	0-1	
Nov	15	A	Newcastle United	2-0	Byfield 2
Dec	6	A	Liverpool	1-3	Walker
Jan	12	**H**	**Sheffield Wednesday**	2-2	Walker 2
Jan	19	**H**	**Sunderland**	2-0	Thompson 2 (1pen)
Feb	1	**H**	**Bradford City**	1-4	Hendrie (pen)
Feb	15	A	Everton	1-1	Bartelt
Feb	23	**H**	**Newcastle United**	0-2	
Mar	1	A	Blackburn Rovers	1-4	Bartelt
Mar	6	A	Sunderland	0-1	
Mar	13	**H**	**Leeds United**	3-5	Hendrie 3 (2pens)
Mar	22	**H**	**Everton**	1-1	Evans S.
Mar	29	A	Middlesbrough	4-1	Evans S., Ghrayib, Thompson, Walker
Apr	3	**H**	**Manchester United**	1-2	Fahey
Apr	12	**H**	**Barnsley**	3-1	Evans S., Marfell, Blackwood
Apr	26	A	Bolton Wanderers	1-2	Walker

Goalscorers:
Richard Walker 9;
Lee Hendrie 4; Stephen Evans 3, Alan Thompson 3;
Gustavo Bartelt 2, Darren Byfield 2, Najwan Ghrayib 2, Aaron Lescott 2;
Michael Blackwood 1, George Boateng 1, Mark Draper 1, Keith Fahey 1, Andrew Marfell 1,
John McGrath 1, Gavin Melaugh 1, Steve Stone 1, Darius Vassell 1, Own goals 1.

YOUTH TEAM RESULTS & GOALSCORERS

YOUTH ACADEMY (UNDER-17)

Aug 28	A	Arsenal	3-3
Moore, Debolla (2)

Sept 4	A	Queen Park Rangers	2-2
Moore, Bewers

Sept 11	A	Wimbledon	4-0
Smith A. (3), Jackman

Sept 18	H	**Queens Park Rangers**	5-3
Debolla, Moore, Willetts, Husbands, Bewers

Sept 25	H	**Arsenal**	2-2
Bewers, Moore

Oct 2	H	**Birmingham City**	3-0
Bewers, Hylton, Debolla

Oct 16	H	**Watford**	2-2
Bewers, Moore

Oct 23	H	**Coventry City**	3-2
Dillon, Edwards, Bewers

Oct 30	H	**Leicester City**	1-0
Jackman

Nov 6	H	**Sunderland**	2-0
og, Moore

Nov 13	A	Tottenham Hotspur	1-1
Hylton

Nov 20	A	Nottingham Forest	3-0
Lewis, Debolla, Moore

Nov 27	A	Birmingham City	3-1
Lewis, Cooke (2)

Dec 4	H	**Manchester United**	2-0
Hylton, Cooke

Jan 14	A	Coventry City	2-1
Moore (2)

Jan 22	A	Watford	2-3
Dillon, Moore

Jan 29	A	Leicester City	1-1
Bewers

Feb 5	A	Millwall	2-1
Bewers, Edwards

Feb 12	H	**Nottingham Forest**	5-1
Moore (5)

Feb 19	H	**Blackburn Rovers**	5-1
Cooke, Debolla, Moore (2), Pawley

Feb 26	A	Manchester United	3-0
Debolla (2), Moore

Mar 4	H	**Crewe Alexandra**	1-5
Husbands

Play-offs:

Mar 18	H	**Bolton W.** (1st Rd)	6-2
og, Moore, Fahey, Dillon, Debolla (2)

Mar 25	H	**Sunderland** (2nd Rd)	2-0
Hylton, Debolla

Apr 8	A	Newcastle Utd (3rd Rd)	3-1
Dillon, Moore, Debolla

Apr 18	A	Crewe Alexandra (SF)	0-1

YOUTH ACADEMY (UNDER-19)

Aug 28	H	**Arsenal**	1-2
Standing

Sept 4	A	Queens Park Rangers	1-1
Curtolo

Sept 11	A	Wimbledon	0-1

Sept 18	H	**Norwich City**	4-0
Evans S. (3), Smith A.

Sept 25	A	Everton	0-1

Oct 2	A	Birmingham City	1-1
Evans S.

Oct 16	H	**Derby County**	2-1
Melaugh (2)

Oct 23	A	Coventry City	0-5

Oct 30	A	Leicester City	1-1
Smith A.

Nov 6	H	**Stoke City**	3-1
Smith J, Melaugh, Evans S.

Nov 13	H	**Peterborough United**	4-0
Evans S. (2), og, Samuel

Nov 20	A	Nottingham Forest	0-3

Nov 27	H	**Birmingham City**	3-1
Samuel, Evans S. (2)

Dec 4	A	Derby County	4-2
Harding, Curtolo, Standing, Evans S.

Jan 14	H	**Coventry City**	1-3
Folds

Jan 22	A	Stoke City	3-1
Walters, Standing, Prince

Jan 29	H	**Leicester City**	3-0
Prince, Melaugh, Smith J.

Feb 5	A	Peterborough United	1-2
Prince

Feb 12	A	Nottingham Forest	0-3

Feb 19	H	**Blackburn Rovers**	0-0

Feb 26	A	Manchester United	1-1
Walters

Mar 4	H	**Crewe Alexandra**	1-1
Standing

Play-offs:

Mar 25	A	Middlesbrough (2nd Rd)	2-2
Evans S., Standing (aet-Villa won 5-4 on pens)

Apr 1	A	Blackburn Rovers (3rd Rd)	1-4
Haynes

RESERVE & YOUTH TEAM APPEARANCES

	PREM. RESERVE LGE		YTH ACC. U19		YTH ACC. U17		FA YTH CUP	
	Apps	Gls	Apps	Gls	Apps	Gls	Apps	Gls
Ryan Amoo	- (-)	-	- (-)	-	1 (5)	-	- (-)	-
David Andrewarthur	- (-)	-	- (-)	-	8 (2)	-	- (-)	-
Gareth Barry	1 (-)	-	- (-)	-	- (-)	-	- (-)	-
Gustavo Bartelt	6 (-)	2	- (-)	-	- (-)	-	- (-)	-
David Berks	1 (-)	-	3 (7)	-	- (-)	-	- (-)	-
Jonathan Bewers	9 (3)	-	1 (-)	-	24 (1)	8	2 (-)	-
Michael Blackwood	4 (3)	1	- (-)	-	- (-)	-	- (-)	-
George Boateng	1 (-)	1	- (-)	-	- (-)	-	- (-)	-
Darren Byfield	2 (1)	2	- (-)	-	- (-)	-	- (-)	-
Colin Calderwood	7 (-)	-	- (-)	-	- (-)	-	- (-)	-
Stan Collymore	2 (-)	-	- (-)	-	- (-)	-	- (-)	-
Stephen Cooke	1 (9)	-	- (-)	-	21 (1)	4	2 (-)	-
Jamie Cunnington	- (-)	-	- (-)	-	7 (5)	-	- (-)	-
David Curtolo	10 (1)	-	23 (-)	2	- (-)	-	- (-)	-
Neil Cutler	11 (-)	-	- (-)	-	- (-)	-	- (-)	-
Mark Debolla	3 (2)	-	2 (-)	-	24 (-)	12	2 (-)	3
Mark Delaney	4 (-)	-	- (-)	-	- (-)	-	- (-)	-
Marco Di Guiseppi*	1 (-)	-	- (-)	-	- (-)	-	- (-)	-
Sean Dillon	- (-)	-	- (-)	-	22 (-)	4	2 (-)	-
Mark Draper	10 (-)	1	- (-)	-	- (-)	-	- (-)	-
Robert Edwards	1 (4)	-	- (-)	-	26 (-)	2	1 (1)	-
Peter Enckelman	6 (-)	-	- (-)	-	- (-)	-	- (-)	-
Graham Evans	- (2)	-	- (-)	-	- (-)	-	- (-)	-
Stephen Evans	10 (6)	3	24 (-)	11	- (-)	-	- (-)	-
Keith Fahey	2 (1)	1	- (1)	-	5 (-)	1	- (-)	-
Liam Folds	1 (1)	-	14 (3)	1	- (-)	-	2 (-)	-
Matthew Ghent	1 (-)	-	19 (-)	-	- (-)	-	- (-)	-
Najwan Ghrayib	13 (-)	2	- (-)	-	- (-)	-	- (-)	-
David Harding	- (-)	-	17 (1)	1	- (-)	-	- (-)	-
Danny Haynes	4 (-)	-	20 (2)	1	- (-)	-	2 (-)	-
Wayne Henderson	1 (-)	-	1 (-)	-	15 (-)	-	2 (-)	-
Lee Hendrie	4 (1)	4	- (-)	-	- (-)	-	- (-)	-
Robert Hughes*	- (-)	-	1 (-)	-	- (-)	-	- (-)	-
Michael Husbands	- (-)	-	- (-)	-	3 (14)	2	- (2)	-
Leon Hylton	2 (2)	-	1 (-)	-	21 (1)	4	2 (-)	-
Cedric Itonga*	- (-)	-	1 (-)	-	1 (-)	-	- (-)	-
Danny Jackman	- (1)	-	- (-)	-	17 (1)	2	- (1)	-
Tommy Jaszczun	13 (-)	-	- (-)	-	- (-)	-	- (-)	-
Karl Johnson	- (-)	-	6 (1)	-	- (-)	-	- (-)	-
Morten Karlsen*	- (1)	-	- (-)	-	- (-)	-	- (-)	-

RESERVE & YOUTH TEAM APPEARANCES (cont.)

	PREM. RESERVE LGE		YTH ACC. U19		YTH ACC. U17		FA YTH CUP	
	Apps	Gls	Apps	Gls	Apps	Gls	Apps	Gls
Jamie Kearns	2 (1)	-	22 (-)	-	- (-)	-	- (-)	-
Martyn Lancaster*	1 (-)	-	- (-)	-	- (-)	-	- (-)	-
Aaron Lescott	18 (-)	2	- (-)	-	- (-)	-	- (-)	-
Stuart Lewis	- (-)	-	- (-)	-	7 (-)	2	- (-)	-
Andrew Marfell	2 (1)	1	2 (2)	-	- (-)	-	- (-)	-
John McGrath	13 (5)	1	- (-)	-	- (-)	-	- (-)	-
Lee McGuire	- (-)	-	- (-)	-	11 (4)	-	- (-)	-
Gary McSeveney	- (-)	-	8 (-)	-	- (-)	-	- (-)	-
Gavin Melaugh	4 (8)	1	17 (2)	4	- (-)	-	- (-)	-
Paul Merson	4 (-)	-	- (-)	-	- (-)	-	- (-)	-
Stefan Moore	- (2)	-	- (-)	-	23 (-)	20	2 (-)	-
Darren Moss*	1 (-)	-	- (-)	-	- (-)	-	- (-)	-
Boaz Myhill	- (-)	-	3 (-)	-	11 (3)	-	- (-)	-
Alexis Nicholas	- (-)	-	- (-)	-	3 (-)	-	- (-)	-
Isaac Nkubi	- (-)	-	- (1)	-	- (-)	-	- (-)	-
Michael Oakes	5 (-)	-	- (-)	-	- (-)	-	- (-)	-
Jamie Pawley	- (-)	-	- (-)	-	2 (1)	1	- (-)	-
Michael Price	- (-)	-	1 (1)	-	- (-)	-	- (-)	-
Luke Prince	- (-)	-	15 (3)	3	- (-)	-	- (-)	-
Keiron Richardson	- (-)	-	- (-)	-	- (1)	-	- (-)	-
Liam Ridgewell	- (-)	-	- (-)	-	- (1)	-	- (-)	-
Adam Rundell*	- (-)	-	- (-)	-	2 (-)	-	- (-)	-
Jlloyd Samuel	14 (1)	-	5 (-)	2	- (-)	-	- (-)	-
Adam Smith	- (-)	-	7 (6)	2	4 (2)	3	- (-)	-
Jay Smith	1 (5)	-	22 (1)	2	- (-)	-	2 (-)	1
Michael Standing	11 (3)	-	22 (2)	5	- (-)	-	- (-)	-
Steve Stone	7 (-)	1	- (-)	-	- (-)	-	- (-)	-
Neil Tarrant	1 (4)	-	- (-)	-	- (-)	-	- (-)	-
Ian Taylor	2 (-)	-	- (-)	-	- (-)	-	- (-)	-
Alan Thompson	11 (-)	3	- (-)	-	- (-)	-	- (-)	-
Stuart Thornley	- (-)	-	- (4)	-	- (-)	-	- (-)	-
Darius Vassell	1 (-)	1	- (-)	-	- (-)	-	- (-)	-
Richard Walker	20 (-)	9	- (-)	-	- (-)	-	- (-)	-
Greg Walters	- (-)	-	7 (2)	2	- (-)	-	- (-)	-
Steve Watson	12 (-)	-	- (-)	-	- (-)	-	- (-)	-
Andrew Wells	- (-)	-	- (-)	-	8 (5)	-	- (-)	-
Ben Willetts	- (-)	-	- (-)	-	20 (1)	1	1 (-)	-
Alan Wright	3 (-)	-	- (-)	-	- (-)	-	- (-)	-
Own Goals		1		1		2		-

* Triallist.

VILLA'S ALL-TIME LEAGUE RECORD – SEASON BY SEASON

Season	Div	Teams	Pos	P	W	D	L	F	A	W	D	L	F	A	Pts	Cup Honours
1888-89	1	12	2nd	22	10	0	1	44	16	2	5	4	17	27	29	*(FAC Winners in 1886-87)*
1889-90	1	12	8th	22	6	2	3	30	15	1	3	7	13	36	19	
1890-91	1	12	9th	22	5	4	2	29	18	2	0	9	16	40	18	
1891-92	1	14	4th	26	10	0	3	63	23	5	0	8	26	33	30	*FAC Runners-up*
1892-93	1	16	4th	30	12	1	2	50	24	4	2	9	23	38	35	
1893-94	**1**	**16**	**1st**	**30**	**12**	**2**	**1**	**49**	**13**	**7**	**4**	**4**	**35**	**29**	**44**	
1894-95	1	16	3rd	30	12	2	1	51	12	5	3	7	31	31	39	***FAC Winners***
1895-96	**1**	**16**	**1st**	**30**	**14**	**1**	**0**	**47**	**17**	**6**	**4**	**5**	**31**	**28**	**45**	
1896-97	**1**	**16**	**1st**	**30**	**10**	**3**	**2**	**36**	**16**	**11**	**2**	**2**	**37**	**22**	**47**	***FAC Winners***
1897-98	1	16	6th	30	12	1	2	47	21	2	4	9	14	30	33	
1898-99	**1**	**18**	**1st**	**34**	**15**	**2**	**0**	**58**	**13**	**4**	**5**	**8**	**18**	**27**	**45**	
1899-00	**1**	**18**	**1st**	**34**	**12**	**4**	**1**	**45**	**18**	**10**	**2**	**5**	**32**	**17**	**50**	
1900-01	1	18	15th	34	8	5	4	32	18	2	5	10	13	33	30	*FAC Semi-finalists*
1901-02	1	18	8th	34	9	5	3	27	13	4	3	10	15	27	34	
1902-03	1	18	2nd	34	11	3	3	43	18	8	0	9	18	22	41	*FAC Semi-finalists*
1903-04	1	18	5th	34	13	1	3	41	16	4	6	7	29	32	41	
1904-05	1	18	4th	34	11	2	4	32	15	8	2	7	31	28	42	***FAC Winners***
1905-06	1	20	8th	38	13	2	4	51	19	4	4	11	21	37	40	
1906-07	1	20	5th	38	13	4	2	51	19	6	2	11	27	33	44	
1907-08	1	20	2nd	38	9	6	4	47	24	8	3	8	30	35	43	
1908-09	1	20	7th	38	8	7	4	31	22	6	3	10	27	34	38	
1909-10	**1**	**20**	**1st**	**38**	**17**	**2**	**0**	**62**	**19**	**6**	**5**	**8**	**22**	**23**	**53**	
1910-11	1	20	2nd	38	15	3	1	50	18	7	4	8	19	23	51	
1911-12	1	20	6th	38	12	2	5	48	22	5	5	9	28	41	41	
1912-13	1	20	2nd	38	13	4	2	57	21	6	8	5	29	31	50	***FAC Winners***
1913-14	1	20	2nd	38	11	3	5	36	21	8	3	8	29	29	44	*FAC Semi-finalists*
1914-15	1	20	13th	38	10	5	4	39	32	3	6	10	23	40	37	
First World War																
1919-20	1	22	9th	42	11	3	7	49	36	7	3	11	26	37	42	***FAC Winners***
1920-21	1	22	10th	42	11	4	6	39	21	7	3	11	24	49	43	
1921-22	1	22	5th	42	16	3	2	50	19	6	0	15	24	36	47	
1922-23	1	22	6th	42	15	3	3	42	11	3	7	11	22	40	46	
1923-24	1	22	6th	42	10	10	1	33	11	8	3	10	19	26	49	*FAC Runners-up*
1924-25	1	22	15th	42	10	7	4	34	25	3	6	12	24	46	39	
1925-26	1	22	6th	42	12	7	2	56	25	4	5	12	30	51	44	
1926-27	1	22	10th	42	11	4	6	51	34	7	3	11	30	49	43	
1927-28	1	22	8th	42	13	3	5	52	30	4	6	11	26	43	43	
1928-29	1	22	3rd	42	16	2	3	62	30	7	2	12	36	51	50	*FAC Semi-finalists*
1929-30	1	22	4th	42	13	1	7	54	33	8	4	9	38	50	47	
1930-31	1	22	2nd	42	17	3	1	86	34	8	6	7	42	44	59	

VILLA'S ALL-TIME LEAGUE RECORD – SEASON BY SEASON

Season	Div	Teams	Pos	P	W	D	L	F	A	W	D	L	F	A	Pts	Cup Honours
1931-32	1	22	5th	42	15	1	5	64	28	4	7	10	40	44	46	
1932-33	1	22	2nd	42	16	2	3	60	29	7	6	8	32	38	54	
1933-34	1	22	13th	42	10	5	6	45	34	4	7	10	33	41	40	*FAC Semi-finalists*
1934-35	1	22	13th	42	11	6	4	50	36	3	7	11	24	52	41	
1935-36	*1*	*22*	*21st*	*42*	*7*	*6*	*8*	*47*	*56*	*6*	*3*	*12*	*34*	*54*	*35*	
1936-37	2	22	9th	42	10	6	5	47	30	6	6	9	35	40	44	
1937-38	**2**	**22**	**1st**	**42**	**17**	**2**	**2**	**50**	**12**	**8**	**5**	**8**	**23**	**23**	**57**	*FAC Semi-finalists*
1938-39	1	22	12th	42	11	3	7	44	25	5	6	10	27	35	41	
Second World War																
1946-47	1	22	8th	42	9	6	6	39	24	9	3	9	28	29	45	
1947-48	1	22	6th	42	13	5	3	42	22	6	4	11	23	35	47	
1948-49	1	22	10th	42	10	6	5	40	36	6	4	11	20	40	42	
1949-50	1	22	12th	42	10	7	4	31	19	5	5	11	30	42	42	
1950-51	1	22	15th	42	9	6	6	39	29	3	7	11	27	39	37	
1951-52	1	22	6th	42	13	3	5	49	28	6	6	9	30	42	47	
1952-53	1	22	11th	42	9	7	5	36	23	5	6	10	27	38	41	
1953-54	1	22	13th	42	12	5	4	50	28	4	4	13	20	40	41	
1954-55	1	22	6th	42	11	3	7	38	31	9	4	8	34	42	47	
1955-56	1	22	20th	42	9	6	6	32	29	2	7	12	20	40	35	
1956-57	1	22	10th	42	10	8	3	45	25	4	7	10	20	30	43	***FAC Winners***
1957-58	1	22	14th	42	12	4	5	46	26	4	3	14	27	60	39	
1958-59	*1*	*22*	*21st*	*42*	*8*	*5*	*8*	*31*	*33*	*3*	*3*	*15*	*27*	*54*	*30*	*FAC Semi-finalists*
1959-60	**2**	**22**	**1st**	**42**	**17**	**3**	**1**	**62**	**19**	**8**	**6**	**7**	**27**	**24**	**59**	*FAC Semi-finalists*
1960-61	1	22	9th	42	13	3	5	48	28	4	6	11	30	49	43	***LC Winners***
1961-62	1	22	7th	42	13	5	3	45	20	5	3	13	20	36	44	
1962-63	1	22	15th	42	12	2	7	38	23	3	6	12	24	45	38	*LC Runners-up*
1963-64	1	22	19th	42	8	6	7	35	29	3	6	12	27	42	34	
1964-65	1	22	16th	42	14	1	6	36	24	2	4	15	21	58	37	*LC Semi-finalists*
1965-66	1	22	16th	42	10	3	8	39	34	5	3	13	30	46	36	
1966-67	*1*	*22*	*21st*	*42*	*7*	*5*	*9*	*30*	*33*	*4*	*2*	*15*	*24*	*52*	*29*	
1967-68	2	22	16th	42	10	3	8	35	30	5	4	12	19	34	37	
1968-69	2	22	18th	42	10	8	3	22	11	2	6	13	15	37	38	
1969-70	*2*	*22*	*21st*	*42*	*7*	*8*	*6*	*23*	*21*	*1*	*5*	*15*	*13*	*41*	*29*	
1970-71	3	24	4th	46	13	7	3	27	13	6	8	9	27	33	53	*LC Runners-up*
1971-72	**3**	**24**	**1st**	**46**	**20**	**1**	**2**	**45**	**10**	**12**	**5**	**6**	**40**	**22**	**70**	
1972-73	2	22	3rd	42	12	5	4	27	17	6	9	6	24	30	50	
1973-74	2	22	14th	42	8	9	4	33	21	5	6	10	15	24	41	
1974-75	2	22	2nd	42	16	4	1	47	6	9	4	8	32	26	58	***LC Winners***
1975-76	1	22	16th	42	11	8	2	32	17	0	9	12	19	42	39	
1976-77	1	22	4th	42	17	3	1	55	17	5	4	12	21	33	51	***LC Winners***

VILLA'S ALL-TIME LEAGUE RECORD – SEASON BY SEASON

Season	Div	Teams	Pos	P	W	D	L	F	A	W	D	L	F	A	Pts	Cup Honours
1977-78	1	22	8th	42	11	4	6	33	18	7	6	8	24	24	46	
1978-79	1	22	8th	42	8	9	4	37	26	7	7	7	22	23	46	
1979-80	1	22	7th	42	11	5	5	29	22	5	9	7	22	28	46	
1980-81	**1**	**22**	**1st**	**42**	**16**	**3**	**2**	**40**	**13**	**10**	**5**	**6**	**32**	**27**	**60**	
1981-82	1	22	11th	42	9	6	6	28	24	6	6	9	27	29	57	*EC Winners*
1982-83	1	22	6th	42	17	2	2	47	15	4	3	14	15	35	68	*ESC Winners*
1983-84	1	22	10th	42	14	3	4	34	22	3	6	12	25	39	60	*LC Semi-finalists*
1984-85	1	22	10th	42	10	7	4	34	20	5	4	12	26	40	56	
1985-86	1	22	16th	42	7	6	8	27	28	3	8	10	24	39	44	*LC Semi-finalists*
1986-87	*1*	*22*	*22nd*	*42*	*7*	*7*	*7*	*25*	*25*	*1*	*5*	*15*	*20*	*54*	*36*	
1987-88	2	23	2nd	44	9	7	6	31	21	13	5	4	37	20	78	
1988-89	1	20	17th	38	7	6	6	25	22	2	7	10	20	34	40	
1989-90	1	20	2nd	38	13	3	3	36	20	8	4	7	21	18	70	*FMC Area Finalists*
1990-91	1	20	17th	38	7	9	3	29	25	2	5	12	17	33	41	
1991-92	1	22	7th	42	13	3	5	31	16	4	6	11	17	28	60	
1992-93	P	22	2nd	42	13	5	3	36	16	8	6	7	21	24	74	
1993-94	P	22	10th	42	8	5	8	23	18	7	7	7	23	32	57	*LC Winners*
1994-95	P	22	18th	42	6	9	6	27	24	5	6	10	24	32	48	
1995-96	P	20	4th	38	11	5	3	32	15	7	4	8	20	20	63	*LC Winners/FAC SF*
1996-97	P	20	5th	38	11	5	3	27	13	6	5	8	20	21	61	
1997-98	P	20	7th	38	9	3	7	26	24	8	3	8	23	24	57	
1998-99	P	20	6th	38	10	3	6	33	28	5	7	7	18	18	55	
1999-00	P	20	6th	38	8	8	3	23	12	7	5	7	23	23	58	*FAC Runners-up*

VILLA'S COMPLETE LEAGUE RECORD

	P	W	D	L	F	A	Pts
Home	1988	1143	435	410	4121	2255	2910
Away	1988	543	476	969	2525	3545	1666
Total	3976	1686	911	1379	6646	5700	4576

2pts for a win up to season 1980-8, 3pts for a win from season 1981-82

Other honours:

World Club Championship runners-up 1982-83

FA Charity Shield joint winners 1981-82

FA Charity Shield runners-up 1910-11, 1957-58, 1972-73

FAC = FA Cup; LC = League Cup; FMC = Full Members' Cup; EC = European Champions' Cup; ESC = European Super Cup.
Championship seasons in **bold** type, relegation seasons in *italics*.

INTO INTERTOTO

Villa's defeat in the FA Cup Final left the InterToto Cup as their last chance of a place in Europe next season, and made for some quick rearranging of diaries and training schedules, as their maiden InterToto campaign begins at the third round stage, as early as 15th July.

The identity of their first opponent was unknown as we went to press, save that it would be a club from either Austria, the Czech Republic or Israel.

The three clubs remaining after the competition has been completed, proceed into next season's UEFA Cup. If Villa are among the survivors, their sixth and final InterToto game will take place on 22nd August, after the domestic season has begun.

VILLA'S ALL-TIME LEAGUE RECORD – CLUB BY CLUB

		Home					Away			
	P	W	D	L	F	A	W	D	L	F	A
Accrington	10	4	0	1	26	12	1	2	2	9	10
Arsenal	142	38	16	17	141	99	20	15	36	81	117
Barnsley	12	3	2	1	9	3	5	1	0	16	2
Birmingham City	96	23	13	12	82	60	16	12	20	68	74
Blackburn Rovers	134	35	17	15	139	90	18	12	37	90	144
Blackpool	62	16	9	6	65	39	10	7	14	44	51
Bolton Wanderers	130	35	15	15	139	84	17	13	35	67	126
Bournemouth	4	1	1	0	3	2	1	0	1	2	4
Bradford Park Avenue	10	4	0	1	12	4	1	2	2	8	16
Bradford City	30	10	2	3	33	12	4	5	6	18	24
Brentford	6	2	1	0	12	4	3	0	0	8	3
Brighton & Hove Albion	16	6	2	0	16	4	3	2	3	8	7
Bristol City	32	10	3	3	27	19	5	6	5	18	14
Bristol Rovers	8	3	1	0	8	3	2	1	1	4	4
Burnley	94	28	12	7	109	47	11	8	28	71	113
Bury	52	17	6	3	59	31	10	6	10	39	39
Cardiff City	44	14	3	5	39	20	8	2	12	23	30
Carlisle United	10	4	1	0	5	1	2	2	1	6	6
Charlton Athletic	40	10	6	4	44	22	6	6	8	23	33
Chelsea	106	27	13	13	104	75	17	10	26	64	78
Chesterfield	8	2	1	1	7	4	3	0	1	8	3
Coventry City	52	15	10	1	41	16	13	6	7	38	31
Crystal Palace	24	8	2	2	22	9	2	6	4	6	10
Darwen	4	2	0	0	16	0	1	1	0	6	2
Derby County	112	37	10	9	137	59	19	11	26	76	94
Doncaster Rovers	4	1	1	0	4	3	0	0	2	1	3
Everton	170	42	19	24	161	114	22	22	41	103	151
Fulham	34	8	5	4	30	22	2	5	10	20	34
Gillingham	2	1	0	0	2	1	0	1	0	0	0
Glossop	2	1	0	0	9	0	0	0	1	0	1
Grimsby Town	20	5	3	2	29	19	5	1	4	16	20
Halifax Town	4	1	1	0	2	1	1	0	1	2	2
Huddersfield Town	64	20	9	3	74	31	7	10	15	32	51
Hull City	16	4	3	1	21	8	2	2	4	7	12
Ipswich Town	40	11	6	3	40	17	5	4	11	20	30
Leeds United	72	18	10	8	60	42	7	13	16	34	58
Leicester City	76	17	9	12	78	59	6	10	22	51	94
Leyton Orient	10	4	1	0	8	3	1	2	2	3	6
Lincoln City	2	0	1	0	1	1	0	1	0	0	0
Liverpool	150	37	17	21	152	97	13	15	47	79	169
Luton Town	32	10	1	5	29	15	1	3	12	8	24
Manchester City	124	32	19	11	114	67	14	15	33	79	118

TO THE END OF SEASON 1999 - 2000

	P	W	D	L	F	A	W	D	L	F	A
			Home						Away		
Manchester United	134	32	17	18	135	97	10	15	42	62	138
Mansfield Town	4	0	0	2	0	2	0	1	1	1	3
Middlesbrough	110	32	10	13	125	60	19	15	21	74	81
Millwall	18	4	4	1	14	8	3	2	4	9	12
Newcastle United	124	32	14	16	118	67	13	9	40	80	136
Northampton Town	2	0	0	1	1	2	0	0	1	1	2
Norwich City	46	14	6	3	42	25	4	7	12	28	41
Nottingham Forest	108	34	10	10	110	53	16	17	21	76	99
Notts County	66	23	7	3	83	29	12	8	13	49	52
Oldham Athletic	30	9	3	3	34	8	7	6	2	29	17
Oxford United	14	4	2	1	9	3	1	3	3	8	11
Plymouth Argyle	14	5	1	1	19	9	2	2	3	12	12
Portsmouth	60	19	7	4	73	39	8	7	15	42	65
Port Vale	4	2	0	0	3	0	0	1	1	4	6
Preston North End	98	37	3	9	108	44	13	11	25	64	90
Queen's Park Rangers	38	8	4	7	32	26	3	3	13	14	29
Reading	4	2	0	0	4	2	2	0	0	7	3
Rochdale	4	2	0	0	3	0	0	1	1	1	2
Rotherham United	8	3	0	1	8	3	2	1	1	6	3
Scunthorpe United	2	1	0	0	5	0	1	0	0	2	1
Sheffield United	120	40	12	8	145	55	17	16	27	85	111
Sheffield Wednesday	128	45	9	10	159	67	18	8	38	89	132
Shrewsbury Town	6	3	0	0	6	0	1	1	1	4	4
Southampton	50	13	8	4	41	18	6	7	12	25	42
Stockport County	2	1	0	0	7	1	1	0	0	3	1
Stoke City	88	31	7	6	108	36	13	13	18	54	66
Sunderland	142	46	12	13	145	89	14	21	36	89	137
Swansea City	14	7	0	0	19	0	4	0	3	12	10
Swindon Town	10	3	1	1	10	5	2	2	1	6	4
Torquay United	4	1	0	1	5	2	0	1	1	2	3
Tottenham Hotspur	114	25	15	17	91	79	19	9	29	92	114
Tranmere Rovers	4	2	0	0	3	0	1	1	0	2	1
Walsall	4	0	2	0	0	0	0	1	1	1	4
Watford	14	4	2	1	15	6	1	2	4	10	16
West Bromwich Albion	124	39	8	15	118	74	19	15	28	86	99
West Ham United	74	19	8	10	73	47	6	12	19	46	80
Wimbledon	26	6	2	5	22	12	3	5	5	20	21
Wolverhampton Wan.	96	26	10	12	109	64	15	12	21	67	86
Wrexham	4	1	0	1	5	4	2	0	0	5	2
York City	4	2	0	0	5	0	1	1	0	2	1
TOTALS	3976	1143	435	410	4121	2255	543	476	969	2525	3545

The Villa team that started the 2000 FA Cup Final: Back row (left to right) - Mark Delaney, Dion Dublin, Paul Merson, David James, Ian Taylor, Ugo Ehiogu. Front row - George Boateng, Gareth Southgate (captain), Alan Wright, Benito Carbone, Gareth Barry.

SUBSCRIBERS ROLL CALL

001	Neil Gallagher	057	Angela Mead
002	Michael Bates	058	Jim Stelfox
003	Aden Cole	059	Robin D. Wilkes
004	Diane Cole	060	Gavin Harris
005	Bill Willcox	061	Andrew Collins
006	Michael Halaj	062	Martyn Thomas
007	John (Villa) Power	063	Wendy Jordan
008	Brian C. Seadon	064	Neil Byrne
009	Rev. L. E. Osborn	065	Andy Perry
010	David Hodges	066	Antony McAllister
011	Paul Rostance	067	Dean Shepherd
012	Damian Barrow	068	Joseph Shepherd
013	Mark Barrow	069	Karen Ellis
014	David G. Hitchens	070	Nigel & Ross Iwanski
015	Barry Silver	071	Gary Weaver
016	Ben Scarle	072	Ross Griffith
017	Pauline Joyner	073	Alison Jones
018	Paul Hands	074	Lee Stewart Anderson
019	Sonia Butler	075	Paul Edwards
020	Lynsey Dunbar	076	Keith Gleadall
021	Elizabeth Dunbar	077	Richard, Sue & Dan Ford
022	Paul & Jenny Bailey	078	Sarah Mills
023	Joe Dennis	079	Brian & Vicki Griffin
024	B. R. Veal	080	Andrew Holden
025	Adam Probert	081	Rob Wardle & Family
026	Tony Dacey	082	Simon Kerr-Edwards
027	Derek T. Hough	083	Alexander, Daniel & Paul Berwick
028	J. T. O'Brien	084	Geoff Clarke
029	Victoria Yandall	085	Nigel Renshaw
030	Keith Potter	086	Norman Renshaw
031	Mr V. A. P. Kiely	087	Stephen (Rennie) Renshaw
032	Glyn & Lorraine Richards	088	Dan (The Villaman) Renshaw
033	Caerwyn & Celyn Richards	089	Simon Renshaw
034	M. A. Thackeray	090	John Murphy
035	David, Susan & Oliver Eagle	091	Lesley Smith
036	Steven Cox	092	Geoffrey Wright
037	Andrew Cox	093	Vincent J. McKenna
038	Leanne Sharpe	094	Craig Vigurs
039	Simon (Wilf) Wheeler	095	Paul Ford
040	Doug Sinclair	096	Kevin Larkin
041	David Grimble	097	Malcolm Cooper
042	Michael, Thomas & Joshua Greaves	098	Jon Noden
043	Michele & Clive Platman	099	Adam Treeby
044	Robert Gough	100	R. E. Garratt
045	Peter Lee Maddocks	101	Gareth C. Jones (Bones)
046	Neil Strevens	102	Vassos Alexander Georgiadis
047	McDivitt Family	103	Rachel Townsend
048	D. S. Willetts	104	David Woodley
049	James Flynn	105	Frank MacDonald
050	Kenneth J. Marriott	106	Simon Booker
051	Katie Turner	107	Richard Burton
052	Mark Pearce	108	Martin Greenslade
053	Stewart James-Dyke	109	Stuart T. Swann
054	D. C. Aust	110	John Hitchman
055	Carol Maguire, Kingstanding	111	Andrew Morgan
056	Philip Gray	112	Philip Chandler
		113	James Villans & Mathew 99

114	Terry Wright
115	Leni & John Ward
116	Charles Wheadon
117	Emily & Martin Kender
118	Kevin Gledhill
119	Richard Gledhill
120	Peter Gledhill
121	Andrew Gledhill
122	R. L. Elwell
123	Stephen James Allison
124	Robert John Lee Allison
125	Alan James Smith (Holte End)
126	Louise Roberts
127	The Fairfield Family (Lancaster)
128	Roger (Tamworth) Nicklin
129	Tony Joyner
130	Julie N. Davies
131	Mark Whitehouse
132	Matthew Dale
133	Mark Lench
134	Miss Alice Kirk
135	Rob Till
136	Charlie Stanley
137	Sheena Meredith
138	Y. A. Graves
139	Teresa Meredith (Shropshire)
140	Dean Morris (Burford)
141	Stephen Paul & Angela Mary Naylor
142	Martin Lockley
143	Martin & David George
144	Sarah Kinsman
145	John Peter Reidy
146	Charles R. Nelson
147	Dr. Mark Wilson
148	Nicholas J. Sanders
149	Bernard Dain
150	Stanley A. Chambers
151	Graham N. Willetts
152	Steven Chapman
153	Robert Chapman (Chip)
154	Colin Brown
155	Cheryl Matthews
156	Philip R. Haynes
157	D. H. Perry
158	Robin & Oliver Peck
159	Antony Millas
160	Sherralyn Scott
161	Jason (Nobby) Crowley
162	G. C. Carlin
163	David J. Barron
164	Adam Hackett
165	Ian Tate
166	Bridget Tate
167	Adrian Chamberlain
168	Martin J. Watson
169	Sophie Louise Wiseman

170 James Plester	224 Adrian Goddard	279 Andrew John Francis
171 Paul Merson	225 Joe, Keith, Emily & Renarta	280 Michael Bloore
172 Jim & Thomas McDonald	Ridout	281 Christopher Bloore
173 David James Watson & Family	226 Geoff Allman	282 Justyn John Alexander Percival
174 H. (Hoppy) Holman	227 David Knight	283 Adam O'Connor
175 Andrew, Stephen & Judith	228 Peter John Ross (Belbroughton)	284 Dan Holmes
Maddern	229 Mark Napier	285 Andrew Webster
176 Steve Solomon	230 Gerald H. Lodwick	286 Richard E. Manley
177 Pete Lancaster &	231 Dr. Stephen C. Tovey	287 Ian Drew
Caroline Woollard	232 Edward Knott	288 S. J. Lavery
178 Antonio Durante (Rome, Italy)	233 Antony Ibbotson	289 Ben & Ian Sutherland
179 Gary & Natalie	234 Ralph & Wendy Willis	290 Mark & Simon Deeley
180 Mark C. Hall	(Middlesbrough)	291 Darren & Debbie
181 Daren Reynolds	235 Chris, Simon & Matt Michell	292 Tom Sedgwick
182 Adam Rooke	236 Steve Crump	293 Patrick May
183 John Adkins (Billericay)	237 Neil Harvey	294 Brig Flounders
184 Jason Russell Perry	238 Stephen Cowburn	295 Mark E. J. Jenkins
185 Barry Geddis (Chester)	239 Neil Shayle	296 Neil Hunt
186 John A. Gould (1934)	240 Jason Davis	297 Raymond Warr
187 Steve Gould	241 Roy & David Scrivens	298 Kerry (30 Years Old) Eades
188 Mark Underwood	242 Sophie Louise Parkin	299 Helen L. Sutton
189 Malcolm Philip Price	243 Dean Strange	300 Samuel York
190 Gordon Wilfred Price	244 Michelle Diggins	301 Peter Griffiths
191 James Dagley	245 Mark (Skully) Rowland	302 James & Colin Daly
192 Carl Lewis	246 James Powell	303 Karen Barlow
193 Ross James Waterhouse	247 Charlotte & Ashley Davis	304 S. Boddy
(Ardens Grafton)	248 Andrew Mason	305 Chris Russell
194 Ian R. Wilson	249 Graham Jackson	306 Kimberly Wiltshire
195 Neil Jones (Holte End)	250 Richard M. Merker	307 Sue & Mick Tilt
196 W. J. Mottram	251 N. M. Salter	308 Andrew Brooks
197 Jon Jones	252 Michael Carey	309 Tony & Andrew Friel
198 Susan Pudge	253 Philip Taylor	310 M. A. King
199 David Tansey	254 Geoff Underhill	311 Dave Banner
200 T. Goode	255 Bob Daniels	312 Mark Bradshaw
201 G. Day	256 Ken, Paul & Peter Noon	313 Stephen Evans
202 Mark David Goodwin	257 Kevin A. Williams	314 Gweedore Villa
203 Richard A. Hales	258 Rory Smith	315 Kevin Stratford
204 Murray V. Tamplin	259 Emma Gregory & Joshua Adams	316 Mike Jehan
205 T. D. Measey	260 Colin & Travis Smith	317 Ralf Schulz
206 Kenton C. Bryant	261 Ben Goldspink	318 Daniel Blake Strange
207 Adam France	262 Claire Cooper	319 Frank McNally
208 Phillip John Wall	263 Chris & Veronica McCormack	320 Andrew R. Owen
209 Tony Spraggon	264 Beryl Stanyard	321 Lauren Clare Duff
210 Julian Smith	265 Roger & Liz Bailey	322 B. Harte
211 Lee Day	266 Gemma & Becky Bailey	323 Tony, Matthew & Andrew Kenny
212 Ted Geary	267 Vikki Lee	324 Allen Souch
213 G. F. Barker	268 James Cooke	325 Gingerpud & Cadbury
214 Scott Davidson	269 Steve Mullins	326 Mark Whorton
215 Malcolm Taylor	270 Mathew Kendrick	327 Richard R. Carter
216 Douglas Talbot	271 Derek, Kerry, Carly & Jean Day	328 Jack & Leo Pinnock
217 Carol Grove J.P.	272 Peter William Giles	329 Diane Swales
218 David Poole	273 M. Asson (Fordbridge)	330 Michael Rose
219 Warren Carvell	274 Gordon Cull	331 J. R. Meek
220 Alan F. Jasper	275 Gordon Parton	332 Tina Rees
221 Gerald Leek	276 Adam & Robert Tilsley	333 Alun Llywelyn Parish
222 John S. Brown	277 Michael James Bateson	334 Natalie Langford
223 Peter Boam	278 Pete Abrahams	335 Dominic 'Pongo' Moore

SUBSCRIBERS ROLL CALL

336	Leslie Hobson	393	Derek Wisdom	450	Esther Gilks
337	Jennie Taylor	394	Paul Duffin	451	Julie Abbott
338	Geoffrey Turner	395	Mark Jenkins	452	randle14 @ hotmail.com
339	Mark Wheeler	396	Rich, Andy, Tony	453	Dejan Tomic
340	R. A. Jones	397	Michael Shrimplin	454	Steven Withers
341	Vera Ellen Ragsdale	398	'The Boy Leese'	455	Nigel Ainge
342	Graham Coggins	399	Nathan Collins	456	Richard, Steven & Jenny Baker
343	Barrie Bailey (Plymouth)	400	Philip Williams	457	Lucy Hawkes
344	D. P. Bedford	401	N. Becerra	458	Rob Vincent
345	Malcolm Blackwell (Culham, Oxon)	402	James Davis	459	Rick Vincent
346	Robert Moss	403	Neil & Julie Edwards	460	Stanley Frank Randle
347	Jamie Wild	404	Adrian Batsford	461	Mark Thomas Randle
348	Steve Thorne	405	Guto Siôn Williams	462	Dave Alan Turner
349	Ray Geary	406	Stephanie Attenborough	463	Matthew Lydon
350	Alan Percival	407	Thomas Johansson	464	The Doyle Family
351	John Clayton	408	Ruth Simmons	465	Mr Sean Christopher Starrs
352	R. K. Pearson	409	Paul Perry	466	H. John Desaulles
353	Carla Kathleen Kirby	410	Adam Thomas Barrett	467	Charles Southby
354	David Yeomans	411	David John Edward Clayton	468	Richard Guy Shutt
355	Julia Greenfield	412	Amanda Evans	469	Ian Smith
356	Neal Sawyer	413	Tony Broadhurst	470	Cheryl Bowditch
357	Stephen Morris (France)	414	Mark Farmer	471	Jason Freeman
358	Keith Puttick	415	Paul McKenna	472	Bob Watler
359	Bob Hughes	416	Ted Osborn	473	Daniel Watler
360	Lisa, Paul & Thomas Palmer	417	Anthony Woolley	474	Dave Shipley
361	Dave, Marg & Paul Buet	418	Hayden Wakeling	475	Paul Anthony Webb
362	Alex Groemminger	419	John Cullen (Wexford)	476	John Mace
363	Dr. Robert Tighe	420	Glenn Douglas	477	Zosia Mace
364	Owen Suter	421	Gwenfyl Royles	478	Richard Prvulovich
365	C. Derrick Dewsbery	422	Alison Royles	479	Frank & Ben Antram
366	Andrew Webb	423	Nicola Royles	480	Adrian H. Mullis
367	David England	424	Nigel Groves	481	Patrick & Gabrielle Fenelon
368	John Foster	425	Karen Cook	482	Chris Bale
369	Matthew Mayne	426	Rod Snelson	483	Nigel & Harry Follos
370	Philip R. Jones	427	Derek Anthony Price	484	John Brealey
371	Kevin Barry O'Neill	428	R. Hemus	485	Brian Harris
372	Robert Cooper	429	Carl, Sylvia & Charlotte Morris	486	Matthew & Nicholas Harris
373	Matthew Idoine	430	Keith Andrew Taylor	487	Carl & Luke Davies
374	Richard Bennett	431	Jason Wardle	488	Martin Green
375	Andrew Gerrard	432	Tom, Rob & Dom Ryan	489	Oliver Simon Stringer
376	Nicholas Cox (Water Orton)	433	Jeff Corfield	490	Sacha Molin
377	John Nicholls	434	Scott Hamblett	491	Nicholas Jones
378	E. Mills (Weoley Castle Villa)	435	Trevor Fisher	492	Roy Stringer
379	Darran Boulter	436	Gerard Murphy	493	Mike & Chrissy
380	Gordon Reynolds	437	Craig Scott Nixon	494	David John Peachey
381	Paul Aldhouse	438	Ciâran Allen John Farley	495	David Beament
382	Mark A. Wheeler (Shard End)	439	Gido Kirfel	496	Ann Gonoude
383	Clive, Gary & David Foster	440	Rein Bladh (Sweden)	497	Robert F. Rea
384	Nick Yates	441	Henrik Blad (Sweden)	498	Paul & Jack Hughes
385	J. I. D. Cox	442	Lewis James Robinson	499	Patiphan Nakwarnon
386	Andrea Warren	443	The Cash Family (Streetly)	500	Dave & Steve Silver
387	Kev Buttery	444	Lars Nilsson	501	Thomas James Knibb
388	Paul Jarvis (Torpoint, Cornwall)	445	Chris Deakin	502	Simon A. J. Burley
389	James Michael Deeley	446	Carl Pell	503	Jamie Taylor
390	Angus David Rae	447	John & Mary Smith	504	Carol Smith
391	Caroline James	448	Gareth Tidey	505	Trevor John Baker
392	John Lacey	449	Andy Campkin	506	Daniel John Baker

507	Liam Matthew Baker	562	Daniel & Kayleigh Evans	617	Callum Fenlon
508	John W. Daw	563	Glyn Howell	618	Abbie & Hollie Horton
509	Martin Hodson	564	Michael O'Brien	619	Ewan Jay Magan
510	Alex Ashford	565	Graham & Liz Jinks	620	Roger Levicki
511	Tom O'Neill	566	Adrian Thorne	621	Tim Levicki
512	John Mitchell	567	Martin Colin Roberts	622	Andrew Levicki
513	James Matharu	568	Charlotte Louise Briggs	623	Michael David Bromwich
514	Maria, Emma & Clare Ganner	569	K. W. Powell	624	Andrew & Daniel Haigh
515	Adrian, Lisa & Charlotte Hill	570	Steve Matthews	625	Sarah & Karen Haigh
516	Jane Dormer	571	Dave Skinner (London)	626	Ian J. Walker
517	The Cleminsons	572	Iris Barford	627	Julie Richardson (Up The Villa)
518	Robert Cooley	573	Andrew C. Dawes	628	Nicki Davies
519	Matthew Robert Oakes	574	The Ray Family & Grand Kids	629	Peter & Kate (at the Semis)
520	Mr S. W. Walton	575	Brendan Shields	630	Gary M. Hayes
521	Philip J. Etheridge	576	Paul Ward	631	Tommy Hayes
522	Simon, Jess, Luke - 99/00	577	Patrick Few	632	Ken Hayes
523	Steve, Claire & Lauren Hill	578	Mick Plant	633	Phyllis Hayes
524	Keith, Natalie & Vickie Stubbs	579	Andrew Wibberley	634	Kevin Wheatly
525	Terence Anthony Barker	580	Kasper Holst (Denmark)	635	John Donohoe
526	Matthew Joseph Monks	581	Adam Paul Howlett	636	Martin K. James
527	Nigel Sadler	582	Tracey & Roy Hatfield	637	Bill Marron
528	Tony A. Bill	583	Shirley & Geoff Blizard	638	R. A. Clarkson
529	Mark Ford	584	Ian Edward Beesley	639	Philip John & Thomas
530	Nick Hampson	585	Darryl M. Sankey		Shakespeare
531	Roger & Judith Bellingham	586	H. J. McCranor	640	Simon Giles
532	Jake Wilcox	587	Matthew John Collinge	641	John Thornton (61-99)
	(Shanklin, Isle of Wight)	588	Jonathan Handley	642	Edmund Gajny
533	Helen Hollywell	589	Mark Thornley	643	Janet Parkinson
534	Ian & David Symes	590	Michael Hoole	644	Andrew Harris (next time)
535	Adrian Paul Rogers	591	Norman D. Crandles	645	Dr. Timothy N. Jackson
536	Steve Hughes	592	Stephen Lammas	646	Craig Ramsey
537	Alexander & Thomas Berry	593	Roger Fullbrook	647	Bob Nicholls
538	The Blythe Family	594	Mark Fullbrook	648	Clive Nicholls
539	Bernard Day	595	Graeme & Cameron Reid	649	Ann Geraghty & Paul Geraghty
540	Morten Esbjerg	596	Baby Rickett	650	N. C. Geldard-Williams
541	Roy Joyner	597	A. A. Bent	651	Paul Robert Eccles
542	Daniel Reeves (Gibraltar)	598	Russell Spiers	652	Sarah Jane Wall-Power
543	Geoff Baker	599	Desiree St. Laurent	653	Jonathan Simon Power
544	Michael & Nicholas English	600	Philip Dennis William & Lynsey	654	Richard, Christopher & Mary
545	Will Alexander		Clover		Henman
546	David Warman	601	Patrick F. J. O'Reilly	655	Dave Cox (Unionville, Canada)
547	Rod Evans	602	Matthew Bond	656	Frank & Edie Beach
548	Richard Hinton	603	W. A. Harvey	657	Pam & Dave Bridgewater
549	Pamela Wood	604	Phil Innamorati	658	Phil Lees
550	Scott Bradley (Evesham)	605	Charles J. Hughes	659	Nadine Goldingay
551	Mr Jason Webb	606	Suzy Wilkinson	660	Vic & Jan Millward
552	Kevin John Williams	607	Tracy Newbold	661	John & Ruth Millward
	(Lower Holte End)	608	Jenny Balmforth	662	Bethany & Adam Millward
553	Christopher Homewood	609	Callum Brown	663	Jansen & Julie King
554	Chris Newton	610	Robert, Matthew & Ashley	664	Heather, Jamie & Brandon King
555	Michael David Ault		Shakespeare	665	Roy, Debbie & Emma Sanders
556	Carl Badham	611	Simon Harrison	666	Paul & George Sanders
557	Derek, Graham, Karl & Nicola Mills	612	Ian Harrison	667	Trevor, Catherine, David &
558	Deacs 2K	613	Mr & Mrs S. Pride		Andrew Hartley
559	Leigh McTiernan	614	Gregory Upton	668	Steve & Martin Farr
560	Michael J. R. Page	615	P. D. J.	669	James & Claire Allsop
561	Michael Shelton	616	Eddie H.	670	Ben Smith